"Reading this will allow you to better understand and support your children, setting them up for success through achievable strategies and tools - it's a game changer! This book is a must have for all educators!" - **Susie Robbins**, Behaviour Consultant and Founder of Resolve to Play

"Finally, a book that demystifies sensory processing and offers practical, easy-to-implement strategies for teachers. With clear explanations, classroom examples, and creative actionable adaptations & strategies, this book empowers educators to create an environment where all children can thrive. A must-read for educators who want to meet the diverse needs of their students with confidence and skill!" - **Hayley Winter**, All About Early Years, EYFS Teacher and Leader

NAVIGATING COMMUNICATION AND SENSORY DEVELOPMENT
for Every Child

Drawing on the authors' combined expertise in both occupational and speech and language therapy, this essential guide is designed to empower teaching staff in their mission to create inclusive learning environments that support every child.

The book offers an accessible exploration of the connection between sensory processing and speech and language difficulties. Illustrated by real-life examples and helpful reflection opportunities, each chapter includes practical strategies and evidence-based interventions to equip the reader with the tools needed to navigate complex challenges with confidence and compassion. With clear guidance on designing inclusive classroom environments, which promote sensory regulation, foster speech and language development, and cultivate collaboration with professionals and families, this book serves as a trusted compass for educators.

Navigating Communication and Sensory Development for Every Child provides a roadmap for creating a welcoming and supportive classroom where every child can thrive. It is valuable reading for early years educators, classroom teachers, teaching assistants, SENCOs, and other allied professionals working in both specialist and mainstream settings.

Joanne Jones is a Consultant Speech and Language Therapist with more than 25 years' experience of working with early years children in the NHS and as the founder of her own preschool. She has helped more than 6,000 families in 32 countries, giving them the knowledge and tools needed to support their child's speech, language and communication needs. Famous for her empowering speech therapy programme for late-talking children, 'Can-Do', Joanne also authored the Amazon bestseller *Ditch the Dummy: The Gentle Way.*

Vicky Robinson is a children's Occupational Therapist, specialising in supporting children with sensory processing difficulties. She has worked with thousands of families over the last 20 years within both the NHS and private therapy services, helping parents to meet their child's sensory needs. Vicky has worked collaboratively with early years settings, mainstream and special schools, to educate and support staff in the implementation of sensory processing strategies within the school environment.

NAVIGATING COMMUNICATION AND SENSORY DEVELOPMENT
for Every Child

The Inclusive Classroom Compass

Vicky Robinson and Joanne Jones

Designed cover image: Getty Images

First published 2026
by Routledge
4 Park Square, Milton Park, Abingdon, Oxon OX14 4RN

and by Routledge
605 Third Avenue, New York, NY 10158

Routledge is an imprint of the Taylor & Francis Group, an informa business

© 2026 Vicky Robinson and Joanne Jones

The right of Vicky Robinson and Joanne Jones to be identified as authors of this work has been asserted in accordance with sections 77 and 78 of the Copyright, Designs and Patents Act 1988.

All rights reserved. No part of this book may be reprinted or reproduced or utilised in any form or by any electronic, mechanical, or other means, now known or hereafter invented, including photocopying and recording, or in any information storage or retrieval system, without permission in writing from the publishers.

Trademark notice: Product or corporate names may be trademarks or registered trademarks, and are used only for identification and explanation without intent to infringe.

British Library Cataloguing-in-Publication Data
A catalogue record for this book is available from the British Library

ISBN: 978-1-032-76138-1 (hbk)
ISBN: 978-1-032-76139-8 (pbk)
ISBN: 978-1-003-47726-6 (ebk)

DOI: 10.4324/9781003477266

Typeset in Interstate
by Apex CoVantage, LLC

CONTENTS

CHAPTER 1 — 1
Introduction – The Inclusive Classroom Compass

CHAPTER 2 — 11
Understanding Sensory Processing

CHAPTER 3 — 27
Exploring Speech and Language Challenges Through the Can-Do Approach

CHAPTER 4 — 53
Creating an Inclusive Classroom Environment

CHAPTER 5 — 81
Enhancing Speech and Language Skills: The Interaction-Rich Classroom

CHAPTER 6 — 105
The Interplay of Sensory Regulation and Communication in the Classroom

CHAPTER 7 — 127
Taking a Fresh Look at Sensory and Communication

CHAPTER 8 — 163
Collaborating with Professionals and Families

CHAPTER 9 — 187
Looking Ahead: Future Directions and Resources

Index — 197

CHAPTER 1
INTRODUCTION – THE INCLUSIVE CLASSROOM COMPASS

LET ME TELL YOU ABOUT HENRY ...

Let's start with a story about Henry, a little boy we worked with earlier this year. Henry attends a mainstream school. He's classed as non-verbal and has a diagnosis of autism. The school had one-to-one support, a speech and language therapist, and an occupational therapist in place, and a carefully structured plan to help Henry make progress.

Despite this support, the school was struggling to meet Henry's needs. He resisted cooperating with the set targets, his teacher and teaching assistant didn't know how to change things up to mean they were achievable and the therapists found it difficult to move forward as Henry hadn't met his previous goals. Henry's behaviour was unpredictable, varying from day to day, and it became increasingly challenging for his teachers to manage him in the classroom. He was spending more and more time outside the classroom in the playground or in a small one-to-one room. Everyone wanted to help Henry succeed, but they found themselves just getting by, reacting to his behaviours as they arose and taking each day as it came, without seeing any meaningful progress.

This is where Vicky and I stepped in. Before I go any further let's do some introductions.

ABOUT THE AUTHORS

My name is Joanne Jones, and I've been a speech and language therapist for over 25 years, working across the NHS and in private practice. My professional journey has taken me from owning a nursery to working as a postnatal doula, and I've combined all these experiences to develop programmes that support both parents and educators in helping children reach their potential.

Over the last four years, I have developed an ethos and programme called The Can-Do Approach, which supports parents and childcare/education practitioners to focus on what children can do rather than what they can't. This approach has helped thousands of families across the world, enabling children to make significant strides in their communication.

My co-author, Vicky Robinson, is an occupational therapist specialising in sensory integration. With over 25 years of experience, Vicky has worked extensively within the NHS, for charities, and in private practice, supporting schools and families to create sensory-friendly environments where children can flourish. Her passion for paediatric occupational therapy, particularly in sensory processing, has driven her to develop tailored interventions that empower both families and educators to foster supportive, inclusive spaces that celebrate each child's unique strengths.

Together, we've spent the last few years combining our expertise, helping children with sensory and communication needs flourish in educational settings. We are passionate about using our knowledge to support educators like you in creating environments where children can not only succeed but truly thrive.

OUR ETHOS: FOCUS ON STRENGTHS AND SUPPORT ALL DAY, EVERY DAY

At the heart of our approach is the belief that children's strengths should guide how we support them. Instead of focusing on what they can't do or where they don't meet "age-related expectations", we must look at what they can do, what makes them unique, and what they need to feel safe, supported, and understood. This approach isn't about ticking off developmental boxes; it's about celebrating individuality and providing the right support for each child to be their best self.

Supporting a child's development isn't something that happens in isolated moments or during therapy sessions alone. It's an all-day, everyday commitment. The small interactions—how we talk to children, how we listen, how we set up the environment - are just as crucial, if not more so than formal interventions. Every moment offers an opportunity to support communication, sensory needs, and emotional well-being.

Educators and childcare providers are among the most influential figures in a child's life, especially for those with additional needs. When they take the time to understand the impact they and their environment have on the children in their care, the possibilities for growth and progress become immense.

By shifting focus to how we can change the environment and our interactions, we move from managing behaviours to supporting children as whole, capable individuals.

So applying this ethos we helped Henry's school shift their focus from managing Henry's behaviours to understanding him - his sensory needs, his communication, and how the environment was impacting him. By changing the classroom environment and interactions, the staff began to see a transformation. Henry started to feel supported, and the behaviours that were once seen as barriers became clues to understanding his needs.

This is what we mean by inclusion.

INTRODUCTION

REDEFINING INCLUSION

Inclusion isn't about managing a child's behaviour in the moment or being reactive with "discipline" and "consequences". It's about creating an environment where that child can flourish, where the adults around them fully understand their needs, and where the focus is on the adults and the environment getting it right for the child.

We shift the focus to supporting success rather than fixing differences. We look at children through a lens that sees them as wanting to be successful, and when they are not, it is up to the adult to work out what they need to thrive.

Today, more children with additional needs are attending mainstream schools, but the resources and services to support them are often stretched thin. Teachers are under immense pressure to teach these children. It can feel completely overwhelming for many teachers and child carers and they may find themselves managing rather than empowering the children to succeed.

When we shift our approach, children show us what they are capable of. We have seen this time and time again. These are not huge cataclysmic shifts we are talking about, they are often little tweaks that make all the difference.

This book is about making the first steps to making that shift. We want to help you create classrooms where children are not just managed, but where they are truly understood, supported, and empowered to thrive.

Our ethos is simple: focus on what children can do, not on what they can't. Set goals that challenge us, the adults, to create environments where they succeed, rather than expecting the children to meet arbitrary goals that mean nothing to them.

BACK TO HENRY'S SCHOOL

So before we move on let's circle back to Henry's school, how did we help?

We gave the school a screening tool to be able to identify exactly where Henry's sensory profile and communication skills sat. We were able to explain that Henry needed his body waking up in order to be ready to learn, that he understood routines when objects were used rather than symbols, and that he enjoyed interacting with familiar adults when they gave him space and followed his lead.

We showed the school that by adding in some basic equipment, giving Henry movement breaks and gathering activities and objects he could already engage with, he was much calmer and more engaged.

We taught the school how to recognise when things were not optimum for Henry and how to listen to what he was telling us (non-verbally) and tweak things to help him focus and resettle. We empowered his teacher and teaching assistant to see Henry through a lens that focused on his strengths and unique personality rather than a list of the things he could not do or boxes he didn't tick.

We taught them about their interaction, how what they said impacted more than anything else on how Henry developed his language. We showed them that speech therapy for

Henry was not about taking him into a side room and doing specific activities. It was about spotting moments in the day that could be moulded into language facilitation moments.

We showed them how to check back in to the screening tools to reassess and measure progress and gave them permission to celebrate tiny inch-stones rather than waiting for the milestones.

We watched the adults in the school gain confidence, connect with what was really important for Henry, and relax about having him in their class. This meant they were better able to communicate with Henry's parents, they were more empowered in the day to day and no longer had to just focus on Henry's behaviour management. Henry quickly started to feel more secure, his behaviour was less challenging and he found ways to successfully communicate his needs throughout the day.

The whole team now, including Henry and his family, would describe his education as successful, happy, and thriving. Everyone feels more confident to tackle anything that might be thrown at them in the future.

THE IMPORTANCE OF ADDRESSING SENSORY AND COMMUNICATION CHALLENGES

We all know that in today's classrooms, you will find children with a wide range of sensory and communication needs in both children and adults. We all sit somewhere on the sensory spectrum, and as educators, we have our own sensory needs. Have you ever considered yours? We will be diving into this later in the book.

Communication is a two-way street. If a child is struggling with speech, language, or communication, can we really put all the responsibility on them to improve? As adults we are part of that communication and we need to take responsibility for the success of the messages being sent.

As more children enter school with speech and language delays and sensory processing challenges, the support systems to help them often seem overwhelmed and inadequate.

Traditionally, interventions are delivered in isolated moments, often outside the classroom and by certain adults. This leaves the educators in the room to manage the rest of the time. Those lucky enough to receive training are often left with a good foundational knowledge of the processes behind sensory and communication development but still don't feel equipped to manage in the moment and support the children all day, every day.

Communication and sensory processing are the foundations of everything else – cognitive development, social-emotional learning, and even academic achievement depend on getting this right. By separating them out and seeing them as a specialism that is addressed in specific exercises or sessions away from the classroom, is to miss the point and miss the opportunity to help many children succeed at school.

Without a strong foundation in sensory and communication support, behaviour becomes the default mode of communication. This then leads to behaviour being managed and seen as something that needs to be stopped. When sensory and communication are thought about first, the situation changes and everyone is more successful.

This book will help you recognise and address those needs in a way that promotes growth, reduces behavioural challenges, and enhances the overall learning experience for all children.

INTRODUCTION

CREATING AN ENVIRONMENT FOR GROWTH

Our ethos centres around building environments where children can flourish – not just survive. When we create classrooms that are attuned to children's sensory and communication needs, we unlock their potential. We want to move away from the idea of children coming to school only to be managed and controlled. Instead, let's create spaces where they are joyful, confident, communicative, and capable of managing the sensory demands around them.

This means paying attention to the sensory landscape of your classroom. How loud is it? How bright? How cluttered or organised? These seemingly small details can have a huge impact on a child with sensory sensitivities. It also means being mindful of how we communicate with children. Are we speaking in a way they can process? Are we giving them time to respond? When we make these adjustments, children feel safer, more secure, and more willing to engage.

In this book, we'll guide you through the steps you can take to create this type of environment in your classroom. It's about more than meeting goals or following a plan; it's about understanding the child's world and making the necessary changes so that they feel included and supported.

THE POWER OF EARLY AND HOLISTIC SUPPORT

Research consistently shows that early intervention makes the biggest difference in long-term outcomes for children with sensory and communication challenges. But we know that early intervention isn't always available when it's needed. Waiting for diagnoses or formal support can take months or even years. That's why it's so important to take action now, with the resources and knowledge you already have.

By focusing on the sensory and communication needs of the children in your care, you can make a lasting impact, even in the absence of formal support. Sensory processing and communication are the foundations for all other areas of development. When we get sensory and communication right, we set children up for success in every area of their lives.

A COLLABORATIVE APPROACH

We believe in the power of collaboration. As educators, you are the key to creating change in your classroom. But you don't have to do it alone. We're here to offer practical tips, ideas, and strategies to help you along the way. This book is designed to be your companion, whether you read it cover to cover or dip in and out when you need advice.

In the following chapters, we'll cover everything from understanding sensory processing and communication challenges to creating inclusive environments and collaborating with professionals and families. Along the way, we'll share stories, examples, and practical tools to help you make your classroom a place where all children can thrive.

By the end of this book, we hope you feel empowered to take a fresh approach to inclusion - one that celebrates strengths, prioritises understanding, and creates lasting, positive change for the children in your care.

So, let's begin this journey together, ready to make a difference in the lives of children with the greatest needs.

INTEGRATING SENSORY AND COMMUNICATION SUPPORT: WHY IT MATTERS

It's easy to compartmentalise a child's needs. We think about a physiotherapist for physical skills, a speech therapist for language, and an occupational therapist for sensory processing. But real progress comes when we stop separating these aspects and look at the child holistically. Sensory processing affects communication; communication affects learning. Everything is interconnected. Ben's story helps us to see this In action.

LET ME TELL YOU ABOUT BEN ...

Ben is a child in a special school who struggled with staying in the classroom, often running around or stripping his clothes off. His teachers didn't know how to engage him because his behaviour seemed unpredictable. But once we looked at Ben through a sensory and communication lens, it became clear that he wasn't misbehaving - he was communicating. His behaviour was his way of telling the adults around him that the sensory environment was overwhelming, and he didn't have the words to explain it.

The adults around him had tried to support Ben by getting looser clothes, trying clothes that buttoned up so he couldn't remove them and sourcing clothes with no seems.

These solutions assumed that the problem was the clothes themselves. But when we encourage the team to think about the wider context, the timing of when this happened and the times when Ben was calm, they began to uncover a different story.

Ben was finding the noise and excessive movement in the classroom at certain times difficult to cope with. He was giving subtle communication gestures to communicate his discomfort such as touching his ears, and disengaging with staff. When these messages were missed in the busy classroom Ben used a different way to communicate, one that wouldn't be missed.

When we addressed Ben's sensory challenges, looked at his movement needs, and zoned in on his more subtle communication, the behaviours lessened.

His behaviour was never the problem - it was the end result of an unmet need.

Behaviour is communication, and it's up to us to decode that message and make the necessary changes to help the child thrive.

This is what this book is all about. Changing the lens and helping children succeed.

THE STRUCTURE OF THE BOOK

This book is designed to be practical and accessible. Here's how it's structured:

1. **Understanding Sensory Processing:** You'll gain a solid foundation in sensory processing and how it impacts learning.
2. **Speech and Language Challenges:** We'll explore how communication issues present in the classroom and how to identify them.
3. **Creating an Inclusive Environment:** Learn how to set up your classroom to support every child's sensory and communication needs.
4. **Supporting Sensory Processing in the Classroom:** Discover strategies for helping children with sensory challenges.
5. **Enhancing Speech and Language Skills:** We'll show you how to adjust your interactions to support language development.
6. **Collaborating with Professionals and Families:** We'll discuss how to build a strong team and write meaningful goals for children.
7. **Looking Ahead: Future Directions and Resources:** Explore emerging trends and resources for continued learning.

HOW TO USE THIS BOOK

Whether you prefer to read cover to cover or dip into sections as needed, this book is packed with practical tips you can implement immediately. Our tone is friendly and informal, but everything we share is grounded in years of professional experience and best practices. We've eliminated jargon to make the concepts easy to understand and apply. This is less a book about sensory and communication foundations and more about how to apply this knowledge to your setting and help the children in you care.

EMPATHY AND UNDERSTANDING: THE KEY TO SUCCESS

Working with children who have additional needs can be challenging. It requires empathy, patience, and persistence. It's not about quick fixes - it's about seeing the world through the child's eyes and creating an environment where they feel safe, understood, and supported. When you lead with empathy, the progress will come.

We hope this book encourages you to take a fresh look at your classroom and the children in it. Together, we can create inclusive environments where all children have the opportunity to shine.

LOOKING AHEAD

This book is just the beginning. We invite you to join our community, continue learning, and collaborate with others who share your passion for inclusion. We look forward to seeing the difference you will make in your classroom.

Let's get started!

REFERENCES AND RESOURCES

American Speech-Language-Hearing Association (ASHA). (2021). *Practice portal: Autism.* Retrieved from www.asha.org/practice-portal/clinical-topics/autism/

Barton, E. E. & Harn, B. A. (2012). Educating young children with autism spectrum disorders. *SAGE Open, 2*(4), 1-14. https://doi.org/10.1177/2158244012458939

Booth, T. & Ainscow, M. (2016). *The Index for Inclusion: Developing Learning and Participation in Schools.* Centre for Studies on Inclusive Education.

Carter, E. W. & Hughes, C. (2006). Including high school students with severe disabilities in general education classes: Perspectives of general and special educators, paraprofessionals, and administrators. *Research and Practice for Persons with Severe Disabilities, 31*(2), 174-185.

Case-Smith, J. & Arbesman, M. (2008). Evidence-based review of interventions for autism used in or of relevance to occupational therapy. *American Journal of Occupational Therapy, 62*(4), 416-429.

Gaertner, B. M. & Parlakian, R. (2019). *Beyond the ABCs: Preparing for Life After Early Intervention.* National Association for the Education of Young Children (NAEYC).

Guldberg, K., Parsons, S., MacLeod, A., Jones, G., Prunty, A., & Balfe, T. (2011). Implications for practice from "International Review of the Evidence on Best Practice in Educational Provision for Children on the Autism Spectrum". *European Journal of Special Needs Education, 26*(1), 65-77.

Humphrey, N. & Lewis, S. (2008). "Make me normal": The views and experiences of pupils on the autism spectrum in mainstream secondary schools. *Autism, 12*(1), 23-46.

Koegel, L. K., Matos-Freden, R., Lang, R., & Koegel, R. L. (2012). Interventions for children with autism spectrum disorders in inclusive school settings. *Cognitive and Behavioral Practice, 19*(3), 401-412.

Parsons, S. & Kasari, C. (2013). School-based interventions for children with autism spectrum disorders. *International Journal of Developmental Disabilities, 59*(1), 1-20.

Rogers, S. J. & Dawson, G. (2010). *Early Start Denver Model for Young Children with Autism: Promoting Language, Learning, and Engagement.* Guilford Press.

Sussman, F. (2012). *More Than Words: Helping Parents Promote Communication and Social Skills in Children with Autism Spectrum Disorder.* Hanen Centre.

Underwood, K. & Frankel, E. (2020). Supporting inclusion in early childhood settings. *Journal of Early Childhood Research, 18*(2), 146-158.

Whalon, K. & Hart, J. E. (2011). Children with autism spectrum disorder and literacy instruction: An exploratory study of elementary inclusive settings. *Remedial and Special Education, 32*(3), 243-255.

World Health Organization (WHO). (2018). *International Classification of Functioning, Disability and Health: Children and Youth Version* (ICF-CY). WHO.

CHAPTER 2
UNDERSTANDING SENSORY PROCESSING

WHAT IS SENSORY PROCESSING?

Sensory processing is a fundamental aspect of how the brain interprets and responds to the world through the senses. The importance of sensory processing in child development cannot be overstated, as it forms the basis for various cognitive, emotional, and behavioural functions. This brief overview aims to shed light on the significance of sensory processing and its intricate connection to learning and behaviour in children.

At its core, sensory processing refers to the brain's ability to organise and make sense of the information it receives from the senses – sight, sound, touch, taste, smell, and the sense of body position and movement. This neurological process lays the foundation for higher-level skills and functions, influencing how a child perceives, interacts with, and learns from their environment.

Our Eight Senses

Our sensory system is made up of eight senses, all interconnected to enable us to function effectively. Let's briefly explore those eight senses:

1. **Sight (Vision)**
   This is the ability to perceive the world through light and colour. Vision plays a critical role in learning, as it helps children identify letters, numbers, and visual cues in their environment.
2. **Hearing (Auditory)**
   Hearing allows children to process sounds, including speech, music, and environmental noises. Auditory processing is essential for language development and communication.
3. **Touch (Tactile)**
   The sense of touch involves perceiving sensations through the skin. It helps children explore their environment and is vital for developing fine motor skills, such as writing and using tools.

4. **Taste (Gustatory)**
   Taste refers to the ability to perceive flavours through the taste buds. This sense plays a significant role in nutrition and can affect a child's willingness to try new foods.
5. **Smell (Olfactory)**
   The sense of smell enables children to identify and differentiate between various scents. It can influence taste and evoke memories or emotional responses, impacting a child's engagement in the classroom.
6. **Proprioception (Body Awareness)**
   Proprioception helps children understand their body's position in space. This sense is crucial for coordination, balance, and physical activities, enabling children to perform tasks like catching a ball or climbing stairs.
7. **Vestibular (Balance)**
   The vestibular sense involves the perception of balance and spatial orientation, primarily through the inner ear. It is essential for movement and coordination, helping children stay upright and navigate their surroundings.
8. **Interoception (Internal Sensations)**
   Interoception is the sense that allows individuals to perceive internal body signals, such as hunger, thirst, or the need to use the bathroom. Understanding these cues is important for self-regulation and emotional awareness.

Sensory processing is a cornerstone of overall child development, impacting various areas such as motor skills, emotional regulation, and social interactions. From the earliest stages of infancy, a child begins to explore and make sense of the world through sensory experiences. These experiences, whether positive or challenging, play a crucial role in shaping neural pathways and establishing the groundwork for more complex cognitive functions.

MOTOR SKILLS

One of the primary domains shaped by sensory processing is motor skills. From the earliest stages of infancy, sensory experiences contribute to the development of both gross and fine motor skills. The sense of touch, for example, plays a pivotal role in a child's ability to grasp objects, while the proprioceptive system contributes to spatial awareness and coordination. As children explore their environment, the brain refines these motor skills based on the feedback received through the senses.

COGNITIVE SKILLS

Sensory processing serves as a scaffold for cognitive development. The information gathered through the senses forms the building blocks for cognitive processes such as attention, memory, and problem-solving. For instance, a child who can effectively filter auditory stimuli is better equipped to focus on a teacher's instructions in a bustling classroom environment. Sensory processing lays the groundwork for the cognitive abilities that are integral to academic success.

EMOTIONAL REGULATION

The impact of sensory processing extends to emotional regulation. Sensory experiences can evoke emotional responses, and the brain's ability to interpret and regulate these emotions is closely tied to sensory processing. For example, a child who finds certain textures aversive may experience emotional distress when confronted with those textures. Understanding and navigating these sensory-related emotions are vital components of emotional intelligence.

SOCIAL SKILLS

Sensory processing also plays a pivotal role in the development of social skills. The ability to interpret social cues, such as facial expressions and body language, relies on effective sensory processing. A child who struggles with sensory modulation may find it challenging to navigate social interactions, leading to difficulties in forming relationships and understanding social nuances.

COMMON SENSORY PROCESSING DIFFICULTIES IN PRE-SCHOOL AND SCHOOL-AGED STUDENTS

Understanding and recognising common sensory-processing difficulties in pre-school and school-aged students is crucial for creating inclusive learning environments. Below is an overview of sensory-processing challenges commonly observed in this age group, shedding light on both sensory sensitivities and sensory-seeking behaviours that can impact a child's daily experiences at pre-school and school.

> **Reflective Prompt**
>
> How does sensory processing influence your own student's behaviour and learning in your classroom? Can you identify students who may be experiencing sensory-processing challenges, and how might you adjust your teaching strategies to better support them?

Sensory Sensitivities

Visual Sensitivities

Example: Students who are sensitive to light may exhibit aversion to bright or fluorescent lighting. They might prefer dimly lit environments.

Impact: Visual sensitivities can lead to discomfort, difficulty focusing, and, in extreme cases, may contribute to headaches or visual fatigue during activities that involve prolonged visual attention.

Auditory Sensitivities

Example: Students with auditory sensitivities may react strongly to loud noises, covering their ears or becoming visibly distressed during noisy activities.

Impact: Auditory sensitivities can affect a child's ability to concentrate, participate in group activities, and even lead to anxiety in noisy environments like school cafeterias or playgrounds.

Tactile Sensitivities

Example: Children with tactile sensitivities may avoid certain textures, resist being touched, or exhibit discomfort during activities involving specific fabrics or materials.

Impact: Tactile sensitivities can impact a child's engagement in various activities, from art and play to routine tasks like getting dressed. It may also affect social interactions if the child is averse to physical contact.

Olfactory and Gustatory Sensitivities

Example: Sensitivities to smells or tastes may lead to strong reactions, such as avoidance of certain foods or discomfort in environments with distinct odours.

Impact: These sensitivities can influence a child's eating habits, participation in cooking or sensory activities, and even their willingness to engage in specific social settings.

LET ME TELL YOU ABOUT MAX...

Max, a 7-year-old boy in Year 2, experiences heightened sensitivity to sensory stimuli, particularly to visual and auditory inputs. During whole-class lessons, he would often become agitated when the classroom lights flickered or when the noise from his classmates became too loud. Max's teacher observed these reactions and, after speaking with his occupational therapist, introduced a set of strategies to help him manage his sensory sensitivities. Max was provided with soft lighting and allowed to use noise-cancelling headphones during certain activities. Additionally, the teacher created a quiet corner in the classroom where Max could retreat to when he felt overwhelmed. These simple adjustments allowed Max to stay engaged in the lesson while managing his sensory needs more effectively.

UNDERSTANDING SENSORY PROCESSING

> **Reflective Prompts**
>
> Max's sensory sensitivities were addressed through adjustments like soft lighting and noise-cancelling headphones. How might you recognise similar sensory sensitivities in your students? What environmental changes could you implement to support students with sensory sensitivities?
>
> Max's teacher collaborated with an occupational therapist to create a supportive environment. In your own practice, how might you collaborate with other professionals to address sensory needs in the classroom?

Sensory-Seeking Behaviours

Proprioceptive Seeking

Example: Children who seek proprioceptive input may engage in activities like jumping, crashing into objects, or seeking deep pressure sensations.

Impact: Proprioceptive seeking behaviours can be misinterpreted as hyperactivity, but they often serve as a self-regulation mechanism. Providing opportunities for controlled proprioceptive input, such as through structured movement breaks, can be beneficial.

Vestibular Seeking

Example: Seeking vestibular input may manifest as a constant need for movement, spinning, or rocking back and forth.

Impact: Vestibular seekers may struggle with activities that require sitting still for extended periods, impacting their ability to participate in tasks that demand focused attention.

Tactile Seeking

Example: Children who seek tactile input may touch everything around them, enjoy messy play, or seek out textures for constant touching.

Impact: Tactile seeking behaviours can impact interactions with peers and the environment. Incorporating tactile-rich activities can provide the input these children crave in a controlled and constructive manner.

> **LET ME TELL YOU ABOUT LUCY...**
>
> Lucy, an energetic 8-year-old in Year 3, constantly seeks out sensory input, especially through movement and touch. She would often be seen spinning around or bouncing

in her seat during lessons. Her teacher, noticing her need for sensory stimulation, collaborated with the occupational therapist to create an environment that allowed Lucy to meet her sensory needs without disrupting class. Lucy was given a set of fidget tools and allowed to take regular movement breaks, such as stretching or walking around the room. This not only helped Lucy feel more focused but also improved her engagement in class activities. By understanding Lucy's sensory seeking behaviours, her teacher was able to provide the support she needed to stay calm and engaged.

Reflective Prompts

Lucy's sensory-seeking behaviours were managed by providing movement breaks and fidget tools. How do you currently support students who seek sensory input? Can you think of other strategies, like incorporating more movement-based learning, that might work in your classroom?

Sensory-seeking behaviours are often misinterpreted as disruptive. How do you ensure you understand the underlying sensory needs of students in your classroom? What steps can you take to avoid mislabelling sensory-seeking behaviours?

Sensory Under-Registration Behaviours

Visual Under-Registration

Example: Children who are under-registered to visual stimuli may not notice visual cues in their environment, such as the teacher's facial expressions, a change in the classroom layout, or visual prompts on the board. These children may appear inattentive or disengaged.

Impact: Visual under-registration can lead to difficulties following classroom instructions or engaging in visual tasks like reading or identifying objects. This may cause frustration for both the child and the teacher, as the child may miss important information that others pick up easily, impacting their learning and participation in activities.

Auditory Under-Registration

Example: Children who are under-registered to auditory stimuli may not respond to soft or distant sounds, such as a teacher calling their name or a quiet classroom announcement. They may appear distracted or unresponsive to verbal instructions.

Impact: Auditory under-registration can affect a child's ability to respond to verbal cues, participate in class discussions, or engage in group activities. These children may miss important auditory information, leading to difficulties in communication, following directions, or understanding instructions in both the classroom and social settings.

UNDERSTANDING SENSORY PROCESSING

Tactile Under-Registration

Example: Children who are under-registered to tactile input may not notice when they are touched or may not respond to physical sensations like changes in clothing or discomfort from physical tasks (e.g., a button pressing into their skin).

Impact: Tactile under-registration can result in children not noticing when they are physically uncomfortable, which could affect their ability to regulate their body during various activities. They may also appear unaware of social cues, such as physical proximity to others, which can affect their interactions and comfort in group settings.

Proprioceptive Under-Registration

Example: Children who are under-registered to proprioceptive input may not notice when their body is in awkward or uncomfortable positions, often engaging in uncoordinated movement or showing a lack of awareness of their body in space. They might not respond to feedback about posture or body orientation.

Impact: Proprioceptive under-registration can lead to difficulties with coordination, balance, and body awareness. These children may engage in clumsy or seemingly aimless physical activities, and they may have challenges with tasks that require fine or gross motor skills, such as writing or navigating the classroom environment.

Vestibular Under-Registration

Example: Children who are under-registered to vestibular input may seem less affected by movement and may not respond to changes in balance or orientation. They may not feel disoriented during activities such as spinning or swinging, often engaging in these activities without noticing any impact on their body or coordination.

Impact: Vestibular under-registration can result in children seeking excessive movement or becoming unaware of the physical limits of their bodies. They may appear overly confident or unaware of potential risks when navigating through space or engaging in physically challenging activities.

> **LET ME TELL YOU ABOUT OLIVER...**
>
> Oliver, a 5-year-old in Reception, often appeared oblivious to sensory stimuli around him. He had a low threshold for detecting sensory input and would often miss important cues during group activities. For example, he rarely noticed when his teacher was calling his name or when it was time to transition to the next activity. His teacher, in collaboration with the occupational therapist, introduced strategies to help Oliver become more aware of his surroundings. Oliver was provided with tactile reminders, like a small buzzer that he could feel in his pocket when it was time to switch tasks, and visual schedules that helped him anticipate transitions. With these adjustments, Oliver's responsiveness improved, and he was better able to stay on task and engage with his peers.

> **Reflective Prompts**
>
> *Oliver's under-registration of sensory input was addressed with tactile reminders and visual schedules. What cues or strategies do you use to help students who may be under-registered to sensory stimuli? How might you adjust your classroom environment to better support these students?*
>
> *Oliver's sensory under-registration was not immediately apparent, which is often the case. How can you improve your ability to observe and identify students who may be under-registered to sensory input and provide them with the right level of support?*

These examples provide a deeper understanding of how sensory-processing differences can manifest in children and how tailored interventions can support them in the classroom.

> **Reflective Prompt**
>
> *Think of a student who exhibits sensory-seeking, sensory-avoidant or sensory under-registration behaviours. How might you create a sensory-friendly environment or provide sensory input in a way that helps this student stay engaged and regulate their emotions?*

THE IMPACT OF SENSORY PROCESSING ON LEARNING

Sensory processing is closely linked to a child's ability to learn and engage in educational activities. When sensory processing functions optimally, a child can focus, attend to tasks, and absorb information effectively. For example, a child with well-regulated sensory processing is more likely to sit comfortably during a lesson, actively participate in group activities, and retain instruction from their teacher.

Conversely, difficulties in sensory processing can impede learning. A child who experiences sensory sensitivities may find it challenging to concentrate in a noisy classroom or may be overwhelmed by the feel of their clothes. These challenges can create barriers to effective learning and may lead to frustration and disengagement in the classroom.

Attention and Focus

At the heart of the connection between sensory processing and learning lies attention and focus. The brain's capacity to filter and prioritise sensory information directly influences a student's ability to concentrate on a task. For instance, a child who is hypersensitive to auditory stimuli may struggle to concentrate in a noisy classroom environment. Understanding and addressing these sensory challenges become crucial for creating an optimal learning environment that supports sustained attention.

Memory and Retrieval

Sensory experiences are closely linked to memory formation and retrieval. The brain often encodes information in conjunction with sensory stimuli, creating associations that enhance memory recall. Imagine a student learning about a historical event while engaging in a tactile activity related to that era. The sensory-rich experience becomes a cognitive aid, supporting the retention and retrieval of information during classwork or discussions.

Problem-Solving and Executive Functions

The cognitive processes involved in problem-solving and executive functions, such as planning and organising, also bear the imprint of sensory processing. Students with difficulties in sensory modulation may face challenges in organising their thoughts or adapting to changes in tasks. Recognising these sensory contributors to executive functions is crucial for educators in supporting students in developing effective problem-solving strategies.

Examples of Sensory Experiences Affecting Learning

One of the most powerful strategies you can use as an educator in supporting your students is to consider how they may be experiencing the world and put yourself in their shoes. This perspective shift is crucial in best supporting your students in the classroom. Here are some examples of how sensory experiences can affect students and how simple accommodations can make a huge difference to their learning experience:

Sight

Imagine if you were a child in the classroom: The bright fluorescent lights are overwhelming. You find it hard to concentrate on the board, and the flashing images from a projector are distracting. You feel anxious and frustrated because your eyes hurt.

Now imagine if, as a teacher, you adjusted the lighting to be softer or used natural light instead. This change means your student could now focus on the lesson without the discomfort of harsh lighting, allowing them to engage more effectively with the material.

Sound

Imagine if you were a child in the classroom: The chatter of your classmates and the constant noise of chairs scraping on the floor make it impossible to concentrate. You feel overstimulated and often zone out, missing important instructions.

Now imagine if, as a teacher, you implemented a quiet signal before starting a lesson or used noise-cancelling headphones. This means your student could now concentrate better and feel calmer, enabling them to absorb information more effectively.

Touch

Imagine if you were a child in the classroom: The texture of the classroom chair feels rough and uncomfortable against your skin, causing you to fidget. You struggle to stay still, which distracts you from learning.

Now imagine if, as a teacher, you provided flexible seating options. This means your student could now feel more comfortable and focused, leading to improved participation in class activities.

Taste

Imagine if you were a child in the classroom: You didn't eat breakfast, and your stomach is growling. The smell of food from the cafeteria is distracting, and you find it hard to concentrate on your work.

Now imagine if, as a teacher, you allowed a snack break or provided healthy snacks in class. This means your student could now focus on learning without the distraction of hunger, leading to better engagement and performance.

Smell

Imagine if you were a child in the classroom: The strong smell of cleaning products or food from the lunchroom makes you feel nauseous. It's hard to think clearly, and you become irritable.

Now imagine if, as a teacher, you ensured proper ventilation and avoided using strong-smelling cleaning products during class time. This means your student could now breathe easily and concentrate better, resulting in a more positive classroom experience.

Proprioception (Body Awareness)

Imagine if you were a child in the classroom: You often bump into things or find it hard to control your body, feeling clumsy and embarrassed. You struggle to write neatly, which makes you feel inadequate compared to your peers.

Now imagine if, as a teacher, you incorporated regular movement breaks or provided movement-rich learning activities. This means your student could now develop better body awareness and coordination, boosting their confidence and learning ability.

Vestibular (Balance and Movement)

Imagine if you were a child in the classroom: You feel dizzy when the class is moving around too much, making it hard for you to stay seated and focus on your work. This causes anxiety and frustration, as you worry about drawing attention to yourself.

Now imagine if, as a teacher, you included calming activities like desk push-ups or rocking in a controlled manner. This means your student could now find their balance and feel grounded, allowing them to engage more fully in classroom activities.

Interoception (Internal Body Sensations)

Imagine if you were a child in the classroom: You often feel overwhelmed and don't know why; you may be too hot or too cold, or need to use the restroom but don't realise it until it's too late. This makes you uncomfortable and distracted.

Now imagine if, as a teacher, you encouraged regular check-ins with students about their feelings and needs. This means your student could now learn to identify their internal cues, leading to improved self-regulation and focus during class.

Creating a Supportive Learning Environment

Understanding the impact of sensory processing on learning necessitates a proactive approach to creating a supportive learning environment. Educators can implement strategies that cater to diverse sensory needs, ensuring that each student has equitable access to the learning experience. This may involve offering sensory breaks, providing flexible seating options, and incorporating sensory-friendly materials into the curriculum.

In essence, the impact of sensory processing on learning is profound and multifaceted. From shaping attention and memory to influencing problem-solving and executive functions, sensory experiences lay the foundations of academic success for students. By recognising and addressing these sensory influences, educators can foster an inclusive learning environment where each student can thrive cognitively and academically. The journey towards effective education involves not only nurturing the mind but also understanding and embracing the diverse sensory pathways that shape the learning experience.

The Connection Between Sensory Processing and Behaviour

The link between sensory processing and behaviour is a nuanced interplay that significantly influences a child's experience in the classroom. This exploration delves into the profound connection between sensory processing and behaviour, offering insights into how sensory difficulties may manifest as challenging behaviours. By understanding this link, educators can navigate the complexities of classroom dynamics with a heightened awareness, fostering an environment that supports the diverse sensory needs of all students.

Children express themselves and communicate through behaviour, and when sensory processing is compromised, it can manifest as behavioural challenges. For instance, a child who struggles with sensory regulation might exhibit behaviours such as aggression, impulsivity, withdrawal, or difficulty with transitions.

Understanding the link between sensory processing and behaviour is crucial for educators. It allows them to recognise that disruptive or challenging behaviours may stem from sensory difficulties rather than intentional defiance. This awareness opens the door to more empathetic and effective strategies for managing behaviour and creating a supportive learning environment.

Regulation and Dysregulation

Central to the link between sensory processing and behaviour is the concept of regulation. Sensory processing serves as a key regulator for emotional and behavioural responses. When sensory input is well-modulated, a child can effectively regulate their emotions and behaviours. However, difficulties in sensory processing can lead to dysregulation, where a child may struggle to modulate their responses to stimuli.

Sensory-Seeking and Sensory-Avoidant Behaviours

Sensory-processing difficulties often manifest in two broad categories of behaviour: sensory seeking and sensory avoidant. Sensory-seeking behaviours involve a child actively seeking out sensory input to regulate their system. This might manifest as fidgeting, seeking touch, or moving around the classroom. On the other hand, sensory-avoidant behaviours involve a child attempting to withdraw or escape from sensory stimuli perceived as overwhelming. This could lead to behaviours such as refusal to participate in certain activities, covering ears in response to loud noises, or avoiding certain textures.

How Sensory Difficulties Manifest in Challenging Behaviours

Meltdowns and Shutdowns

One common manifestation of sensory difficulties in the classroom is the occurrence of meltdowns or shutdowns. For a child with sensory sensitivities, an overwhelming sensory experience can trigger an emotional response that goes beyond typical frustration. Meltdowns may involve intense emotional reactions, while shutdowns may result in withdrawal and a disengagement from the environment. Understanding the sensory triggers for these reactions is pivotal in developing strategies to prevent or manage such challenging behaviours.

Disruptions and Agitation

Sensory-processing challenges can also contribute to disruptions and agitation in the classroom. A child experiencing sensory overload may become agitated, leading to impulsive behaviours or difficulties in following instructions. Recognising the connection between sensory stimuli and disruptive behaviours enables educators to create an environment that minimises sensory triggers, promoting a calmer and more focused learning atmosphere.

Avoidance

In some instances, sensory difficulties may be expressed through avoidance behaviours. For example, a child who finds certain tactile sensations aversive may refuse to participate in activities involving those sensations. Understanding that avoidance may stem from sensory challenges rather than intentional defiance is essential for implementing effective strategies to encourage participation and engagement.

Supporting Students with Sensory Difficulties

Individualised Strategies

Recognising the link between sensory processing and behaviour opens the door to individualised strategies to support students with sensory difficulties. Collaboration with occupational therapists and other specialists can provide valuable insights into a child's sensory profile. Implementing personalised sensory breaks, offering alternative seating options, and providing sensory tools are examples of strategies that can help regulate sensory input and promote positive behaviour in the classroom.

Sensory-Friendly Classroom Design

Creating a sensory-friendly classroom environment is a proactive approach to managing behaviour related to sensory-processing difficulties. This involves thoughtful design considerations such as minimising visual and auditory distractions, incorporating sensory-friendly seating options, and providing designated sensory spaces where students can retreat when needed. These environmental adjustments contribute to a more inclusive and supportive learning atmosphere.

In conclusion, the link between sensory processing and behaviour is a crucial aspect of understanding and supporting students in the classroom. Sensory difficulties can manifest in a range of challenging behaviours, from meltdowns to avoidance, making it imperative for educators to approach behaviour management with a sensory lens. By fostering awareness of the sensory needs of each student and implementing targeted strategies, educators can create a learning environment that acknowledges and supports the diverse ways in which sensory processing influences behaviour. In embracing this connection, educators contribute not only to behaviour management but also to the overall well-being and success of every student in the classroom.

CONCLUSION

Understanding sensory processing and its impact on learning is fundamental for creating an inclusive classroom environment. By recognising the diverse sensory needs of students, educators can provide tailored support that promotes engagement, enhances learning outcomes, and fosters emotional well-being. Effective collaboration with therapists and families ensures that strategies are consistent across settings, contributing to the overall success of the child.

KEY TAKEAWAYS

- Sensory processing plays a critical role in child development, influencing learning, behaviour, and emotional regulation.
- Understanding and identifying sensory sensitivities, sensory seeking and sensory under-registration behaviours can help educators better support students in the classroom.
- Collaborative approaches between educators, therapists, and families are essential for ensuring consistent strategies and improving student outcomes.

REFERENCES AND RESOURCES

Ahn, R. R., Miller, L. J., Milberger, S., & McIntosh, D. N. (2004). Sensitivity to sensory stimulation in preschool children: The Short Sensory Profile. *Pediatrics, 113*(2), 274-281. doi:10.1542/peds.113.2.e274.

Brugnone, M. (2023). Differentiating sensory-processing issues from typical behaviours in preschool-aged children. [Capstone poster]. Cleveland State University.

Child Mind Institute. (n.d.). Understanding sensory processing issues. Available at https://childmind.org/article/sensory-processing-issues-explained/.

Dunn, W. (2001). *The Sensory Profile: User's Manual*. Psychological Corporation.

Kranowitz, C. S. (2015). *The Out-of-Sync Child: Recognizing and Coping with Sensory Processing Disorder*. Perigee Books.

Miller, L. J., Anzalone, M. E., Lane, S. J., Cermak, S. A., & Steele, M. (2007). The impact of sensory processing disorder on the daily lives of children and their families. *Journal of Pediatric Nursing, 22*(1), 3-9. doi:10.1016/j.pedn.2006.06.006.

Sensory Processing Disorder Foundation. (n.d.). What is Sensory Processing Disorder? Available at: https://sensoryhealth.org/basic/about-spd.

Sensory Integration Network (UK). (n.d.). *Resources for Understanding Sensory Processing*. Sensory Integration Network.

CHAPTER 3
EXPLORING SPEECH AND LANGUAGE CHALLENGES THROUGH THE CAN-DO APPROACH

WHY COMMUNICATION MATTERS

Communication is the heart of everything we do. It shapes our relationships, how we learn, and how we express ourselves. But it's more than just talking. Communication is about making connections – sharing our ideas, feelings, and needs with the world around us. For children, it's how they start building their independence and self-esteem.

LET ME TELL YOU ABOUT IVY...

Ivy is a little girl who started school with a vocabulary that would impress anyone. Long sentences, interesting facts – she could chatter away for ages. But after a few weeks, her teachers were puzzled. She wasn't engaging with the class, not answering questions, and often looked anxious. It seemed as though this confident, verbal child had suddenly become withdrawn.

When we looked deeper, we realised Ivy wasn't struggling with words; she was struggling with responding in a way the adults expected. Ivy could speak well when she initiated, but when asked to follow instructions or answer questions, the language demands were too much for her to process quickly. She was using her strengths – her memory and her ability to recall – but was overwhelmed when expected to create novel responses on the spot.

Here's how her teachers supported her:

1. **Reducing Language Demands:** Instead of asking Ivy open-ended questions like "What did you do this weekend?" her teachers began offering choices or prompts to help her formulate answers. For example, they would say, "Did you go to the park or stay at home?" This adjustment gave Ivy a structure to respond without feeling overwhelmed by the need to generate entirely new language.

DOI: 10.4324/9781003477266-3

2. **Using Visual Supports:** The teachers incorporated visual aids into Ivy's learning. For multi-step instructions, they used picture cards or written steps to accompany verbal directions. For instance, during an art activity, the instructions "Get your paper, choose a color, and start drawing" were paired with images of each step. This helped Ivy process the information at her own pace.
3. **Slowing the Pace of Interactions:** Recognising Ivy's need for more time to process, her teachers paused after asking questions or giving instructions. They would count silently to five to allow her time to think and respond without pressure. This simple change reduced her anxiety and encouraged her to participate more.
4. **Highlighting and Using Her Strengths:** Ivy excelled in memory and recall, so her teachers designed activities that leveraged these abilities. For example, during group discussions, they invited Ivy to share facts or details she had learned about a topic. Praising her ability to remember and explain information boosted her confidence and allowed her to shine in areas where she felt secure.

Ivy's story reminds us that communication challenges aren't always about what's obvious. Communication is much broader than just speech – it's also about social cues, understanding, processing information, and feeling safe enough to take part. And that's where our Can-Do Approach comes in. We don't just look at what's missing; we focus on what children **can do** and build from there.

COMMUNICATION AS AN UMBRELLA

Think of communication like an umbrella – there are many parts under it, and they all work together. It's not just about talking. It's about listening, understanding social rules, interpreting non-verbal cues, and figuring out how to respond. Some children, like Ivy, may excel in one part but struggle in another. Our job as educators and parents is to look at the whole picture, not just the parts that seem "broken".

For instance, verbal communication is just one part. Ivy had a lot of verbal strengths, but she struggled with social communication – understanding when it was her turn to speak or how to respond to questions. Then there's non-verbal communication, like body language, facial expressions, and gestures, which often say more than words. We must be tuned into these, especially for children who are late talkers or non-verbal, because this is how they communicate before speech.

EMBRACING EVERY WAY OF COMMUNICATING

When we embrace all forms of communication, we send a powerful message to children: **we see you, we hear you, and we value what you're saying**, whether that's through words, gestures, pictures, or behaviours.

Let's go back to Ryley. He was in nursery and not yet speaking. One day, his keyworker asked him to glue leaves onto a picture for an autumn project. But instead of following the instructions, Ryley scrunched the leaves up and threw them on the floor. His keyworker saw this as defiance, thinking Ryley was just refusing to follow the task. But when I watched him, I saw something different. Ryley wasn't being naughty – he simply didn't understand the instructions. The most interesting thing to him was how the leaves felt in his hands.

I showed him how to stick the leaves down, without using words, and he immediately joined in. This moment wasn't about fixing Ryley's behaviour; it was about understanding what he was communicating through his actions. His hands were telling us something, and once we "listened", he could move on to the task.

> **Reflective Prompt**
>
> Think about a recent situation where a child's behavior or actions seemed defiant. Could it have been their way of communicating something else? How might you have responded differently?

THE CAN-DO APPROACH TO COMMUNICATION

The Can-Do Approach encourages us to focus on what a child **can** do right now. It's about building on those strengths, whether that's in verbal or non-verbal communication, and not getting hung up on what they *can't* do. Children with communication challenges often feel overwhelmed in environments where they're expected to keep up with complex language, and their confidence takes a hit.

Here's another analogy: Imagine you're learning to ride a bike. If someone constantly points out what you're doing wrong – "you're wobbling", "you can't steer straight" – you'll soon lose the confidence to try again. But if they praise the bits you're getting right, no matter how small, you'll keep going. Communication is the same. When we focus on the parts a child can manage, we help them grow.

CONTINUOUS COMMUNICATION: IT'S HAPPENING ALL THE TIME

Communication isn't something that only happens during designated times, like when we're asking children to follow instructions or answer questions. It's happening all day, every day, in all kinds of ways. Children are constantly communicating through their actions, their facial expressions, and even their silence. And as educators and parents, it's our job to tune in, notice, and respond.

Imagine you've had a long, hard day at work. You walk into the staff room with a heavy sigh, and one of your colleagues looks up, sees your face, and immediately asks if you're okay. You didn't say anything, but you communicated plenty through your body language. Now, what if no one had noticed? Or worse, what if someone started asking you about some work project instead of checking in on how you're feeling?

Children experience this same disconnect when their non-verbal communication isn't picked up on. They're telling us something, but if we're too focused on their words - or lack of them - we can miss the real message. That's why a huge part of the Can-Do Approach is learning to read the cues children give us throughout the day, even if they're not using speech.

BRINGING COMMUNICATION INTO EVERYDAY MOMENTS

One of the key principles of the Can-Do Approach is integrating communication support into everyday routines and activities. We don't need to set up special speech therapy sessions or create complex interventions. Often, the most powerful opportunities for building communication come from the simplest moments in the day.

Take **lunchtime**, for example. Instead of asking a non-verbal child what they want and waiting in silence for them to answer, we can offer choices visually or with gestures. Hold up two options - "Do you want the apple or the banana?" - and give them the space to communicate in a way that works for them. Whether they point, sign, or use a picture card, the key is they're communicating, and we're giving them the tools to do so confidently.

Then there's **playtime**, which is filled with opportunities for communication. Instead of focusing on getting the child to say specific words, we can join in their play and talk about what they're doing, introducing language in a natural, enjoyable way. If a child is pushing a toy car, we can say, "Wow, your car is going fast!" This kind of back-and-forth interaction is where real language development happens - not in isolated sessions but in the moments that matter to the child.

FINDING MAGIC MOMENTS: COMMUNICATION THROUGH INTERESTS

One of the most effective ways to build a child's confidence in communication is by tapping into their interests. When we meet them where they are - whether they're obsessed with dinosaurs, cars, or anything else - we can use that passion as a springboard for communication.

I've seen this countless times with the children I've worked with. Take **Leo**, for instance. He was a little boy with limited speech but a huge love for trains. His parents were worried because he wasn't using many words and struggled to engage in conversations. But the moment we brought trains into the picture, everything changed. Instead of trying to force language out of him in formal settings, we used his love of trains to spark interactions. We'd set up train tracks together, talk about the colours of the trains, and even make up little stories about where they were going.

These were what I call **Magic Moments** - those times when a child is fully engaged and open to learning because they're doing something they love. It's in these moments that we can sneak in language without it feeling like work. And for Leo, it wasn't long before he started using more words because he felt confident and connected.

The Can-Do Approach teaches us that **every child has something they're passionate about**, and when we find that thing, we've found the key to unlocking their communication potential.

> **Reflective Prompt**
>
> Reflect on the children you work with. What are their "magic moments" - the activities or interests that light them up? How could you incorporate these interests into building their communication skills?

BUILDING COMMUNICATION CONFIDENCE

A big part of what makes communication challenges so difficult for children is the **hit to their confidence**. Imagine being surrounded by people speaking a language you barely understand, and every time you try to join in, it feels like you're getting it wrong. That's what it's like for many children with speech and language difficulties.

When a child's attempts at communication go unnoticed or unacknowledged, their confidence takes a blow. They may stop trying altogether, not because they don't want to communicate, but because they've learned that their attempts aren't successful. That's why it's so important for us to **recognise and celebrate every form of communication**, no matter how subtle.

In the Can-Do Approach, we focus on what the child **can do** right now. If they're pointing, that's fantastic. If they're making sounds or gestures, we respond as if they've communicated perfectly because, in their own way, they have. This doesn't mean we don't encourage progress, but we build from a place of strength, not frustration.

Let's go back to **Ivy**. After her teachers began responding differently - recognising the strengths she did have and reducing the language demands in situations that were hard for her - she started to thrive. The classroom became a place where she could engage on her own terms, and with her confidence growing, her communication skills followed.

SEEING COMMUNICATION IN BEHAVIOUR

Sometimes, the most powerful communication doesn't come in words at all - it comes in behaviour. Many children with communication challenges use their actions to express what they can't yet say verbally. Unfortunately, this often gets misinterpreted as "bad behaviour".

LET ME TELL YOU ABOUT...

George is a five-year-old who struggled with both speech and understanding. During group activities, George would often push other children or get frustrated and throw things. His teachers initially saw this as disruptive behaviour and felt George was lashing out. But when we looked closer, it was clear that George's pushing wasn't aggression - it was communication. He was overwhelmed by the language demands around him and didn't have the words to ask for help or explain his frustration. His behaviour was his way of saying, "I can't cope".

Once we started seeing George's actions as communication, everything shifted. We made sure he had simpler instructions, more time to process, and ways to ask for help that didn't require speech, like pointing to a picture or raising his hand. Almost immediately, the pushing stopped. George didn't need to lash out anymore because he had a way to express himself.

Here's how his teacher supported him:

1. **Simplifying Instructions:** The teacher broke down group activity instructions into smaller, manageable steps and paired them with visual cues. Instead of saying, "Everyone, sit in a circle, take a partner, and start working on this puzzle", they provided step-by-step guidance using pictures: "First, sit here" (with a picture of the circle), "Next, find a partner" (with an image of two children). This clarity helped George understand what was expected and reduced his feelings of overwhelm.
2. **Creating a Visual Schedule:** The teacher introduced a visual daily schedule, showing George what was coming next. For example, during transitions between activities, the schedule included images like a puzzle for group work and a playground for free time. Knowing what to expect helped George feel more secure and prepared, reducing his need to act out.
3. **Introducing Break Cards:** Recognising George's need to step away when he felt overstimulated, the teacher introduced "break cards". George could hold up a card with a picture of a quiet space whenever he needed a moment to regulate himself. This gave him an alternative to pushing or throwing objects and empowered him to communicate his needs non-verbally.
4. **Building Positive Peer Interactions:** The teacher facilitated structured, low-pressure opportunities for George to engage with peers. For example, during activities, they paired him with a buddy who was patient and understanding. They also modeled how to take turns and share materials, helping George feel more confident in social situations.

The Can-Do Approach encourages us to see beyond the behaviour and understand the message behind it. By doing this, we not only support the child's communication development but also help reduce challenging behaviours that stem from frustration.

> **Reflective Prompt**
>
> How might you better recognise a child's behavior as communication in your setting? What strategies could you implement to meet the child's needs?

EMPOWERING CHILDREN THROUGH COMMUNICATION

At the core of the Can-Do Approach is the belief that communication empowers children. It gives them a voice, a way to express who they are, what they need, and what they want from the world around them. And when we help children build confidence in their ability to communicate – whether that's through words, gestures, pictures, or behaviour – we're giving them the tools they need to navigate life with independence and self-assurance.

Take **Sophie**, for example, a child who hadn't spoken much at home or in school. Her parents were understandably anxious, wondering if she'd ever start talking. But instead of focusing solely on speech, we worked on giving Sophie other ways to communicate – using pictures, signs, and even some simple technology. Over time, as she realised she could get her needs met and make herself understood, Sophie's confidence grew. And guess what? The words started coming too, because she felt safe and empowered.

Communication isn't just about language; it's about connection. When children feel connected to the people around them – when they know their efforts at communication are heard and valued – they're more likely to keep trying, to explore, and to grow.

> **Reflective Prompt**
>
> Think about a child who may feel unheard or unsupported. What small changes could you make to give them a voice in everyday interactions?

FOCUSING ON WHAT THEY CAN DO: A SHIFT IN PERSPECTIVE

One of the most fundamental shifts the Can-Do Approach offers is focusing on what children *can* do, rather than what they *can't*. Traditional approaches to speech and language challenges often fixate on deficits – what the child isn't doing yet, how they're falling behind. But this can leave both the child and the adults around them feeling frustrated and disheartened.

Take **Ellie**, for instance. She's a 4-year-old who hadn't yet started talking when she came to us. Her parents were understandably anxious. They'd been to multiple professionals, each one providing lists of what Ellie couldn't do – how far behind she was, how concerning her lack of speech was. This left her parents feeling hopeless and Ellie, though unaware of the specifics, likely sensed the tension around her communication.

When we met Ellie, we flipped the script. Instead of focusing on the absence of words, we looked at what Ellie could already do. She was pointing, using eye contact, making sounds, and engaging in her own unique way. We built on that. We responded to her gestures and sounds as if they were full sentences because, to Ellie, they were. Over time, as her confidence grew, so did her communication. Speech followed when Ellie felt understood and supported in the ways she was already expressing herself.

This change in focus - from deficit to strength - is the cornerstone of the Can-Do Approach. Children like Ellie aren't stuck; they just need the space to communicate in the ways they're already capable of and to build from there. It's about celebrating every small success, knowing that these successes lay the foundation for greater progress.

THE POWER OF ROUTINE: EVERYDAY OPPORTUNITIES FOR COMMUNICATION

Routines are gold mines for communication. Every day, children engage in activities like snack time, getting dressed, or tidying up, and these moments provide natural opportunities to build communication skills. In the Can-Do Approach, we see these daily routines not as mundane tasks but as chances to model language, offer choices, and encourage children to express themselves.

Let's look at **Jasper**, a 3-year-old who had difficulty using words to express his needs. His parents often did everything for him - dressed him, fed him, and chose his toys - because it was faster and easier than waiting for Jasper to figure out how to ask. But this approach wasn't helping Jasper develop his communication skills; it was reinforcing his silence.

By integrating communication into daily routines, Jasper's parents started to offer him simple choices: "Do you want the red shirt or the blue one?" instead of just dressing him without asking. When he pointed, they would say, "Oh, you chose the blue shirt!" By labeling his choices and giving him time to respond, they created countless opportunities for Jasper to practice communicating, even without words.

Snack time became another communication moment. Instead of just giving Jasper his snack, they held up two options - "Do you want a banana or a cracker?" Again, Jasper didn't have to use words, but by pointing or gesturing, he was making decisions and communicating. Over time, as he became more confident, Jasper began to add in words - "cracker" or "banana" - because he felt in control of the process.

The Can-Do Approach encourages us to embed communication into these everyday moments. The beauty of routines is their predictability, which gives children the security to try new things, including communication, in a familiar context.

MAGIC MOMENTS: TAPPING INTO INTERESTS TO SPARK COMMUNICATION

Every child has something that lights them up—whether it's dinosaurs, cars, animals, or dancing. These moments, when a child is fully engaged in their favourite activity, are what we call **Magic Moments**. These are the times when their brains are most open to learning because they're doing something they love.

For **Harry**, it was all about construction. He didn't talk much in school, and when he did, his speech was often unclear. But when the class moved into the building blocks area, Harry came alive. He would spend ages creating elaborate structures, deeply focused and proud of his work. His teacher saw this as an opportunity. She joined him in the play, commenting on what he was doing: "Wow, Harry, your tower is so tall!" or "I love how you've used the red block here". Gradually, Harry began responding, first with gestures, then with single words, and eventually with full sentences like, "I'm building a castle".

Magic Moments are like open doors to communication. When a child is deeply engaged in something they love, they're more likely to interact, and these interactions build confidence. The Can-Do Approach teaches us to seize these moments, join in the child's interests, and use them as stepping stones to communication.

CREATING INTERACTION-FRIENDLY ENVIRONMENTS

An interaction-friendly environment is one where social, collaborative, supportive interactions are valued and championed. It's an environment that respects all forms of communication – spoken words, signs, gestures, pictures, or behaviour – and responds to them in meaningful ways.

Creating this kind of environment doesn't require complicated tools or special equipment. It's about creating a space where children are supported to express themselves. One of the best ways to do this is by giving children plenty of **choices** throughout the day. Choices give children the power to express their preferences and make decisions, which builds confidence and helps them feel understood.

> ### LET ME TELL YOU ABOUT SASHA...
>
> Sasha is a child who has very limited speech but loved music. At school, when it was time to choose songs during circle time, Sasha's teacher gave her a simple choice: "Do you want 'Twinkle Twinkle' or 'Wheels on the Bus?'" Sasha pointed to the picture of "Twinkle Twinkle", and the teacher said, "Twinkle!" By responding to her choice as if she had spoken, the teacher validated Sasha's communication and encouraged her to keep participating.
>
> In a interaction-friendly environment, **all communication is valued**. Whether it's a word, a gesture, or a picture, we respond as if it were a sentence. This helps children feel empowered and understood, which is essential for building their communication skills.

EMPATHY AND PATIENCE: KEYS TO UNLOCKING COMMUNICATION

One of the most important aspects of supporting children with communication challenges is **empathy**. It's about putting ourselves in the child's shoes and imagining what it must feel like to want to communicate but struggle to do so. When we approach communication with empathy, we naturally become more patient, giving the child the time and space they need to express themselves.

Take **Mia**, a little girl who was often misunderstood because her speech wasn't clear. Her classmates would get frustrated when they couldn't understand her, and sometimes, even the adults around her would rush her or finish her sentences for her. This only made Mia more anxious, and soon, she started speaking less.

But when Mia's teacher began practicing more empathy and patience, everything changed. Instead of rushing Mia or asking her to repeat herself, the teacher slowed down, gave her time, and listened carefully. She didn't interrupt or fill in the gaps. And when she wasn't sure what Mia was saying, she would ask gently, "Can you show me?" or "Let's figure it out together". With this new approach, Mia felt less pressure and began to open up more. Her speech improved too, because she wasn't afraid of getting it wrong.

The Can-Do Approach is grounded in empathy. It's about understanding that communication is hard for some children and that our job is to make it easier, not more stressful. **Patience** is one of the greatest gifts we can give a child who is learning to communicate.

LONG-TERM SUCCESS: COMMUNICATION BEYOND THE CLASSROOM

The skills children develop through communication aren't just for the classroom – they're for life. Being able to express themselves, make choices, and connect with others is foundational to their success in all areas of life.

Think about **Anna**, who struggled with communication in her early years but, thanks to the support of her teachers and parents, gradually found her voice. Today, Anna is thriving, not just academically but socially too. She's confident in making friends, sharing her ideas, and asking for what she needs. The foundation laid by focusing on what Anna could do, building her confidence, and giving her the tools to communicate in her own way has carried her far beyond the classroom.

The Can-Do Approach is about preparing children for these long-term successes. It's about helping them build the skills they'll need to navigate the world, form relationships, and advocate for themselves. **Communication is a lifelong skill**, and by giving children the confidence to express themselves, we're setting them up for success, not just today, but for the rest of their lives.

BEHAVIOUR AS COMMUNICATION: UNDERSTANDING THE MESSAGE BEHIND ACTIONS

One of the key tenets of the Can-Do Approach is recognising that **all behaviour is a form of communication**. When a child acts out, it's often because they're trying to tell us something but don't have the words or the means to express it. Understanding this shifts our perspective from managing 'bad behaviour' to understanding the unmet need behind it.

LET ME TELL YOU ABOUT DANIEL . . .

Daniel was a 6-year-old who was constantly getting into trouble at school. He would hit other children, refuse to sit during circle time, and would often run around the room during lessons. His teachers felt frustrated, and Daniel seemed to be getting more isolated from his peers. When I observed Daniel, it became clear that he wasn't being defiant – he was overwhelmed. The noise of the classroom, the constant instructions, and the expectation to sit still were too much for him. Daniel didn't have the language to ask for a break or say he didn't understand, so he used his behaviour to 'speak.'

Once we understood this, we gave Daniel ways to communicate his need for a break. We introduced a simple visual card system: when he felt overwhelmed, he could hold up a picture of a quiet space, and he'd be allowed a few minutes away from the noise. His teachers also started using simpler language and gave him visual prompts to follow instructions. Almost immediately, Daniel's behaviour improved – not because we were 'disciplining' him better, but because we were **listening to what his behaviour was communicating**.

The Can-Do Approach teaches us to look deeper at the behaviour and understand the child's underlying communication. Often, what looks like defiance or disinterest is really frustration, confusion, or sensory overload. By giving children tools to express their needs – whether that's with words, visuals, or gestures – we reduce challenging behaviours and build a more supportive environment.

REDUCING THE PRESSURE: TAKING THE FOCUS OFF 'PERFECT' SPEECH

In many traditional approaches to speech and language therapy, there's a heavy focus on achieving 'perfect' speech. Children are often asked to repeat words or phrases until they get them right, with the idea that practice will make perfect. But this can sometimes backfire, especially for children who are already struggling to communicate. The pressure to speak correctly can make them anxious, leading to avoidance or frustration.

In the Can-Do Approach, we take a different stance: **the message matters more than the delivery**. It's not about whether the child's speech is clear or grammatically correct; it's about whether they're able to express what they need to say. Once children feel heard and understood, the clarity often follows naturally, because the pressure is off.

Take **Tommy**, for instance, a 7-year-old who had difficulty with articulation. His speech was often hard to understand, and his teachers would ask him to slow down and try again. But the more they focused on getting the words 'right,' the more frustrated Tommy became. He started talking less, not because he couldn't, but because he was afraid of getting it wrong.

When we began working with Tommy, we made a conscious effort to **focus on the content of what he was saying** rather than how clearly he said it. Instead of correcting him, we would listen carefully and respond to his message. If we weren't sure what he meant, we'd ask gentle, open-ended questions like, "Can you tell me more about that?" This shift in approach took the pressure off Tommy. He started speaking more because he knew his words were being valued, and over time, his clarity improved as well. It wasn't about drilling him on speech sounds – it was about making him feel confident and heard.

TAILORING SUPPORT: EVERY CHILD'S COMMUNICATION JOURNEY IS UNIQUE

One of the most important aspects of the Can-Do Approach is recognising that **every child's communication journey is different**. There's no one-size-fits-all solution when it comes to supporting speech and language development. Each child has their own strengths, preferences, and challenges, and our role is to tailor the support to meet their individual needs.

For some children, **visual supports** like picture cards or symbols are essential for helping them understand and communicate. For others, **gestures** or **signs** may be their preferred method of expression. Some children, like **Max**, might benefit from a combination of approaches.

Max was a non-verbal 4-year-old with a deep love for animals. His parents were worried that he wasn't talking yet, but Max had other ways of communicating. He would bring picture books with animals to his parents, point to the animals he liked, and make the corresponding animal noises. While his speech was delayed, his understanding of language was strong. Instead of focusing on getting Max to say words, we introduced **visual schedules** and **signs** that helped him communicate what he wanted and needed. Over time, Max's confidence grew, and he began to use words more naturally, alongside his signs and gestures.

The Can-Do Approach embraces the idea that **communication is multi-faceted**. We don't need to force children into one particular method of expression. Instead, we support them in whatever way feels natural and empowering to them, knowing that speech may come, but it's not the only valid form of communication.

COLLABORATION IS KEY: WORKING WITH FAMILIES AND EDUCATORS

One of the most powerful aspects of the Can-Do Approach is the emphasis on **collaboration**. Supporting a child's communication development isn't the responsibility of just one person - it's a team effort. This team includes parents, teachers, speech therapists, and other professionals who work with the child regularly.

Take **Sophie**, for example. Sophie was a non-verbal 5-year-old who used a mix of gestures, pictures, and sounds to communicate. Her parents were doing their best to support her at home, but they felt disconnected from what was happening at school, where Sophie spent most of her day. Her teacher, meanwhile, was using different strategies in the classroom but wasn't sure how to coordinate with the family.

The Can-Do Approach encourages open communication between home and school, ensuring that everyone is on the same page. For Sophie, this meant creating a **communication passport** - a simple document that outlined how Sophie communicated, what strategies worked best for her, and how both her parents and teachers could support her in a consistent way. By sharing this information, Sophie's parents and teacher were able to work together, using the same strategies and reinforcing each other's efforts. This consistency helped Sophie feel more secure and supported, and her communication improved across all settings.

Collaboration also extends to **listening to the child themselves**. Even if a child isn't using words, they have preferences and ways of expressing what works for them. By paying attention to these cues and being flexible in our approach, we can make sure that the support we're providing is tailored to the child's individual needs.

LOOKING FORWARD: BUILDING LIFELONG COMMUNICATION SKILLS

The ultimate goal of the Can-Do Approach isn't just about helping children communicate in the here and now - it's about building skills that will serve them for the rest of their lives. Communication is a tool for independence, for forming relationships, and for advocating for one's own needs. By supporting children's communication development in a way that builds confidence and connection, we're setting them up for success in all areas of life.

For children like **Anna**, who started her journey with significant speech and language delays, the future looks bright because of the strong foundation that was laid early on. Anna may not have been the most verbal child in her early years, but through consistent support, patience, and a focus on her strengths, she developed the skills to navigate school, friendships, and eventually the workplace with confidence.

In the Can-Do Approach, we recognise that communication doesn't stop developing when children leave school. It's a skill that continues to grow and evolve throughout their lives, and the tools we give them today will help them succeed in the future. Whether they become leaders, creators, or carers, the confidence to express themselves will carry them far.

REDUCING THE PRESSURE: LETTING COMMUNICATION FLOW NATURALLY

For some children, the challenge isn't about having the words - they have them, but they struggle to get them out smoothly. This is often the case for children who **stammer**. Stammering, or stuttering, can create anxiety around speaking, as children become hyper-aware of their speech and feel pressured to get it "right". In the Can-Do Approach, we take the pressure off, focusing on the message rather than the delivery.

Let's look at **Jack**, a bright and energetic 8-year-old who loved storytelling but often got stuck when trying to speak. His stammer would cause him to repeat sounds or pause, and he'd often lose his confidence mid-sentence. The more his teachers or peers tried to help - by encouraging him to 'slow down' or 'take a deep breath' - the more anxious Jack became, and the stammer would worsen.

In the Can-Do Approach, we learned that the best way to support Jack was to **reduce the pressure** around his speech. Instead of focusing on the stammer itself, we focused on what he was saying, not how he was saying it. We gave him space to speak without interruption, listened patiently, and responded to his ideas. If Jack got stuck, we didn't finish his sentence for him or ask him to repeat it. We let him know that we were interested in his story, no matter how long it took to tell it.

Over time, Jack began to relax. The stammer didn't disappear overnight, but he felt less anxious about speaking because he knew people were listening to what he was saying, not judging how he was saying it. And as his confidence grew, so did his fluency. The Can-Do Approach teaches us that **patience and understanding** are key to helping children with speech challenges like stammering. When we take the pressure off, we make room for their natural communication to flow.

SUPPORTING GESTALT LANGUAGE PROCESSORS: SEEING THE BIGGER PICTURE

Some children approach language differently - they don't learn it in a linear, step-by-step way. These children are often **gestalt language processors**, meaning they learn language in chunks or phrases rather than individual words. While this might seem unusual at first, it's simply another way of processing the world, and the Can-Do Approach helps us support children by understanding how they learn and communicate.

Maya was a perfect example of a gestalt language processor. At 4 years old, she didn't speak in single words like "juice" or "toy" like her peers. Instead, she would repeat whole phrases she'd heard from TV shows or books, such as "Let's go on an adventure!" or "I can't find my shoes!" At first, her parents and teachers were confused, wondering why Maya wasn't using more typical language. But Maya wasn't behind - she was just learning language differently.

The Can-Do Approach helped us see that Maya was using **echolalia** (repeating phrases) as a way to communicate and make sense of language. Rather than correcting her or trying to get her to speak in single words, we celebrated her use of language chunks and gradually introduced new phrases that were relevant to her experiences. If Maya said, "Let's go on an adventure!" when she wanted to go outside, we responded, "Yes, let's go outside and play!" By acknowledging her way of communicating and building on it, we helped Maya feel understood and gave her the tools to expand her language over time.

With gestalt language processors like Maya, the Can-Do Approach teaches us to **meet them where they are**. Instead of trying to change how they learn, we use their strengths to support their communication development. Over time, as their language grows, they begin to break down these chunks and use more flexible and creative language.

RELUCTANT TALKERS: SUPPORTING SELECTIVE MUTES WITHOUT PRESSURE

Some children are fully capable of speaking but choose not to, especially in certain settings. This is often the case with children who experience **selective mutism**, a form of anxiety where a child is reluctant to speak in specific situations, like school, even though they're verbal at home. In these cases, pressure to talk can make the situation worse, so the Can-Do Approach focuses on creating a safe, low-pressure environment where communication of any kind is encouraged.

Lily was a classic example of a selective mute. At home, she was chatty and expressive, but in the classroom, she was silent. Her teachers were concerned, and some even thought Lily was being stubborn or shy. But this wasn't about willpower - Lily wanted to talk but felt too anxious to do so in school.

Instead of pushing Lily to speak, we created an interaction-friendly **environment** where she felt safe. We encouraged her to communicate in any way she felt comfortable - whether through gestures, nodding, pointing, or even writing things down. Over time, as Lily realised that she wasn't being forced to talk, she began to relax. We also gave her a small buddy group, letting her spend time with just a couple of trusted friends instead of the whole class. These small, supportive interactions built her confidence slowly.

The turning point came when Lily used her voice, almost unexpectedly, to answer a question during a quiet activity. Her teacher responded calmly, as if it were the most natural thing in the world, without making a big deal of it. This calm, pressure-free response allowed Lily to speak more freely in the future, and eventually, her selective mutism began to lift.

The Can-Do Approach teaches us that **pressure creates silence**, and **patience creates safety**. By taking the focus off talking and encouraging other forms of communication, we give children like Lily the space they need to feel confident and safe enough to use their voices when they're ready.

BUILDING CONNECTION: THE HEART OF COMMUNICATION

At the centre of the Can-Do Approach is **connection**. Communication isn't just about words, sentences, or speech - it's about connecting with others, forming relationships, and feeling understood. When we focus on connection, we create an environment where children feel safe to express themselves, even if their communication looks different from what we expect.

Let's think about **Ella**, a 5-year-old who struggled to communicate verbally. She wasn't diagnosed with any specific language disorder, but she found it difficult to connect with her classmates and teachers. Ella wasn't very talkative, and when she did speak, it was often short and abrupt. She felt disconnected, and this led to frustration for both her and the adults around her.

When we started working with Ella, we shifted the focus from getting her to 'talk more' to simply **building connection**. During playtime, instead of asking Ella lots of questions or encouraging her to speak, her teacher began to **follow Ella's lead** - joining in with her play silently, matching her pace, and responding to her non-verbal communication. They built towers together, shared smiles, and laughed when the towers fell. Through this shared activity, Ella began to feel more connected to her teacher. Over time, she started speaking more, but it wasn't because she was being pushed - it was because she felt connected and confident.

The Can-Do Approach recognises that **communication grows out of connection**. When children feel safe and valued for who they are, they are more likely to communicate in ways that feel comfortable to them. By building relationships and focusing on connection, we create a foundation for all other forms of communication to flourish.

CO-REGULATION: SUPPORTING EMOTIONAL AND COMMUNICATION DEVELOPMENT

Another key aspect of the Can-Do Approach is **co-regulation**, which refers to the way adults can help children manage their emotions and behaviours through calm, supportive interactions. When children are dysregulated - whether they're feeling frustrated, anxious, or overwhelmed - their ability to communicate often shuts down. This is where co-regulation comes in.

Think about **Aiden**, a 6-year-old with language delays who would frequently have meltdowns during transitions between activities. He would get upset, cry, and sometimes even throw things when it was time to move from one task to the next. His teachers often responded by asking him to use his words or by reminding him to calm down, but this only seemed to escalate the situation.

Through the Can-Do Approach, we introduced the idea of co-regulation. Instead of asking Aiden to regulate his emotions on his own, we modelled calmness for him. When it was time to transition, his teacher would sit close to him, speak in a calm and soothing voice, and offer a visual schedule to show what was coming next. If Aiden got upset, she didn't push him to speak or follow instructions right away. Instead, she waited with him, breathing slowly and staying with him until he felt ready. This calm presence helped Aiden regulate his emotions, and once he felt calm, he was much more able to communicate his needs.

Co-regulation is essential for children with communication challenges. When adults regulate their own emotions and provide a calm, predictable presence, children feel supported and safe. Over time, they learn to regulate their own emotions and become more confident communicators because they know that they have the space and support to express themselves.

LONG-TERM SUCCESS: COMMUNICATION SKILLS BEYOND THE CLASSROOM

The Can-Do Approach isn't just about immediate progress - it's about setting children up for long-term success in all areas of life. Communication is the foundation for building relationships, navigating social situations, and becoming independent. By focusing on what children can do and helping them develop their strengths, we're giving them tools that will last a lifetime.

Let's take **Sam**, a teenager who had been through years of speech and language therapy. He had always struggled with expressive language, especially in social situations. In school, he rarely raised his hand to participate, even though he often knew the answer. Sam's teachers were concerned that his lack of participation would affect his confidence and social relationships.

Instead of focusing solely on Sam's speech, we began working on **social scripts** - practicing common social interactions and giving Sam the tools he needed to feel more comfortable in conversations. We didn't just focus on 'fixing' his speech; we focused on helping Sam feel more prepared for the real-life situations he would face outside the classroom. By practicing these scenarios in a safe, supportive environment, Sam began to feel more confident in his ability to communicate with others.

Over time, Sam's participation in class improved, and he even began making more friends. His teachers noticed that once Sam felt more confident in his social skills, his expressive language also began to improve. The Can-Do Approach had given him the tools he needed to succeed, not just in school, but in life.

EMPATHY IN ACTION: LISTENING TO THE WHOLE CHILD

At the core of the Can-Do Approach is **empathy** - not just for the child's communication challenges, but for their whole experience. It's about seeing the child as more than their difficulties and understanding that communication is deeply tied to their emotional and social well-being.

Let's talk about **Leah**, a 10-year-old who struggled with both communication and emotional regulation. Leah would often shut down during class, refusing to engage in activities or interact with her peers. Her teachers saw this as defiance, but when we looked closer, we saw that Leah was experiencing deep anxiety about making mistakes. She wasn't refusing to engage; she was overwhelmed by the pressure to get things right.

In the Can-Do Approach, we worked with Leah's teachers to shift the focus from academic performance to **emotional support**. Instead of pushing Leah to complete her work or engage in conversations, her teachers began to focus on creating a calm, supportive environment where Leah could express her feelings in whatever way felt comfortable to her. They used **visual supports**, **calming strategies**, and **quiet spaces** to help Leah regulate her emotions.

Once Leah felt safe and understood, she began to open up. She started participating more in class discussions, and her anxiety about making mistakes gradually lessened. Her communication skills followed as she felt more confident and capable.

The Can-Do Approach reminds us that empathy is the foundation for supporting children's communication development. When we see the whole child and understand the emotional factors that impact their ability to communicate, we can create environments where they feel safe, supported, and empowered to express themselves.

THE POWER OF PLAY: COMMUNICATION THROUGH JOY

Play is one of the most natural ways that children communicate. Through play, they express their thoughts, emotions, and ideas in ways that often go beyond words. The Can-Do Approach recognises the power of play in supporting communication, especially for children who may struggle with more formal language.

For **Tom**, a 3-year-old with delayed speech, traditional speech therapy exercises were frustrating. He didn't enjoy sitting down for structured activities, and asking him to repeat words or practice speech sounds felt like a chore. But when we introduced **play-based communication strategies**, everything changed.

Tom loved building with blocks, so we used this as an opportunity for language development. Instead of asking Tom to say words, we joined in his play, narrating what he was doing: "You're building a tall tower!" or "Oh no, the blocks fell down!" Through this natural, playful interaction, Tom started to pick up new words and phrases without feeling pressured.

Play creates a sense of **joy and freedom**, which is essential for building communication skills. The Can-Do Approach teaches us that when children are engaged and having fun, they're more open to learning new language and expressing themselves. By incorporating play into our communication support, we help children develop their skills in a way that feels natural, enjoyable, and meaningful.

SCAFFOLDING COMMUNICATION: BUILDING ON STRENGTHS

One of the most powerful tools in the Can-Do Approach is **scaffolding** – a method where we build on what a child can already do to help them reach the next level of communication. This means we're always focusing on strengths, not deficits. Instead of highlighting what a child can't do, we look for the small successes and use those as the foundation to keep growing their communication skills.

Take **Zara**, a 7-year-old who used very few words but had a strong understanding of what others were saying. Zara's parents were concerned about her limited speech and felt stuck in how to help her communicate more. They had tried flashcards and repetitive drills, but these felt like chores to Zara, and she began avoiding them.

Through the Can-Do Approach, we focused on **scaffolding**. We used Zara's love for drawing as the starting point. Instead of asking her to say words directly, we started with simple activities where she could draw what she wanted to talk about. As she drew, we provided language that matched her actions – "You're drawing a cat! What a great cat!" Zara didn't need to repeat anything or feel pressure, but over time, as we kept layering in language around her interests, she started using more words herself.

Scaffolding allows us to **meet the child where they are** and then gently encourage them to reach beyond their current abilities. For Zara, this meant using her love of drawing as a way to start building her language in a non-threatening, engaging way. This method can be applied across many different communication challenges, and it always comes back to **starting with the child's strengths**.

CHOICE AND CONTROL: EMPOWERING CHILDREN THROUGH COMMUNICATION

One of the biggest factors that can limit a child's ability to communicate is a feeling of **lack of control**. For children who struggle with language, many daily situations – like snack time, transitions, or group activities – can feel overwhelming because they don't have the words to express their needs or make decisions. The Can-Do Approach teaches us that **giving children choice and control** can significantly reduce frustration and increase their confidence in communication.

Consider **Nina**, a 5-year-old who was mostly non-verbal but fully capable of making decisions. In group settings, Nina would often become agitated and withdraw, which her teachers initially interpreted as disinterest. But when we looked more closely, we saw that Nina was frustrated because she wasn't given a say in what was happening.

We began giving Nina more **choices** throughout her day. During snack time, we used visual cards with pictures of different foods, allowing Nina to point to what she wanted instead of waiting for her to verbalise it. The same approach was used during playtime – Nina could choose which activity she wanted by pointing to a picture or simply bringing the toy she preferred to the group. As her teachers responded to her choices, Nina's frustration eased, and she became more engaged. Over time, as Nina became more comfortable, she started using words to express her preferences.

In the Can-Do Approach, we understand that communication isn't just about words – it's about **agency**. By offering choices, we give children like Nina the chance to take control of their environment and express their needs in ways that feel manageable to them. As they experience success in making choices, their confidence grows, and they are more likely to take communication risks, including using more words.

WORKING AS A TEAM: THE ROLE OF EDUCATORS, PARENTS, AND PEERS

Supporting children with communication challenges isn't a solo job – it's a team effort. Whether we're working in a classroom, at home, or in a playgroup, the **collaborative effort** between adults and peers is vital. The Can-Do Approach encourages all the key players in a child's life – parents, teachers, therapists, and friends – to work together to provide a **consistent, supportive environment** for the child's communication development.

Let's take **Ollie**, a 6-year-old with speech delays, as an example. Ollie's teachers were concerned because he wasn't speaking much at school, even though his parents reported that he was talking more at home. There was a disconnect between what was happening in different environments, which made it hard to build on his progress.

Through the Can-Do Approach, we introduced regular **communication between home and school**. Ollie's parents and teachers began sharing information daily – what worked at home, what happened at school, and how Ollie was progressing in each setting. This simple step made a huge difference. His parents shared that Ollie responded well to visual schedules and prompts, so his teacher introduced these in the classroom. Likewise, his teachers reported that Ollie enjoyed playing with certain toys during free time, so his parents incorporated those toys into their conversations at home.

As everyone started to align their strategies, Ollie's communication skills began to improve in both settings. He became more confident in expressing himself because the **approach was consistent**. Importantly, we also introduced Ollie's peers to simple strategies for supporting him, such as giving him extra time to respond and using gestures along with their words. This made Ollie feel more included, and soon, he began initiating more interactions with his friends.

The Can-Do Approach shows us that when everyone around a child is working together, the impact on the child's confidence and communication is huge. Parents, educators, and peers all play a role in helping the child feel supported and successful.

CELEBRATING SUCCESSES, NO MATTER HOW SMALL

One of the key principles of the Can-Do Approach is **celebrating every success**, no matter how small. Communication can be a long journey for many children, and it's easy to focus on the end goal - clear speech, complete sentences, or perfect articulation. But every step along the way is a victory, and it's crucial to celebrate those moments to build the child's confidence and motivation.

Let's talk about **Emily**, a 4-year-old who rarely spoke in full sentences. Her parents and teachers were focused on getting her to speak more fluently, but this pressure made Emily feel anxious, and she withdrew further. Through the Can-Do Approach, we shifted the focus from long-term goals to **small, everyday wins**.

One day, during a snack break, Emily pointed to her cup and said, "Juice". This might seem like a small thing, but it was a big deal for Emily. Her teacher immediately responded, "Yes, juice! You said 'juice,' Emily - well done!" This small celebration made Emily smile, and from that point, she became more willing to use single words to express her needs. Her teacher didn't push for full sentences right away but instead kept reinforcing and celebrating these small steps.

By **celebrating small victories**, we build a child's confidence. When children feel that their efforts are noticed and valued, they're more likely to keep trying. Over time, these small successes add up to big progress, and the child's communication skills grow naturally.

LOOKING AHEAD: THE LIFELONG IMPACT OF COMMUNICATION SUPPORT

The Can-Do Approach isn't just about helping children communicate today - it's about preparing them for the future. **Communication is a lifelong skill**, and the confidence, strategies, and support we provide children now will have a lasting impact on their ability to navigate the world as they grow.

Think about **Jake**, a teenager who started his journey with significant speech and language delays. Early on, his parents and teachers worked together to build Jake's confidence, focusing on what he could do and giving him the tools he needed to express himself. As Jake entered high school, those early interventions paid off. He was more confident in group discussions, able to advocate for himself in class, and had built strong relationships with his peers.

The Can-Do Approach set Jake up for success because it focused on **building skills from the inside out** - confidence, connection, and communication. By celebrating his small successes, supporting his unique communication style, and giving him control over his communication, Jake learned to navigate both the classroom and social settings with ease.

As children grow, the skills they develop through the Can-Do Approach don't just help them in school - they help them in life. Communication is at the heart of relationships, work, and personal growth. By supporting children's communication development now, we're giving them the tools to thrive in all areas of their future.

COMMUNICATION AS A JOURNEY, NOT A DESTINATION

Throughout this chapter, we've explored the many facets of communication challenges children may face, from stammering and selective mutism to gestalt language processing and behavioural communication. At the heart of these stories and examples is one simple truth: communication is a journey, not a destination.

The Can-Do Approach teaches us that **every child's communication journey is unique**, and our role as parents, educators, and therapists is to support them at each stage of their development. Whether it's by celebrating small wins, reducing pressure, or offering choices, we empower children to express themselves in ways that feel natural and authentic to them.

FOCUSING ON STRENGTHS

One of the key themes of the Can-Do Approach is focusing on what children **can do**. Instead of fixating on deficits, we look for opportunities to scaffold new skills from existing strengths. This approach builds confidence and encourages children to keep pushing their boundaries, whether through words, gestures, or behaviour. Children like Zara, who found her voice through drawing, or Jack, who learned to relax his stammer when the pressure was taken off, remind us that **progress happens when we nurture what's already there**.

REDUCING PRESSURE, BUILDING CONFIDENCE

Throughout this chapter, we've seen how pressure can inhibit communication. For children with stammers, speech delays, or selective mutism, the more they feel scrutinised, the less likely they are to speak. The Can-Do Approach shows us that by focusing on the **message** rather than the **delivery**, we help children feel safe, understood, and capable. Building this kind of confidence is the key to long-term communication success.

COMMUNICATION IS MORE THAN WORDS

We've also explored how communication is not just about words – it's about connection, agency, and self-expression. Children like Nina, who communicated her choices through gestures and visual cards, remind us that **communication comes in many forms**. Our role is to embrace and encourage those forms, whether they involve speech, gestures, signs, or behaviour. By giving children control over how they express themselves, we help them navigate their world with confidence and independence.

LOOKING AHEAD: PREPARING FOR THE NEXT STEP

As we come to the end of this chapter, it's important to remember that the journey of communication doesn't stop here. What we've learned so far about recognising challenges, focusing on strengths, and celebrating small successes is only the beginning. The next step is to explore **practical strategies** that can further support children on this journey.

In the upcoming chapter, we'll dive deeper into specific methods and tools that can be used to help children develop their communication skills. From play-based interventions to visual supports and sensory integration, we'll look at how to create environments and routines that nurture communication and help children thrive.

Communication is a lifelong skill, and with the right support, every child can unlock their full potential. The Can-Do Approach gives us the tools to make that happen, by meeting children where they are and helping them grow from a place of confidence, connection, and capability.

CONCLUSION

The Can-Do Approach is more than a method; it's a way of seeing each child as full of possibility. When we celebrate what they can do, rather than fixating on what they can't, we shift their experience from one of frustration to one of empowerment. Through Ivy's growing confidence, George's reduced frustration, and Sophie's blossoming independence, we see how this approach transforms lives. These successes remind us that every step forward – whether through a gesture, a word, or a shared laugh – is worth celebrating.

By focusing on connection, confidence, and capability, we're not just helping children communicate; we're helping them find their place in the world.

KEY TAKEAWAYS

- The Can-Do Approach focuses on what children can do, celebrating strengths and fostering confidence in communication development.
- It emphasises integrating communication support into everyday routines and activities, ensuring children are supported during naturally occurring moments.
- The approach highlights the importance of recognising all forms of communication, not just verbal, and using them to scaffold further development.
- Empathy and patience are essential in supporting children, ensuring they feel heard and understood regardless of how they communicate.
- Collaboration between parents, teachers, and other professionals is vital in creating a consistent, supportive environment for children's communication growth.
- Magic Moments, which tap into a child's interests, are key to sparking meaningful interactions and boosting communication.
- Creating interaction-friendly environments where all forms of communication are valued promotes children's engagement and confidence in expressing themselves.
- Reducing pressure and focusing on the message rather than speech perfection allows children to communicate freely, fostering growth.

REFERENCES AND RESOURCES

American Speech-Language-Hearing Association (ASHA). (n.d.). *Social Communication Disorders in School-Age Children*. Retrieved from asha.org.

Ayres, A. J. (2005). *Sensory Integration and the Child: Understanding Hidden Sensory Challenges*. Western Psychological Services.

Blakemore, S. J. & Frith, U. (2005). *The Learning Brain: Lessons for Education*. Wiley-Blackwell.

Braun, V. & Clarke, V. (2006). Using thematic analysis in psychology. *Qualitative Research in Psychology, 3*(2), 77-101.

Brinton, B. & Fujiki, M. (2005). Social skills of children with specific language impairment. *Topics in Language Disorders, 25*(1), 29-41.

Burman, D., Booth, J. R., & Bitan, T. (2008). Sex differences in neural processing of language among children. *Neuropsychologia, 46*(5), 1349-1362.

Catts, H. W. & Kamhi, A. G. (2005). *Language and Reading Disabilities*. Pearson.

Dunlap, G. & Fox, L. (2009). Positive behavior support and early intervention for young children with autism: Case studies on the efficacy of proactive treatment of problem behavior. *Topics in Early Childhood Special Education, 29*(1), 22-32.

Dykens, E. M. & Hodapp, R. M. (2001). Strengths and weaknesses in children with intellectual disabilities. *American Journal of Mental Retardation, 106*(1), 70-81.

Fuller, K. & Kaiser, A. P. (2019). A systematic review and meta-analysis of early language interventions for children from low socioeconomic status backgrounds. *Journal of Speech, Language, and Hearing Research, 62*(9), 3456-3471.

Gernsbacher, M. A., Morson, E. M., & Grace, E. J. (2016). Language development in children with developmental disabilities. *Journal of Speech, Language, and Hearing Research, 59*(1), 97-106.

Greenspan, S. I. & Wieder, S. (2009). *Engaging Autism: Using the Floortime Approach to Help Children Relate, Communicate, and Think*. Da Capo Press.

Howlin, P. & Rutter, M. (1987). *Treatment of Autistic Children*. Wiley.

Kaiser, A. P. & Hancock, T. B. (2003). Teaching communication skills to young children with developmental delays. *Infants & Young Children, 16*(3), 236-252.

Klatte, M., Bergström, K., & Lachmann, T. (2013). Does noise affect learning? A short review on noise effects on cognitive performance in children. *Frontiers in Psychology, 4*, 578.

MacKay, T., Knott, F., & Dunlop, A. W. (2007). Developing social interaction and understanding: A theoretical framework. *Educational Psychology in Practice, 23*(4), 315-336.

McCauley, R. J. & Fey, M. E. (2006). *Treatment of Language Disorders in Children*. Brookes Publishing.

Nelson, K. E. & Camarata, S. (1993). Effects of speech and language intervention: Clinical insights and implications. *Journal of Speech and Hearing Research, 36*(2), 267-280.

Prizant, B. M. & Wetherby, A. M. (2005). *The SCERTS Model: A Comprehensive Educational Approach for Children with Autism Spectrum Disorders*. Brookes Publishing.

Rinaldi, C. & Howe, T. (2012). Co-regulation and self-regulation in early childhood: Reflections on a new paradigm. *Early Childhood Education Journal, 40*(4), 301-308.

Rutter, M. & Schopler, E. (1987). *Autism and Developmental Receptive Language Disorder: Similarities and Differences*. Plenum Press.

Sussman, F. (2012). *More Than Words: Helping Parents Promote Communication and Social Skills in Children with Autism Spectrum Disorder*. Hanen Centre.

Tomblin, J. B., Zhang, X., Buckwalter, P., & O'Brien, M. (2003). The stability of primary language disorder: Four years after kindergarten diagnosis. *Journal of Speech, Language, and Hearing Research, 46*(6), 1283-1296.

Warren, S. F., Fey, M. E., & Yoder, P. J. (2007). Differential treatment intensity research: A missing link to creating optimally effective communication interventions. *Mental Retardation and Developmental Disabilities Research Reviews, 13*(1), 70-77.

Weitzman, E. & Greenberg, J. (2002). *Learning Language and Loving It: A Guide to Promoting Children's Social, Language, and Literacy Development in Early Childhood Settings*. Hanen Centre.

Williams, J. E. & Chapman, R. S. (2000). Narrative development in children with specific language impairment. *Journal of Speech, Language, and Hearing Research, 43*(5), 1147-1164.

Yoder, P. J. & Warren, S. F. (2002). Effects of prelinguistic communication intervention on language development in children with developmental disabilities. *Journal of Speech, Language, and Hearing Research, 45*(6), 1158-1174.

Zubrick, S. R., Taylor, C. L., & Rice, M. L. (2007). Late language emergence at 24 months: An epidemiological study of prevalence, predictors, and covariates. *Journal of Speech, Language, and Hearing Research, 50*(6), 1562-1592.

CHAPTER 4
CREATING AN INCLUSIVE CLASSROOM ENVIRONMENT

UNDERSTANDING SENSORY REGULATION IN THE CLASSROOM

Sensory regulation refers to the process by which individuals respond to and manage sensory input from their environment in a way that allows them to function effectively in daily life. Sensory input can come from any of the senses – sight, sound, touch, taste, smell, as well as vestibular (balance) and proprioceptive (body awareness) inputs. Sensory regulation is a critical component of how we engage with the world, including how we focus, respond to stimuli, and interact with others.

In a classroom environment, sensory regulation plays a vital role in determining a child's ability to learn, focus, and behave appropriately. For many students, the classroom can be an overwhelming sensory experience. Bright lights, the buzz of conversation, the feeling of different textures on desks or chairs, or even the scent of cleaning products can contribute to sensory overload. Sensory regulation allows students to filter out these distractions, maintain focus on tasks, and participate actively in lessons. However, when a child has difficulty regulating their sensory input, it can manifest in behaviour that may be misunderstood as disruptive or inattentive.

The impact of sensory regulation on learning is profound. A child struggling with sensory processing issues might find it difficult to concentrate or follow instructions in a typical classroom setting. For instance, a student who is particularly sensitive to noise (auditory over-responsiveness) may be unable to focus during group work if the classroom is loud. Alternatively, a child who craves sensory input (Sensory Seeking) may fidget, move around excessively, or have difficulty sitting still during quiet activities. These behaviours can be misinterpreted as a lack of discipline or attention, but they are often an indication that the child is either overwhelmed or under-stimulated by their environment.

Effective sensory regulation supports the development of self-control, emotional regulation, and cognitive engagement, all of which are essential for academic success. When students are able to manage their sensory input, they can better participate in learning activities, engage with their peers, and meet the behavioural expectations of the classroom. This not only enhances their individual learning experience but also contributes to a more harmonious classroom environment.

RECOGNISING COMMON SENSORY NEEDS IN STUDENTS

Understanding and recognising the diverse sensory needs of students is a crucial step in creating an inclusive classroom environment. Sensory processing varies from student to student, and what is calming for one child might be overwhelming for another. Sensory needs generally fall into three broad categories: Sensory Over-Responsive (SOR), Sensory Under-Responsive (SUR), and Sensory Seeking (SS).

Sensory Over-Responsive (SOR)

Students who are Sensory Over-Responsive are highly sensitive to sensory stimuli. They may perceive everyday sensations as overwhelming or even painful. For example, a student with auditory sensitivity may find it difficult to concentrate in a noisy classroom, becoming distressed by background sounds that other students can easily ignore. Similarly, students with tactile sensitivity might struggle with certain textures, such as the feel of clothing labels, which can cause them to become distracted or anxious.

Signs of Sensory Over-Responsiveness in the classroom may include:

- Covering ears or eyes in response to noise or bright lights.
- Avoiding physical contact or becoming distressed when touched.
- Withdrawal from activities that involve certain textures (e.g., sand, paint).
- Difficulty concentrating in busy environments.

These students may need strategies to help them filter out unwanted sensory stimuli, such as noise-cancelling headphones, seating in quieter areas, or dimmed lighting in certain parts of the classroom.

Sensory Under-Responsive (SUR)

On the opposite end of the spectrum, students who are Sensory Under-Responsive may not register sensory input as readily as their peers. They often appear lethargic or disengaged and may require more sensory stimulation to feel alert and focused. For example, a student with low sensitivity to movement may benefit from more frequent physical activity to remain engaged in learning. Similarly, a student who does not notice visual or auditory cues may seem "tuned out" during lessons.

Signs of Sensory Under-Responsiveness include:

- Appearing tired or unmotivated, even after adequate sleep.
- Sluggish responses to instructions or stimuli.
- Failing to notice when their name is called or when a task is presented.
- Limited engagement with peers or classroom activities.

These students may benefit from regular movement breaks, sensory integration activities, and more pronounced visual or auditory cues during instruction.

Sensory Seeking (SS)

Sensory seekers are students who crave sensory input and may engage in behaviours that provide them with the stimulation they need. This can manifest as fidgeting, touching objects or people excessively, or moving around the classroom. While these behaviours can be misinterpreted as disruptive, they are often a sign that the student is trying to meet their sensory needs in the only way they know how.

Sensory seekers may display the following behaviours:

- Constantly touching objects, people, or their own body.
- Fidgeting or moving around when expected to sit still.
- Making loud noises or engaging in repetitive vocalisations.
- Seeking out strong sensory experiences, such as bright lights or strong flavours.

To support sensory seekers, teachers can incorporate sensory breaks into the school day, allowing the student to engage in activities that provide the input they need without disrupting the flow of the lesson. For example, giving the student access to fidget tools, allowing them to take movement breaks, or using tactile-based learning activities can help them remain focused.

> **Reflective Prompt**
>
> *How do you currently recognise sensory differences in your students? What are some signs that a student may be Sensory Over-Responsive, Under-Responsive, or Seeking? How might you adjust your classroom environment to support these different needs?*

HOW SENSORY NEEDS AFFECT BEHAVIOUR AND LEARNING

The connection between sensory regulation and behaviour in the classroom is often overlooked, but it is a critical factor in a student's ability to engage with the learning process. When sensory needs are not addressed, students may exhibit behaviours that are disruptive or disengaged, which can negatively impact their academic performance and social relationships.

For example, a student who is Sensory Over-Responsive may act out because they are overwhelmed by environmental stimuli, such as loud noises or bright lights. Their behaviour may appear defiant or avoidant, but it is often a coping mechanism to reduce sensory input. On the other hand, a student who is Sensory Seeking might become restless or disruptive, engaging in excessive movement or noise to meet their sensory needs. In both cases, without understanding the root cause of these behaviours, teachers might resort to discipline strategies that further alienate the child, rather than addressing their underlying sensory needs.

Moreover, unaddressed sensory needs can affect not only academic performance but also emotional well-being. Students who struggle with sensory regulation may experience higher levels of anxiety, frustration, or emotional outbursts because they are unable to cope with their environment. In contrast, when their sensory needs are understood and supported, students are more likely to feel calm, focused, and ready to learn.

Incorporating sensory regulation strategies into classroom design and teaching methods is essential for creating an inclusive learning environment. Understanding the sensory needs of students and recognising how these needs influence behaviour and learning can enable teachers to provide appropriate accommodations and interventions. By doing so, educators can support not only the individual student but the overall dynamics of the classroom, fostering an environment where all students can thrive academically, emotionally, and socially.

THE IMPORTANCE OF AN INCLUSIVE ENVIRONMENT

Creating an inclusive classroom environment that supports sensory regulation is not just beneficial for children with identified sensory processing challenges; it benefits all students. A sensory-friendly classroom is one where all students feel comfortable, engaged, and ready to learn, regardless of their sensory preferences or needs. Inclusive classrooms promote a sense of belonging, provide access to equitable learning opportunities, and foster a positive environment where every child can thrive. Additionally, by incorporating strategies that address sensory regulation, educators can enhance communication and language development across the classroom.

WHY SENSORY-FRIENDLY CLASSROOMS BENEFIT ALL STUDENTS

One of the primary advantages of designing a sensory-friendly classroom is that it creates a more predictable, calm, and responsive learning environment for every student. Sensory needs are not exclusive to children with diagnosed conditions such as autism or sensory processing disorder (SPD); every child has sensory preferences and thresholds. Some children may be more sensitive to environmental stimuli, while others may seek additional input to stay alert and focused. By creating a classroom that considers a range of sensory needs, educators can accommodate these preferences, ensuring that all students feel comfortable and ready to engage in learning.

REDUCING DISTRACTIONS AND PROMOTING FOCUS

Classrooms are inherently sensory-rich environments. The sounds of chairs scraping, the hum of conversation, visual stimuli from posters or projectors, and physical sensations such as uncomfortable seating can all serve as distractions that inhibit learning. A sensory-friendly classroom takes these factors into account by minimising distractions. This might include incorporating flexible seating arrangements, providing noise-cancelling headphones, or using dimmable lighting. For example, some students may find bright fluorescent lights overstimulating, while others may be distracted by background noise or a cluttered classroom. Reducing these sensory triggers can help create a more focused and calmer atmosphere for all students, making it easier for them to concentrate on tasks.

For children who do not have specific sensory challenges, a sensory-friendly classroom still offers benefits. Many students experience occasional sensory sensitivities or preferences, especially when they are tired, anxious, or feeling unwell. By designing a classroom that is adaptable to different sensory needs, teachers create a space that is responsive to students' changing emotional and physical states. When students feel that their environment is predictable and comfortable, they are better able to focus, manage their emotions, and engage with their peers and teachers.

PROMOTING SELF-REGULATION AND EMOTIONAL WELL-BEING

Sensory regulation is deeply tied to emotional regulation. When students are overwhelmed by sensory stimuli, they are more likely to experience anxiety, frustration, or distress. In contrast, when they feel comfortable and supported, they are more likely to remain calm, focused, and ready to learn. Creating a sensory-friendly environment helps students develop the skills they need to self-regulate, which is essential for academic success and personal development.

Self-regulation refers to the ability to manage one's emotions, behaviour, and attention in response to sensory input. In a sensory-friendly classroom, students are provided with tools and strategies to help them manage their own sensory needs. For example, giving students access to sensory breaks, fidget tools, or movement opportunities can help them maintain focus and stay engaged in learning. Additionally, creating "calm corners" or quiet spaces where students can retreat when they feel overwhelmed can help them manage their emotional and sensory states.

When students are given the tools and opportunities to regulate their own sensory input, they are also learning valuable life skills. Self-regulation is not only important in the classroom but also in everyday life, helping students navigate challenging situations, manage stress, and interact with others in socially appropriate ways. By teaching these skills in a sensory-friendly classroom, educators are promoting emotional well-being and resilience, which will serve students well beyond the school years.

BUILDING AN INCLUSIVE CLASSROOM CULTURE

One of the most important aspects of creating a sensory-friendly classroom is that it fosters a culture of inclusion and understanding. Inclusive classrooms recognise that every student has unique needs and strengths, and they are designed to ensure that all students have equitable access to learning. By making sensory accommodations a normal part of classroom life, teachers send a powerful message to their students: diversity is valued, and every student's needs are important.

This inclusive mindset can have a profound impact on students' social and emotional development. When children see that their peers' sensory needs are being met – whether through noise-reducing headphones, movement breaks, or alternative seating – they learn to appreciate differences and develop empathy for others. Moreover, when children are given the tools to manage their own sensory needs, they develop a sense of ownership and agency over their learning experience.

In an inclusive environment, children who might otherwise struggle with sensory regulation can participate fully in classroom activities. They are less likely to feel isolated or singled out for their differences, and they are more likely to form positive relationships with their peers. This sense of belonging is essential for building self-confidence, social skills, and a positive attitude towards learning.

THE RELATIONSHIP BETWEEN SENSORY REGULATION AND COMMUNICATION

The ability to regulate sensory input is closely connected to communication and language development. When students are overwhelmed or under-stimulated by sensory input, it can significantly impact their ability to process information, engage with peers, and express themselves effectively. Understanding this relationship is crucial for teachers who want to support both sensory regulation and communication in their classrooms.

SENSORY OVERLOAD AND COMMUNICATION BREAKDOWN

For children who experience sensory overload, communication can become particularly challenging. When the brain is overwhelmed by sensory input – whether from loud noises, bright lights, or uncomfortable textures – it can go into a "fight, flight, or freeze" response. In this state, the child may struggle to focus on what is being said, process verbal instructions, or find the words to express their own thoughts and feelings. This can lead to communication breakdowns, where the child may withdraw, become non-verbal, or exhibit challenging behaviours as a way of coping with their discomfort.

For example, a student who is highly sensitive to noise may find it difficult to concentrate during group discussions or class presentations. They may become agitated, cover their ears, or stop participating in the conversation altogether. In these situations, sensory overload directly impacts the child's ability to engage in communication.

THE IMPACT OF SENSORY SEEKING ON LANGUAGE DEVELOPMENT

On the other hand, sensory-seeking students may also face communication challenges, though for different reasons. Sensory seekers often engage in constant movement, touching, or noise-making to meet their sensory needs. This behaviour can make it difficult for them to sit still and focus on verbal instructions, which in turn affects their ability to follow conversations or develop language skills. Additionally, their sensory-seeking behaviours may distract or disrupt their peers, leading to social difficulties and further communication barriers.

In a sensory-friendly classroom, strategies that address sensory needs can help mitigate these challenges and promote better communication. For example, providing sensory-seeking students with fidget tools or allowing them to stand or move during lessons can help them meet their sensory needs while still participating in the conversation. Similarly, using visual aids, simplified instructions, or alternative communication methods can support students who are struggling to process verbal communication due to sensory overload.

An inclusive, sensory-friendly classroom environment benefits all students by promoting focus, emotional well-being, and a sense of belonging. By supporting sensory regulation, teachers can enhance communication and language development, ensuring that every student has the opportunity to succeed. In this way, sensory-friendly classrooms not only meet the needs of individual students but also create a more equitable, supportive, and engaging learning environment for everyone.

DESIGNING A SENSORY-FRIENDLY CLASSROOM

A sensory-friendly classroom is an environment that acknowledges the diverse sensory needs of students and seeks to accommodate them through careful design choices. These classrooms are intended to help children self-regulate their sensory inputs, providing an environment where they can thrive academically, socially, and emotionally. Creating such an inclusive space requires a focus on the physical layout, calming and alerting zones, as well as key elements such as lighting, noise control, and furniture choices. Each of these aspects plays a significant role in how students interact with their environment and how conducive the space is to their sensory regulation.

CLASSROOM LAYOUT AND PHYSICAL ENVIRONMENT CONSIDERATIONS

The layout of a sensory-friendly classroom is foundational to supporting sensory regulation needs. It requires intentional design, with zones for different activities and levels of stimulation to accommodate the varied sensory profiles of the students. An ideal layout ensures that the space is organised, decluttered, and visually structured to reduce potential distractions. For students with sensory sensitivities, an overly cluttered or chaotic environment can be overwhelming, leading to anxiety and difficulty concentrating.

1. **Clear Pathways:** Classrooms should have clearly defined pathways for movement. Some children, particularly those who are Sensory Seeking or have vestibular (movement-related) needs, may benefit from regular movement breaks. Providing easy access to open areas where children can move freely without disruption is essential. Circulation around the room should be smooth, with distinct areas for group activities, quiet individual work, and play or sensory exploration.
2. **Flexible Seating Options:** Different types of seating can help meet diverse sensory needs. Some children may prefer sitting on traditional chairs, while others may benefit from alternative seating options such as wobble stools, bean bags, or floor cushions. Sensory-sensitive students may need a designated space that feels enclosed or secure, such as a small cubicle or a corner with soft furnishings, where they can withdraw when they feel overwhelmed.
3. **Visual Organisation:** Clear labelling and visual schedules can help students feel more in control and less anxious about transitions and expectations. For example, using symbols or photos to denote areas for specific activities can provide students with a predictable routine, which is especially helpful for autistic students or students with sensory processing challenges. The use of neutral tones or soft colours on walls and furniture can also prevent visual overstimulation.

CREATING CALMING AND ALERTING ZONES

A key aspect of designing a sensory-friendly classroom is providing both calming and alerting zones. These designated areas allow students to seek out either sensory input that helps them stay alert and engaged or calming input to help them self-regulate when feeling overstimulated.

Calming Zones

Calming zones are spaces where students can retreat when they are feeling overwhelmed or dysregulated. These areas should be designed to be soothing and free from distractions. Elements that can be incorporated include:

- Soft furnishings such as bean bags, cushions, or weighted blankets that provide deep pressure, which can help children feel grounded and secure.
- Quiet activities such as books, puzzles, or soft tactile materials (e.g., fidget toys or textured fabrics) to engage children in a calming manner.
- Dim lighting or the use of soft, non-intrusive lights such as salt lamps or fairy lights, which can create a calming atmosphere and reduce sensory overload.

Alerting Zones

In contrast, alerting zones are designed to provide sensory input that helps students who are under-stimulated become more engaged and attentive. These areas might include:

- Movement-based activities such as a balance board, trampoline, or even swings (if space allows). These activities can provide proprioceptive and vestibular input that is essential for students who are Sensory Seeking.
- Tactile and manipulative resources like putty, sand, or sensory bins can also provide the sensory stimulation needed to boost alertness and engagement.
- Brightly coloured visuals or more intense lighting may be appropriate for alerting zones, as they can help stimulate focus and attention.

Having both calming and alerting zones in the classroom ensures that children with different sensory needs have access to a variety of spaces that help them modulate their sensory inputs according to their needs at any given moment.

THE ROLE OF NATURAL LIGHTING, NOISE CONTROL, AND FURNITURE CHOICES

Several other key environmental factors play a role in designing a sensory-friendly classroom, with lighting, noise levels, and furniture choices being some of the most impactful.

Natural Lighting

The use of natural light is one of the most effective ways to create a sensory-friendly environment. Natural light is less harsh than artificial lighting, making it easier for students, particularly those with sensory sensitivities, to tolerate. Where natural light is not possible, soft, ambient lighting should be used in place of bright, fluorescent lights, which can cause discomfort for some children, particularly those who are visually sensitive. Adjustable blinds or curtains can help manage light levels throughout the day, depending on the classroom activities and individual student needs.

Noise Control

Noise levels are another critical factor in a sensory-friendly classroom. For students who are auditory-sensitive, even everyday sounds like chatter, the hum of air conditioners, or movement around the room can be overwhelming. Creating a quiet environment can be achieved through the use of sound-absorbing materials such as carpets, soft furnishings, and acoustic wall panels. Additionally, noise-cancelling headphones or ear defenders can be provided for students who need to block out noise to focus or self-regulate. Teachers should also be mindful of their tone and volume when speaking, using visual cues to support verbal instructions wherever possible.

Furniture Choices

The type of furniture used in the classroom can either support or hinder sensory regulation. Heavy, solid furniture that stays in place can provide stability and predictability, which is reassuring for many children with sensory needs. Meanwhile, adjustable desks or standing desks can help meet the physical and sensory preferences of individual students. Allowing for movement, whether through flexible seating or standing options, is essential for students who need to fidget or move to stay focused.

Incorporating sensory-friendly furniture such as rocking chairs or sensory cushions can also help students with sensory-seeking behaviours or those who need additional proprioceptive input.

Designing a sensory-friendly classroom is about more than just accommodating students with sensory processing challenges – it creates a nurturing and inclusive environment for all students. By considering the classroom layout, creating calming and alerting zones, and paying attention to factors like lighting, noise, and furniture choices, educators can create a space that supports sensory regulation and promotes positive learning outcomes. A well-designed sensory-friendly classroom benefits not only students with specific sensory needs but also contributes to a more focused, calm, and engaging learning environment for every child.

Accommodating Diverse Sensory Needs

Accommodating diverse sensory needs in a classroom is essential to creating an inclusive environment where all students can thrive. Students with sensory processing challenges, such as those seen in autistic children, children with ADHD, and/or SPD, may have unique reactions to everyday stimuli. These responses can influence their ability to focus, participate, and learn effectively in a traditional classroom setting. Recognising and addressing these needs through practical strategies and classroom adaptations can benefit not only students with sensory difficulties but all students, by fostering a more supportive and accommodating learning environment.

CREATING AN INCLUSIVE CLASSROOM ENVIRONMENT

> *Reflective Prompt*
>
> *Think about a time when a student in your class exhibited sensory behaviours that affected their learning. What strategies could you implement to help this student manage sensory input more effectively? How might you create a more sensory-friendly classroom to prevent these issues?*

Understanding Sensory Profiles

Sensory profiles describe how individuals perceive and respond to sensory stimuli, such as sounds, touch, light, and movement. Students generally fall into one or more of the following sensory categories:

Sensory Over-Responsive (SOR): These students are hypersensitive to sensory input and may be easily overwhelmed by loud noises, bright lights, or tactile sensations. For example, a fire alarm or crowded, noisy environments may cause distress, leading to withdrawal, anxiety, or outbursts.

> ### LET ME TELL YOU ABOUT TOM...
>
> Tom, an 8-year-old in Year 3, has heightened sensitivity to visual stimuli. During lessons, he would often cover his eyes or look away from bright lights, especially when the classroom lights were switched on too brightly. His teacher initially thought he was being inattentive or distracted, but after consulting with his parents and an occupational therapist, they realised Tom's discomfort was due to visual sensitivity. To help him, Tom's teacher dimmed the classroom lights and allowed him to use soft lighting near his desk. Additionally, Tom was given sunglasses to wear when the light became overwhelming. These changes allowed Tom to feel more comfortable, and he became more engaged in his learning.

> *Reflective Prompt*
>
> *How might Tom's visual sensitivity have been overlooked if his teacher had not consulted with his parents and an occupational therapist? What steps can you take to ensure that you identify and address sensory sensitivities, like visual or auditory sensitivities, in your students?*

Sensory Under-Responsive (SUR): These students have an under-response to sensory input. They may appear indifferent to stimuli that others find obvious, such as not noticing when their name is called or when they're bumped in a busy hallway. These students might seem disengaged or lethargic and may require more stimulation to become alert.

LET ME TELL YOU ABOUT OLIVER...

Oliver, a 5-year-old in Reception, often seemed disengaged during class activities and missed important cues. For example, he rarely responded when his teacher called his name and struggled to focus on tasks, especially during seated activities. His teacher initially thought he was distracted, but after discussing his behaviour with his parents and an occupational therapist, they discovered that Oliver had sensory under-registration. He had difficulty registering auditory and visual input, which made it challenging for him to stay alert and respond to cues.

To help Oliver engage more effectively in class, his teacher introduced short, structured movement breaks throughout the day. These breaks allowed Oliver to move around the classroom, stretch, or do simple exercises that helped activate his sensory system. After each break, Oliver appeared more alert and ready to focus on the next task. His teacher also used gentle tactile reminders, such as a soft tap on the shoulder, to help him refocus when needed. These adjustments helped Oliver "wake up" and become more aware of his surroundings, significantly improving his participation and learning outcomes.

Reflective Prompt

Oliver's teacher used movement breaks to help him become more alert and engaged. How might you incorporate movement breaks or other strategies to support students who may be under-registered to sensory stimuli? How can you ensure these students are receiving the necessary stimulation to stay engaged in class activities?

Sensory Seeking (SS): These students actively seek out sensory experiences. They might enjoy running, jumping, fidgeting, or touching various objects. These children often appear as though they have an excess of energy, and they may exhibit behaviours such as fidgeting, climbing, or making noise to satisfy their sensory needs.

LET ME TELL YOU ABOUT MIA...

Mia, a 9-year-old in Year 4, often displayed sensory-seeking behaviours, particularly through excessive movement. She would constantly move around the classroom, rocking in her chair or even spinning when she was supposed to be working. Initially, her teacher believed Mia was being disruptive, but after collaborating with an occupational therapist, they found that Mia was seeking vestibular input to help her focus. The teacher provided Mia with opportunities for short, structured movement breaks throughout the day, such as stretching or walking around the classroom, and gave her a balance ball chair to sit on. These strategies helped Mia regulate her need for movement and allowed her to focus better on her lessons.

> **Reflective Prompt**
>
> Mia's need for movement was addressed with structured movement breaks and a balance ball chair. How might you identify and support students who exhibit sensory-seeking behaviours? What changes could you make in your classroom environment to allow for movement or tactile input in a way that helps them stay engaged?"

Sensory Modulation Disorder (SMD): A broader category, SMD describes difficulties in regulating sensory input, leading to inconsistent responses depending on the sensory domain. A child might be over-responsive to sound but under-responsive to touch, for example, complicating classroom support.

PRACTICAL STRATEGIES FOR ACCOMMODATING SENSORY DIFFERENCES

Effective accommodations for students with diverse sensory needs require a flexible and adaptive approach. Tailoring classroom activities and the physical environment to account for these differences can significantly enhance students' ability to learn, regulate, and participate. Below are practical strategies to support students with each sensory profile.

Creating Predictable Routines with Sensory Breaks

Students who struggle with sensory regulation often benefit from clear, predictable classroom routines. Knowing what to expect reduces anxiety, particularly for over-responsive children who may feel overwhelmed by sudden changes. Implementing a daily schedule that includes sensory breaks can help all students maintain a sense of calm and focus.

For sensory seekers, including short, high-energy breaks that allow them to move around and exert energy can prevent restlessness. Movement activities such as stretching, yoga poses, or using a sensory pathway can help them reset before returning to more sedentary tasks. For over-responsive students, quieter breaks that offer an opportunity to retreat to a calm, low-stimulus environment can help them regulate their responses to overwhelming sensory input.

Providing Sensory Tools

Sensory tools can be used to help students self-regulate throughout the day. These tools can include:

- ✦ Fidget spinners, stress balls, or textured objects can offer sensory stimulation for students who need tactile input to maintain focus.

- Weighted lap pads or cushions can provide deep pressure, which can be calming for Sensory Over-Responsive children, particularly during seated activities to provide grounding and a sense of security.
- For students who are sensitive to auditory stimuli, noise-cancelling headphones or earplugs can help reduce overwhelming noise levels, especially in busy classrooms or during loud activities like assemblies.
- Chewing gum, chewable necklaces, or similar items can provide proprioceptive input for sensory seekers who need oral stimulation to focus.

Offering a selection of sensory tools in the classroom allows students to choose the ones that best meet their individual needs. It is important to teach students how to use these tools appropriately to ensure they serve their purpose without becoming a distraction.

Flexible Seating Arrangements

Traditional desks and chairs may not suit all sensory profiles, particularly for students who need to move frequently. Providing flexible seating options allows students to select seating that best supports their sensory needs. This might include:

- Wobble stools or stability balls: These options provide students with the opportunity to move while seated, which can be beneficial for sensory seekers or under-responsive students who need more movement to stay alert.
- Bean bags or soft chairs: For students who need a calm, sensory-friendly space, soft seating options can create a soothing environment where they feel more comfortable and less overwhelmed.
- Standing desks or movement areas: Some students may benefit from the option to stand or move while working, rather than remaining seated for extended periods. Providing areas where students can stand, pace, or even walk while completing tasks can help sensory seekers stay focused.

Adjusting Sensory Input During Activities

Teachers can adjust the sensory demands of activities to match students' sensory profiles. For example, during art or hands-on learning activities, students who are over-responsive to tactile input may benefit from using tools that reduce the need to directly touch materials, such as brushes or gloves. Conversely, sensory seekers may enjoy activities that provide rich sensory input, such as working with clay, sand, or textured materials.

In group activities, considering a student's auditory sensitivities is crucial. Some students may benefit from being seated farther away from loud group discussions or having smaller group sizes to reduce overwhelming noise levels. Offering individual workspaces or quiet zones can help students who become overstimulated during collaborative work.

Visual and Auditory Modifications

Visual and auditory stimuli in the classroom environment can significantly affect sensory-sensitive students. Simple adjustments can create a more inclusive atmosphere:

- Harsh fluorescent lighting can be overstimulating for some students. Consider using natural lighting where possible or adding dimmable lights. For students who are sensitive to bright lights, offer sunglasses or visors as a tool for regulating their visual input.
- Excessive visual stimuli, such as crowded walls or chaotic displays, can be distracting. Simplifying classroom displays and keeping visual information organised and clear can benefit students with sensory sensitivities.
- Reducing background noise by closing windows, using noise-cancelling machines, or positioning students away from high-traffic areas can improve focus for sensory-sensitive students. Teachers should also consider speaking at a calm, consistent volume, and minimising unnecessary loud activities.

TAILORING CLASSROOM ACTIVITIES TO DIFFERENT SENSORY PROFILES

While the physical classroom environment plays a critical role in supporting sensory regulation, the way activities are structured can further enhance students' ability to engage and learn.

Sensory Enrichment for Sensory Seekers

For sensory seekers, classroom activities that incorporate movement, touch, and sound can be highly beneficial. Integrating movement breaks into lessons or allowing students to use manipulatives during instruction can keep them engaged. Hands-on learning experiences, such as building models, conducting experiments, or role-playing activities, provide the sensory input these students crave.

Low-Stimulus Alternatives for Sensory Over-Responsive Students

In contrast, students who are over-responsive to sensory input may benefit from quieter, more structured activities. Offering options for independent work or creating quiet zones within the classroom allows these students to complete tasks in a less stimulating environment. Using written instructions or visual aids can reduce the need for verbal communication, which may overwhelm some students.

Providing Multiple Learning Modalities

Every student learns differently, and providing a variety of learning modalities - such as auditory, visual, tactile, and kinaesthetic activities - helps meet the diverse needs of all students. This multi-sensory approach ensures that all students, regardless of their sensory profiles, can access the curriculum and participate fully.

Accommodating diverse sensory needs in the classroom requires thoughtful planning, flexibility, and a willingness to adapt. By providing sensory tools, offering flexible seating arrangements, adjusting sensory input during activities, and tailoring classroom activities to match students' sensory profiles, educators can create an environment where all students, regardless of their sensory needs, feel supported and included. These strategies not only support children with sensory processing difficulties but also enhance the learning experience for all students, creating a more inclusive, effective classroom environment.

SUPPORTING SENSORY REGULATION FOR COMMUNICATION DEVELOPMENT

Effective communication is fundamental to a child's academic and social success, but for many children with sensory processing difficulties, their ability to communicate is intricately tied to how their sensory systems function. Sensory regulation refers to the ability to manage and respond to sensory input from the environment and one's own body in a way that is appropriate to the situation. When a child's sensory system is well-regulated, they are better able to engage with their surroundings, including interacting and communicating with others. Conversely, difficulties in sensory regulation can hinder communication development and result in challenges in both verbal and non-verbal forms of communication.

In this section, we will explore how sensory regulation affects communication development, and we will outline strategies for supporting students with diverse communication needs in the classroom.

THE IMPACT OF SENSORY REGULATION ON COMMUNICATION

Sensory regulation plays a crucial role in shaping a child's ability to communicate. A well-regulated sensory system allows for an optimal level of arousal and attention, which are prerequisites for effective communication. When a child can process sensory information effectively, they can focus on listening, understanding, and responding appropriately in conversations. However, when sensory input is overwhelming or insufficiently stimulating, it can affect communication in several ways:

Attention and Focus

Sensory regulation directly affects a child's ability to maintain attention, which is essential for communication. For example, a child who is overstimulated by noise or visual input in the classroom may struggle to focus on what the teacher or peers are saying. As a result, they may miss out on important communication cues and instructions. Similarly, a child who is under-stimulated may appear withdrawn or disinterested in interactions, leading to challenges in engaging in conversations or understanding social expectations.

Processing Language and Non-Verbal Cues

Sensory regulation affects how children process auditory and visual information, both of which are critical for communication. Children with sensory processing difficulties may struggle to filter out background noise, making it difficult for them to focus on a speaker's words. This can lead to misunderstandings or a delay in their ability to respond. Furthermore, difficulty in processing non-verbal cues, such as facial expressions or body language, may hinder their ability to interpret and participate in social interactions effectively.

Speech Production

The physical act of speaking relies on motor planning and coordination, which are influenced by sensory input. For instance, children with poor body awareness or proprioceptive issues may have difficulty regulating the strength and clarity of their speech. They might speak too loudly or too softly or struggle with articulation because of the sensory feedback they receive from their own bodies. Sensory dysregulation can also lead to behaviours like stimming (self-stimulatory behaviours), which can interfere with a child's ability to focus on producing clear speech.

Emotional Regulation and Social Interaction

Sensory regulation and emotional regulation are closely linked. A child who is sensory dysregulated may become easily frustrated, anxious, or withdrawn, which can impact their willingness or ability to communicate. For example, a child who is overwhelmed by tactile or auditory stimuli might avoid group activities or interactions with peers, reducing their opportunities to develop social communication skills. These emotional responses can create barriers to forming meaningful connections with others and participating in collaborative learning activities.

STRATEGIES TO SUPPORT STUDENTS WITH VARYING COMMUNICATION NEEDS

Supporting communication development in children with sensory regulation difficulties requires a holistic approach that takes into account their sensory needs as well as their communication abilities. Here are several strategies that teachers and educators can implement to support sensory regulation and communication development in the classroom:

Create a Sensory-Friendly Environment

The first step in supporting communication development is ensuring the classroom environment is conducive to sensory regulation. Minimising distracting sensory input, such as excessive noise or harsh lighting, can help students stay focused and engaged. Consider providing noise-cancelling headphones or quiet spaces where children can retreat if they feel overwhelmed. Visual schedules and communication boards can also help children who struggle with auditory processing, allowing them to follow instructions more easily and reduce anxiety.

Use Visual Supports

Visual supports, such as pictures, symbols, or written words, can enhance communication for children with sensory processing difficulties. These tools help students who have trouble processing verbal information by providing a concrete reference point. Visual timetables, for example, allow children to see the structure of their day, reducing anxiety and enhancing their ability to communicate their needs. Additionally, visual cues can help children understand social expectations and routines, making it easier for them to participate in conversations and activities.

Incorporate Sensory Breaks

Sensory breaks are short periods during which students can engage in activities that help them regulate their sensory systems. These breaks allow students to either increase or decrease sensory input, depending on their needs. For example, a child who is under-responsive to sensory input might benefit from a physical activity break that includes jumping or using resistance bands, which can help them feel more alert and ready to engage in communication. Conversely, a child who is overstimulated might need a quiet break with a calming activity, such as deep breathing or squeezing a stress ball, to help them refocus on conversations and learning tasks.

Adapt Teaching Strategies to Match Sensory Profiles

Tailoring teaching methods to a child's sensory profile can significantly improve their ability to communicate and engage in the classroom. For example, for a child with auditory sensitivity, consider speaking in a calm, quiet tone and providing written instructions alongside verbal directions. For children who seek sensory input, hands-on learning activities that involve movement or tactile exploration can help them stay engaged and focused on the communication tasks at hand. Offering multiple modes of communication—such as spoken language, gestures, and written text—gives students more ways to express themselves and understand others.

Encourage Peer Interaction with Sensory Supports

Peer interaction is a key part of communication development, but children with sensory processing difficulties may need support to engage in social interactions. Providing sensory tools, such as fidget toys or weighted lap pads, can help these children feel more comfortable in social situations. Teachers can also facilitate small group activities that encourage collaboration and conversation, allowing students to practice their communication skills in a structured, supportive environment. Pairing children with communication difficulties with understanding and patient peers can further encourage positive social exchanges.

Collaborate with Speech Therapists and Occupational Therapists

For students with significant sensory and communication challenges, collaboration with speech and occupational therapists is essential. These professionals can provide targeted interventions that address both sensory regulation and communication needs. Speech therapists can support communication, interaction, language comprehension, and social communication, while occupational therapists can focus on sensory regulation strategies that support these communication goals. Regular communication between teachers and therapists ensures that the strategies used in the classroom align with the child's individual therapy goals.

Sensory regulation is a fundamental aspect of communication development, as it affects a child's ability to focus, process information, and interact with others. By creating sensory-friendly environments, providing sensory breaks, and adapting teaching strategies to suit sensory profiles, educators can support the communication needs of all students. Encouraging peer interactions and collaborating with specialists further enhances the classroom experience, promoting both sensory regulation and effective communication. When sensory needs are addressed, children are better able to express themselves, understand others, and thrive academically and socially.

IMPLEMENTING MOVEMENT BREAKS

Incorporating movement breaks throughout the school day is crucial for supporting sensory regulation. Movement breaks offer students an opportunity to engage in physical activity, which can help to regulate their sensory systems and improve overall attention and focus. These breaks can be implemented in various ways:

Structured Movement Breaks

Schedule short, structured movement breaks between lessons or during transitions. Activities may include stretching, jumping jacks, or dancing to music. These breaks should last no more than five to ten minutes and should be followed by a brief return to focused tasks.

Sensory Circuits

Establishing sensory circuits involves creating a designated area in the classroom where students can engage in specific sensory activities. This can include jumping on a trampoline, balancing on a wobble board, or engaging with tactile materials. Sensory circuits can be tailored to individual sensory profiles, allowing students to choose activities that best meet their needs.

Use of Classroom Movement

Integrating movement into classroom instruction can be beneficial. For example, when reviewing phonics, students can participate in a scavenger hunt around the classroom or engage in role-playing activities that require movement. This active involvement can help keep students engaged and facilitate sensory processing.

CREATING SENSORY BREAKS

In addition to movement breaks, implementing sensory breaks is essential for supporting students' sensory needs. Sensory breaks provide students with the opportunity to take a step back from overwhelming stimuli and engage in calming activities that help them regulate their sensory systems. These breaks can take various forms:

Quiet Corners

Designate a quiet corner in the classroom equipped with calming items such as cushions, soft lighting, and calming visuals. This space can serve as a retreat for students who feel overwhelmed or overstimulated. Providing a visual timer can help students understand how long they can spend in this area before returning to class activities.

Breathing Exercises

Teaching students breathing exercises can be an effective strategy for managing sensory overload. Simple techniques, such as inhaling deeply for a count of four, holding for a count of four, and exhaling for a count of four, can help students regain focus and calm themselves during stressful moments.

Mindfulness Activities

Incorporating mindfulness activities into the classroom can be a valuable tool for enhancing sensory regulation. Simple practices such as guided imagery, progressive muscle relaxation, or mindful walking can provide students with techniques to manage stress and anxiety while promoting self-awareness and emotional regulation.

EVALUATING AND ADJUSTING THE CLASSROOM ENVIRONMENT

Creating a sensory-friendly classroom environment is an ongoing process that requires careful evaluation and adjustment. As educators implement sensory-friendly modifications and strategies, it is essential to assess their effectiveness and make necessary changes based on student feedback and individual needs. This section will discuss the importance of evaluating the success of sensory-friendly modifications and provide practical strategies for making ongoing adjustments to create an optimal learning environment for all students.

THE IMPORTANCE OF EVALUATION

The first step in evaluating the effectiveness of sensory-friendly modifications is to understand the diverse needs of students within the classroom. Every child has a unique sensory profile, and their experiences in the classroom can significantly impact their engagement, behaviour, and learning outcomes. Evaluation allows educators to determine whether the modifications made are effectively addressing students' sensory needs and facilitating their participation in classroom activities.

1. To evaluate the success of sensory-friendly modifications, educators should establish clear criteria. These may include observing changes in student behaviour, attention levels, engagement during lessons, and overall well-being. For example, a decrease in sensory-seeking behaviours, such as fidgeting or disruptive movements, may indicate that the modifications are effectively meeting students' needs.
2. Evaluation should encompass both quantitative and qualitative data. Quantitative data can include academic performance, attendance rates, and behaviour incidents, while qualitative data can be obtained through observations, student feedback, and conversations with parents. Collecting a comprehensive dataset allows educators to gain a well-rounded understanding of the impact of sensory-friendly modifications.
3. Educators can engage in self-reflection to assess their own perceptions of the classroom environment and the effectiveness of the modifications. Reflective practice can help teachers identify areas for improvement and highlight successful strategies that positively impact students. Educators may consider keeping a reflective journal where they document observations, insights, and changes in the classroom dynamics.

CONDUCTING OBSERVATIONS

Regular observations are a critical component of evaluating sensory-friendly modifications. Observations allow educators to gain real-time insights into how students interact with their environment and the modifications made.

1. Observe how students respond to sensory tools, movement breaks, and calming zones. Are they using the tools effectively? Do they seem calmer or more focused? Recording observations using a checklist or anecdotal notes can help track progress over time.
2. Inviting another educator to observe and provide feedback can help identify strengths and areas for improvement in sensory-friendly practices. This collaborative approach encourages a culture of support and professional development among staff.

3. Ask your students to feedback on what they find challenging in the classroom. Do they have any suggestions for strategies? Which of the strategies have they found most helpful? What would they like more or less of? Questions can focus on whether students feel supported in their sensory needs, how effective they find the tools provided, and any suggestions for improvement. Remember, we all experience and process sensory input differently, so it is important to brainstorm with your students where possible.

MAKING ONGOING ADJUSTMENTS

The process of evaluating and adjusting the classroom environment is dynamic and should evolve based on the changing needs of students. Educators should remain flexible and open to making ongoing adjustments to sensory-friendly practices.

1. Schedule regular review meetings with the teaching team, support staff, and specialists to discuss the effectiveness of sensory-friendly modifications. These meetings can serve as a platform for sharing observations, student feedback, and data gathered from evaluations. Collaboratively brainstorming ideas for improvement encourages a team-oriented approach to creating an inclusive environment.
2. Recognise that not all modifications will yield immediate success. It may take time for students to adjust to new tools or strategies. Educators should adopt a mindset of trial and error, where they can experiment with different approaches and assess their impact. Maintaining a flexible attitude allows educators to adapt quickly to students' evolving sensory needs.
3. Engage in ongoing professional development to stay informed about best practices in sensory integration and inclusive education. Participating in workshops, training sessions, and webinars can provide educators with new strategies, tools, and insights into supporting sensory regulation in the classroom.

Evaluating and adjusting the classroom environment to meet the sensory needs of students is an essential aspect of fostering an inclusive learning atmosphere. Through observations, gathering student feedback, and making ongoing adjustments, educators can create a sensory-friendly classroom that supports all students in achieving their potential. By remaining responsive to individual needs and engaging in collaborative practices, teachers can create an optimal learning environment where every student can thrive.

CREATING A CLASSROOM CULTURE OF INCLUSIVITY

Fostering an inclusive classroom culture is essential for promoting understanding, empathy, and respect among students. An environment that values diversity and inclusion not only benefits neurodiverse students but enhances the learning experience for all. This section will explore strategies for encouraging empathy among students, building a community that values diversity, and teaching neurotypical students about the needs of their neurodiverse peers. The emphasis will be on creating a culture where differences are recognised, valued, and respected, rather than expecting neurodivergent students to conform or mask their true selves to fit in.

ENCOURAGING EMPATHY AND UNDERSTANDING AMONG STUDENTS

Empathy is a cornerstone of an inclusive classroom environment. When students learn to understand and share the feelings of others, they develop meaningful connections that foster a sense of belonging.

Model Empathy in Action

Teachers play a crucial role in modelling empathetic behaviour. By demonstrating empathy in their interactions with students, educators set an example for the class. This can be done through active listening, validating students' feelings, and addressing conflicts with kindness and understanding. For instance, sharing personal experiences that illustrate vulnerability can encourage students to open up and support one another.

Empathy-Building Activities

Implement activities that promote empathy among students. Role-playing scenarios where students must navigate situations from the perspective of a neurodiverse peer can deepen their understanding of diverse experiences. Additionally, literature that highlights diverse characters and their challenges can facilitate discussions about feelings and perspectives. Stories about neurodiverse characters can be powerful tools for fostering empathy and challenging stereotypes.

Encouraging Open Dialogue

Create a safe space for students to express their feelings and thoughts openly. Encourage discussions about emotions, challenges, and differences. Establishing a routine where students can share their experiences - such as a "feelings circle" - allows them to practice articulating their emotions and listening to others. This practice can cultivate a sense of community where students feel comfortable discussing their experiences.

BUILDING A CLASSROOM COMMUNITY THAT VALUES DIVERSITY AND INCLUSION

A strong sense of community is vital for creating an inclusive classroom. When students feel they belong, they are more likely to support one another and celebrate their differences.

Create Class Norms and Values

Collaboratively establish classroom norms that emphasise respect, kindness, and inclusion. Involve students in the process of creating these norms, allowing them to voice their ideas and expectations. This engagement fosters a sense of ownership and accountability, making students more likely to uphold the community's values.

Celebrate Diversity

Regularly celebrate the diversity within the classroom through activities, discussions, and events that recognise different cultures, abilities, and experiences. For instance, organise "diversity days" where students can share aspects of their backgrounds or interests. These celebrations can include food, music, and stories, allowing students to learn from one another and appreciate the richness of diversity in their classroom.

TEACHING NEUROTYPICAL STUDENTS ABOUT NEURODIVERGENT PEER'S NEEDS

Educating neurotypical students about the needs of their neurodivergent classmates is essential for fostering understanding. Often, the emphasis is placed on the neurodivergent child to "fit in" or learn "how to" socialise with their peers. This education should focus on recognising and valuing differences rather than expecting neurodivergent students to conform.

Curriculum Integration

Integrate lessons about neurodiversity into the curriculum. Use age-appropriate resources to teach students about different neurological conditions, such as autism, ADHD, and sensory processing difficulties. This education can help demystify neurodiversity and promote acceptance. For example, discussing how different brains process information can create a deeper understanding of neurodiverse experiences.

Emphasising Strengths and Contributions

Highlight the strengths and contributions of neurodivergent individuals in various fields, such as science, art, and technology. By showcasing successful neurodiverse role models, students can see the value of diverse perspectives and talents. This recognition shifts the focus from limitations to capabilities, reinforcing the idea that every individual has something unique to offer.

Encouraging Respect for Differences

Foster an understanding that differences should be celebrated rather than viewed as deficiencies. Engage students in discussions about respect and kindness, focusing on how everyone has unique strengths and challenges. Encourage them to think critically about how their actions and words affect others. Use scenarios and case studies to facilitate these discussions, allowing students to explore and articulate their thoughts on inclusion.

CHALLENGING THE NOTION OF CONFORMITY

It is crucial to challenge the expectation that neurodivergent students must conform to neurotypical standards or mask their identities to fit in. This mindset can be detrimental to their self-esteem and overall well-being.

- Encourage students to embrace their authentic selves. Reinforce the idea that everyone has a right to express themselves in ways that feel comfortable and true to them. By creating an environment where differences are accepted, students can feel empowered to be themselves without fear of judgement.
- Involve neurodivergent students in discussions about their experiences and needs. Allow them to share their insights with their peers, fostering a sense of pride in their identities. This empowerment not only benefits neurodivergent students but also enriches the classroom environment as all students gain a broader perspective on diversity.
- Establish a classroom culture where students actively support one another. Encourage acts of kindness, such as celebrating each other's achievements and

CREATING AN INCLUSIVE CLASSROOM ENVIRONMENT

offering help when needed. This support creates a sense of belonging, enabling neurodivergent students to feel valued for who they are rather than for how well they conform to neurotypical norms.

Creating a classroom culture of inclusivity requires intentional effort and commitment from educators and students alike. By fostering empathy, building a strong community, educating neurotypical students about the needs of their neurodiverse peers, and challenging the notion of conformity, educators can create an environment that values diversity and promotes mutual respect. Ultimately, an inclusive classroom benefits all students, creating a richer learning experience that prepares them for a diverse world. The journey towards inclusivity is ongoing, but with dedication and a shared vision, every student can thrive in a supportive and accepting classroom community.

CONCLUSION

Creating an inclusive classroom that supports sensory regulation is essential for fostering an environment where all students can thrive. By understanding sensory processing needs and making simple yet effective modifications, educators can provide a space that supports the diverse needs of all students, both neurodivergent and neurotypical. Sensory regulation not only aids in emotional and behavioural management but also enhances communication and language development, creating a more engaged and focused learning environment for everyone.

KEY TAKEAWAYS

- Sensory regulation is vital for student's ability to focus, engage, and participate in class activities.
- Recognising the sensory needs of students and adapting the classroom environment can improve both learning and behaviour.
- A sensory-friendly classroom benefits all students by creating a calm, inclusive, and supportive environment.
- Collaboration between teachers, therapists, and parents is essential in addressing sensory processing challenges.

CHAPTER 5
ENHANCING SPEECH AND LANGUAGE SKILLS
THE INTERACTION-RICH CLASSROOM

HELPING ALL CHILDREN BECOME GREAT COMMUNICATORS

It's important to remember that communication isn't just about words – it's about connection. When we create communication-rich environments, we're not only helping late talkers, but we're building a foundation for all children to become confident communicators. This focus on communication fosters their ability to express thoughts, ask questions, share ideas, and interact with others. Even children who speak fluently benefit from adults who model good communication practices, like slowing down speech, giving time for processing, and allowing space for responses.

The Power of Slow Pace

Imagine a busy nursery setting. You notice one child, **Charlie**, who speaks fluently and quickly dominates conversations. Next to him is **Mia**, a quieter child who listens intently but doesn't speak as much. It's easy to focus on Charlie's verbal confidence, but for Mia, offering slower-paced interactions will invite her into the conversation too. Slowing down allows both children, the talkative and the quiet, to reflect and respond thoughtfully. This is especially powerful when we wait and give space, as we're not rushing to fill silences.

> **Reflective Prompt**
>
> *How do you currently balance the needs of talkative and quieter children in your setting? What small changes could you make to ensure everyone has a chance to contribute?*

THE IMPORTANCE OF SELF-AWARENESS IN COMMUNICATION

One of the key principles we often overlook in early childhood education is the role of *self-awareness* in adult-child communication. As educators, our habits, tone, body language, and the way we speak all influence the way children learn to communicate. Self-awareness doesn't mean being critical of every word you say, but rather, reflecting on how your language impacts children's development.

Listening to Yourself: Becoming Self-Aware

Reflect on the way you naturally speak to children. Many of us have habits we don't realise, like asking too many questions, or even speaking in a rushed or impatient manner because the day is busy. Taking a step back to evaluate your own communication style can be transformational. For example, you might discover that you default to giving instructions rather than engaging in conversations, or that you rush through interactions without meaning to.

> **Reflective Prompt**
>
> *Reflect on your tone, pace, and interaction style. Are there habits you could adjust to foster more open communication with children in your classroom?*

Noticing the Impact of Adult Talk

In one nursery, a practitioner named Emily often found herself instructing children throughout the day: "Put your coat on", "Don't forget your bag", "Time for snack". While these are necessary directions, Emily noticed that this style limited her engagement with the children. After reflecting on her interactions, she decided to slow down and switch some instructions into more conversational interactions. Instead of "Put your coat on", she tried, "Shall we put your coat on together? It's a bit chilly outside". This opened space for dialogue, where children had the opportunity to contribute and communicate more openly.

BUILDING FACE-TO-FACE INTERACTIONS: A FUNDAMENTAL STRATEGY

One of the simplest, yet most effective universal strategies for fostering communication is getting down to the children's level. When adults position themselves face-to-face with children, it creates a more equal interaction. Children can focus on our facial expressions, watch our mouths as we speak, and feel like communication partners rather than being spoken down to.

Face-to-Face Encourages Participation

> **LET ME TELL YOU ABOUT SOPHIE...**
>
> Sophie, a practitioner in an early years setting, noticed that her tall frame often meant she loomed over children during interactions. Determined to foster stronger connections, she made a conscious effort to kneel down or sit at their level during activities and conversations. One day, during free play, Sophie joined a group of children building with blocks. By positioning herself at their eye level and engaging naturally, she created an atmosphere of equality and trust. Jamie, a usually hesitant child, pointed to a block and whispered, "Blue one". Sophie mirrored his gesture and said, "You've chosen the blue block – where does it go?" Jamie's face lit up as he placed the block carefully, his confidence growing with each turn he took. Over time, he began initiating conversations more often, building his communication skills in a safe, supportive environment.

Here's how Sophie adjusted her approach to support children like Jamie:

1. **Positioning at the Child's Level:** Sophie consistently knelt or sat at the children's eye level during interactions. This made her more approachable and helped children feel like equals in the conversation. By physically aligning herself with the children, she encouraged them to engage more openly, reducing any power imbalance.
2. **Mirroring and Responding Positively:** Sophie mirrored the children's actions and verbal attempts. For example, when Jamie pointed at a block, Sophie reflected his choice verbally ("blue block") and waited for his response. This simple act of acknowledgement validated his effort to communicate and encouraged him to take the next step.
3. **Creating Low-Pressure Interaction Opportunities:** During free play, Sophie avoided quizzing or correcting children. Instead, she commented on their activities, such as saying, "Wow, you're building such a tall tower!" This approach reduced performance anxiety and invited children to share their thoughts naturally.
4. **Encouraging Turn-Taking:** Sophie facilitated back-and-forth exchanges during play. When Jamie responded with "blue block", Sophie followed up with, "Building with the blue block?" This turn-taking not only strengthened Jamie's confidence but also built his conversational skills by modelling the rhythm of communication.

Outcome:
Through these intentional strategies, Sophie transformed her interactions with children. Jamie, who had previously hesitated to communicate, began speaking more frequently

and with greater confidence. By prioritising connection and creating an inclusive environment, Sophie was able to empower all children in her care to express themselves and feel valued in their communication journey.

> **Reflective Prompt**
>
> *Are there opportunities in your setting to adjust your physical positioning during interactions? How might this change the way children engage with you?*

ATTENTION AS CURRENCY

Children crave attention, not just from a place of neediness, but because it is how they measure their worth and importance. Every interaction - whether it's a verbal response, a nod, or even eye contact - signals to a child that their attempts to communicate are valued. In busy settings, some children might seek attention more than others, while others remain quiet, not demanding that same level of focus. Balancing this is challenging, but awareness of who is receiving attention and who is being overlooked can help address this disparity.

Balancing Attention in a Busy Setting

Take the example of Luke, who often seeks attention by calling out and tugging on his teacher's arm. In contrast, his peer, Sarah, tends to stay on the edges of the group, quietly watching but not engaging much. The practitioner noticed that while Luke's attention-seeking behaviour was often met with quick responses, Sarah was inadvertently left with fewer interactions. By deliberately including Sarah in conversations and ensuring she had moments of focused attention too, the practitioner was able to help balance the dynamic and encourage more participation from her.

CREATING OPPORTUNITIES FOR MEANINGFUL INTERACTIONS

We know that language doesn't develop in a vacuum. Creating meaningful opportunities for interaction, where children need to communicate to get what they want or participate, fosters natural development. Often we think about helping language development as talking to children, repeating words and asking questions but meaningful interactions always start with stopping talking, slowing down, listening, and responding to the child.

Another way to create opportunities is by setting up situations to allow the child to come forward and communicate, maybe offering choices, leaving something out, doing the "wrong thing" or giving less than is anticipated. These changes we call Routines Reinvented and it allows children to use their communication to advocate for themselves.

Encouraging Language through Play

In one classroom, toy cars were deliberately placed on a higher shelf where children had to ask for them. Oliver, a child who rarely spoke unless prompted, had to request the car he wanted. Over time, this simple adjustment led him to practice asking more often, and soon he was initiating requests in other areas of play too. It's a reminder that small changes in the environment can lead to significant developments in communication.

INNER VOICE: THE POWER OF POSITIVE COMMUNICATION

Children internalise the way we speak to them, and it becomes their inner voice. When adults use kind, supportive language, it nurtures confidence and self-esteem. However, when language is critical or dismissive, even in a joking way, it can leave lasting effects. Every interaction is an opportunity to contribute to a child's inner dialogue - so it's essential that we speak with kindness, even in moments of frustration.

Shaping the Inner Voice

Think of **Thomas**, a little boy I visited in a nursery, he was always a bit messy with his art projects. His teacher used to laugh and say, "Oh, look, Thomas is at it again with the glue everywhere!" While said in good humour and with a gentle voice, you could see on Thomas' face the feeling of dejection. Over time Thomas started to believe he was clumsy and not very good at art. His confidence dropped, and he started avoiding the craft table. When the teacher realised this, she shifted to saying, "Look at all the effort you're putting in - great job on using that glue so carefully today!" Over time, Thomas started to take more pride in his work and became more willing to try new tasks.

UNIVERSAL STRATEGIES: SUPPORTING ALL CHILDREN TO BECOME GREAT COMMUNICATORS

We know that language skills develop in a dynamic, interaction-rich environment. While we often focus on late talkers, it's essential to recognise that all children benefit from a communication-supportive environment. Whether a child is a confident speaker or someone who hesitates to engage verbally, they all need opportunities to enhance their communication abilities. Our role as educators and caregivers is to create spaces that promote language for everyone - not just those who need additional support but for all learners.

CLASSROOM SETUP: CREATING AN ENVIRONMENT FOR COMMUNICATION

A thoughtfully designed environment can make an enormous difference in how children communicate. One of the first steps to establishing a communication-rich space is making sure it encourages interaction. The classroom should be a place where children feel comfortable to explore, ask questions, express ideas, and engage in back-and-forth communication with peers and adults.

Designing Communication Zones

In Sarah's nursery, she set up small, themed zones like a role-play area, a sensory corner, and a reading nook. The design of these spaces encouraged natural communication. For instance, in the role-play corner, children acted out stories, sharing ideas and collaborating with peers. In the sensory area, children described textures or asked questions about what they were experiencing. Each zone became a place where language was organically woven into their play.

Communication zones also take into account the need for small spaces for small children. Big open spaces with harsh acoustics can negatively impact on child's communication, such as making quieter children more reluctant to talk and loud children, use a louder voice.

Physical Layout: Inviting Interactions

When the aim becomes interactions and not language-rich, we see the environment change, cosy, comfortable areas, nooks, and space become the priority over visuals, lots of language and small group "speech therapy".

SETTING EXPECTATIONS: BALANCING STRUCTURE WITH FLEXIBILITY

Clear expectations are vital for children's communication development. A well-structured routine provides predictability, which helps children feel secure and confident to express themselves. However, it's equally important to build in flexibility, allowing children the space to engage on their terms, make choices and impact their day.

Predictable Routines: Providing a Sense of Security

If we are looking towards better interactions being the key to all children's learning we can begin to make changes within the routine to include this. Children thrive when they know what to expect, and this includes knowing when they will have opportunities to use language in which way. Use names for times in the routine and help children know what they are for: for example, Circle Time is about telling a story to the class, whether that is the teacher telling the story or the children telling their own accounts of things; Chinwag is time for children to talk to each other about whatever they want; the Problem Solving panel is a structured talking time to help children problem solve in a group; Feedback Friday is a time where children can tell each other things they have done well. All these structured times help to build communication and interaction for all children.

Example: Predictable Story Time Discussions

Every day after reading a story, Nina, a year 1 teacher, made it a point to ask open-ended questions like: "What do you think will happen next?" or "What would you do if you were the character?" Over time, even the quieter children started to anticipate this routine and began offering responses without being prompted. Knowing they would have a chance to share helped them feel prepared and less anxious about speaking.

Flexibility: Allowing Room for Child-Led Conversations

While routines are important, it's equally crucial to allow flexibility. Child-led interactions, where children decide the topics or how conversations unfold, are powerful because they are more meaningful to them. These moments of spontaneity offer opportunities for genuine engagement and development of communication skills.

Following the Child's Lead

During outdoor play, **Louis**, a typically quiet child, found a snail and started talking to himself about it. Instead of interrupting or redirecting the activity, his teacher, **Amy**, knelt down beside him and waited to see what Louis had to say about his treasure. Louis quickly opened up and was thrilled to share his observations. This small moment, initiated by Louis, became a rich interaction opportunity that wouldn't have been possible if Amy had jumped in with questions, teaching opportunities, and a lot of language.

SPEED OF DELIVERY: SLOWING DOWN FOR COMMUNICATION

The pace at which we speak and expect children to respond is another critical aspect of fostering communication. Often, adults rush interactions, either because of time pressures or simply out of habit. But slowing down is essential - children need time to process what they've heard, think about what they want to say, and then find the words to express themselves. This is particularly true for children with language delays, but it benefits all learners.

Giving Time to Think and Respond

Pausing after asking a question or making a comment gives children the processing time they need. If we rush to fill the silence, we risk taking away their chance to engage. Children need those extra seconds to gather their thoughts, and when given that time, they are more likely to participate and respond with confidence.

Using the Power of the Pause

In a busy reception setting, **Julie** noticed that children often gave brief, one-word answers during group discussions. After reflecting on her own practice, she realised she was moving on too quickly after asking questions and sometimes asking more than one question at a time. She began intentionally pausing for five to ten seconds after asking each question, giving children more time to process. As a result, their responses became more thoughtful and detailed, and even the less confident children started to contribute more frequently.

FACILITATION VS. DIRECT TEACHING: ENCOURAGING LANGUAGE DEVELOPMENT

One of the fundamental principles of our approach is the emphasis on *facilitating* language rather than directly teaching it. Instead of focusing on questions and corrections, which can put children on the spot, facilitation means walking beside the child, guiding them, and allowing them to come forward with their own words.

Facilitating Conversations: Walking Beside the Child

Facilitation involves creating space for the child to communicate without the pressure of being quizzed or corrected. It's about making comments, observing, and giving the child space to respond or initiate the next part of the conversation.

Commenting Instead of Questioning

Instead of asking, "What are you making?" during craft time, **Ruby** began saying, "Wow, you're working really hard on that - look at all the colours you've used!" She then stops and waits for the child to take their part. This simple change from a question to a comment invited children to share more about what they were doing without feeling tested or put on the spot.

STRATEGIES FOR FACILITATING COMMUNICATION IN GROUP SETTINGS

When working with groups of children, it's easy for the louder or more confident children to dominate discussions. Ensuring that every child has the chance to contribute, especially those who are quieter or more hesitant, requires a mindful approach.

Giving Every Child a Voice

Children who don't actively seek attention are often overlooked in busy classrooms. These quieter children benefit from being included in structured communication opportunities where they are given the space and encouragement to share their thoughts. Start by encouraging non-verbal participation such as "stand up if you need the toilet" or "thumbs up if you think the girl in the story was happy".

Turn-Taking in Group Discussions

During circle time, **Kelly** used a "talking stick" to ensure that every child had the chance to speak. The simple act of passing the stick gave each child, including the quieter ones, a clear signal that it was their turn to speak. This strategy reduced the tendency for more vocal children to dominate and encouraged everyone to participate.

UNIVERSAL STRATEGIES: BUILDING GREAT COMMUNICATORS FOR ALL CHILDREN

When we think about communication development, it's easy to focus solely on children who are late talkers or have noticeable speech and language delays. However, **every child** - whether they're meeting their language milestones or not - benefits from intentional, thoughtful strategies that support their communication skills. This is where **universal strategies** come into play. These are approaches designed for use with all children, not just those with identified communication challenges, and they help every child to become a confident communicator.

Confidence and Connection: The Foundation of Communication

Ultimately, communication is about connection, and that's why confidence plays such a critical role. A child who feels unsure of their abilities, or who has been frequently corrected, is less likely to experiment with language. They might say fewer words or avoid speaking altogether. On the other hand, a child who is confident, who knows that their words are heard and valued, will engage more, speak more, and try new things.

Think of a garden. Children are like seeds - each has the potential to grow into something wonderful. The way we communicate with them is like the water and sunlight that helps them grow. Too much correction (or "bad weather") can stunt their growth, while nurturing and patient communication allows them to flourish.

By combining these universal strategies - interaction-rich environments, face-to-face interactions, self-awareness, and fostering confidence and connection - we create an environment where all children can grow into great communicators. These approaches aren't just for children who need extra support; they are for every child, every day, in every interaction.

In the next section, we'll explore how these strategies can be adapted to meet more specific needs, but the universal principle remains: great communication begins with us. Every child, regardless of their starting point, benefits from an environment where communication is valued and nurtured.

EARLY SCREENING: SPOTTING THE SIGNALS AND TAKING ACTION

Early screening is essential for identifying children at risk of language delays. By actively observing a child's behaviour, educators and caregivers can notice subtle signs of communication struggles, such as limited vocabulary or difficulty following instructions. These early indicators allow us to intervene with tailored support before challenges become deeply ingrained, giving children the best chance to catch up to their peers.

There is an important distinction to make at this stage between children who have had limited linguistic exposure in their formative years, children who are in bilingual environments, and children who have a language delay independent of the environment they have been raised in.

Typical advice such as "talk more to the children" "read daily to improve language" and "immerse children in language" works well for children who are late talkers because of limited exposure to language and for very young bilingual children. But this does not work for children who are struggling to learn language despite a typical environment.

The latter group and older bilingual children do not respond well to the "everyday advice" of narrate the day or talk more. They actually need the opposite. They need space, time, and opportunity to come forward with their communication.

In a classroom, a teacher observes a child, **Mia**, who seldom joins group activities and only uses a few basic words when communicating. Rather than waiting for Mia to develop her language skills independently, the teacher documents Mia's interactions and shares observations with the local speech and language therapy team. The waiting list for an assessment is long, but rather than wait and see, the teacher begins to implement strategies to support Mia's communication straight away.

SUPPORTING LATE TALKERS: ENCOURAGING PARTICIPATION

In an interaction-rich environment, all communication is accepted. It becomes more about what the message the child is sending rather than about how they are sending the message. When caregivers and educators look for the message and respond to it, they build confidence in their late talkers to keep sending messages.

When the children gain confidence that they will be heard and understood they naturally find more reasons to communicate, particularly when interactions are prioritised in the setting.

In a reception class in the Midlands, interaction is prioritised and all communication is accepted for the message. **Talia** is 4 and not yet talking but she has many ways that she communicates. Her teacher told me Talia uses eye pointing, body language and vocalisations to send messages. She was able to tell me a specific example of one day when Talia's cup had fallen behind the cupboard unnoticed by staff. Talia was hot and thirsty and the teacher had said to her "You are hot". She had given a sad look to the teacher and put her hand to her mouth. The teacher understood: "You want a drink". She scanned the room for Talia's cup but couldn't see it. Talia looked worried. "Let's find your cup", the teacher said, and went over to where the cups should be. Talia stood by the cupboard. The teacher thought about why Talia was doing this. She approached her and said: "Cup, where are you?" Talia glanced to the back of the cupboard. The teacher then found her cup and got her a drink. Talia was able to convey this complex message without talking and the interaction with her teacher was successful.

Think of the environment as an adventure course, where each child is a brave explorer. Instead of providing everything at the start, like a guided adventure, place "clues" and choices along the way that encourage children to ask questions, make requests, and share their ideas. This makes language the map that guides them through their day, helping them to find what they want and communicate their needs. And remember to accept all forms of communication not just talking.

SLOWING DOWN: GIVING CHILDREN TIME TO PROCESS AND RESPOND

For children with language delays, fast-paced interactions can be overwhelming. Slowing down our speech, simplifying language, and providing longer pauses after questions or prompts gives children a comfortable window to process and respond. This approach not only demonstrates respect for their pace but also reassures them that their voice is valued.

A nursery practitioner, observing that **Sophie**, a late talker, often hesitates before responding, implements a "count-to-five" strategy. When she asks Sophie a question, she counts silently to five before prompting again. Over time, Sophie becomes more responsive, as she realises she won't be rushed. Her increased confidence in communicating gradually extends beyond the nursery, with Sophie even sharing a story about her favourite toy with her family. This simple patience technique builds her assurance that her words are worth waiting for, allowing her to thrive in her communication efforts.

To think about how overwhelming language can be, I like this analogy: imagine learning to drive on a winding mountain road. If you drive too fast, you risk missing important signs or making mistakes. Similarly, rushing communication with children who find language tricky can make it hard for them to "read the road" and respond comfortably. Slowing down is like lowering the speed limit, giving them time to feel confident and in control.

PERSONALISING INTERACTION: BUILDING CONNECTION THROUGH INDIVIDUAL ATTENTION

Individual attention is a powerful way to engage children who may feel overshadowed or unsure in group settings. One-on-one time allows us to adapt language, tailor responses, and build the child's confidence in a personalised way, all while reinforcing that their unique voice is heard and valued.

This can often feel overwhelming to educators and caregivers, but individual interactions do not need to be taking the child into a small room and doing "specific speech therapy sessions". It is much more about taking time to share focus with the child in their everyday moments. We call these Magic Moments, and it is about joining the child's focus without taking over and spending a few seconds with them.

Jake, a four-year-old awaiting a speech and language assessment, struggles with group activities, often hiding behind his peers. His teacher noticed and started using Magic Moments with him and finding opportunities to join him in his interest without taking over and talking. She noticed he gained confidence in her and she could feel their connection growing. Jake started seeking her out to share moments. These few seconds sprinkled throughout the day paid dividends without the teacher feeling as though she was fitting in speech therapy.

Imagine each child as a flower with unique sunlight needs. While some thrive in the group's shared light, others need dedicated time in the sun to open up fully. Giving individual attention to children with delayed language is like directing a special beam of light toward them, allowing their confidence and skills to blossom uniquely and beautifully.

IN THE MOMENT STRATEGIES TO HELP LATE TALKERS

Let's look in more depth at ways to support late talkers in those moments sprinkled within the day.

Airspace: Creating Room for Expression

Why It Matters: Airspace is about giving children the time and freedom to think, process, and respond at their own pace. Young children, particularly those with language delays, may require more time to gather their thoughts before verbalising them. In high-paced environments, they may otherwise be unable to contribute meaningfully.

How to Implement:

- **Introduce Deliberate Pauses:** After asking a question or making a comment, count silently to five or even ten. This silent pause creates a low-pressure environment, encouraging children to respond without feeling rushed.
- **Designate Quiet Times:** Integrate "quiet time" periods throughout the day, especially during group activities, where only children's voices are encouraged to fill the space. This approach encourages children to notice one another and the opportunity to engage.
- **Reduce Adult Conversation Overload:** In high-activity settings, adult conversations can unintentionally overshadow children's voices. Make a conscious effort to keep adult discussions minimal in shared spaces, encouraging children's voices to take priority.
- **Lead with Airspace:** Enter all interactions with an airspace first approach. Go in listening with your eyes and ears first before speaking.

Imitate and Respond: Encouraging Natural Interaction

Why It Matters: Children learn by observing and mimicking. Imitation - whether it's repeating a sound, copying a gesture, or following a child's lead - reinforces language naturally and builds reconnection.
How to Implement:

- **Reflect and Build:** Shift from focusing on the words, sentences and sounds and think about the conversational turns you take with the child. Go into the interaction not to teach words but to build turns in conversation. Imitating their sounds and actions is a great way to build turns.
- **Follow Their Lead in Play:** When a child initiates play, mimic their actions. If they start stacking blocks, join in. This "mirroring" makes them feel heard and seen and shows that their communication, even non-verbal, has value.
- **Echo Emotions with Empathy:** If a child expresses excitement or frustration, reflect it back using expressions and a tone of voice that matches. This helps children feel understood and promotes social-emotional skills alongside language.

5CS APPROACH IN TARGETED SUPPORT

The Can-Do Approach's 5Cs - *Connection, Confidence, Consistency, challenge, and Consolidation* - serve as a core framework for supporting children. Here's how each principle can guide practitioners to create an environment conducive to language development.

1. **Connection: Building Relationships as a Foundation**

Building connections with children encourages them to engage. When children feel valued and secure, they are more likely to communicate and explore their environment.
Strategies for Connection:

- **Prioritise Daily Check-ins:** Small gestures, such as greeting each child by name in the morning and making time to connect individually, convey respect and interest.
- **Use Physical Proximity:** Sit on the floor, join their play, and ensure your eye level matches theirs. This closeness promotes engagement.
- **Observe Non-Verbal Communication:** A child's body language, gestures, or gaze can offer cues about their interests or needs. Responding appropriately to these cues nurtures a stronger sense of connection.
- **Lead with airspace:** Go in to interactions with airspace rather than teaching words or asking questions.

2. Confidence: Cultivating Self-Assuredness in Communication

Confidence comes when children feel safe to try out their voices without fear of correction or judgement. Confidence-building for at-risk children focuses on fostering comfort within their abilities.

Strategies for Building Confidence:

- **Acknowledge All Attempts:** A simple nod or smile when a child tries to communicate - verbally or through gesture - reinforces their effort, boosting confidence.
- **Provide Choices:** Let children make small choices, such as picking between two snacks or toys. Empowering them to choose enhances self-assurance in expressing preferences.
- **Use Imitate:** Reinforce children's efforts to engage by copying their verbal and non-verbal communication.

3. Consistency: Providing Predictability and Reassurance

Children with language delays thrive on consistent routines and predictability. Knowing what to expect enables them to feel secure, which is essential for confident communication.

Strategies for Consistency:

- **Maintain Routine Language:** Use the same language for recurring activities. For example, "It's snack time - time to wash our hands!" provides familiar phrasing that becomes easy to understand.
- **Establish Visual Schedules:** Visual aids with pictures representing daily routines offer children a sense of what's happening next. This support reduces anxiety and encourages involvement in transitions.
- **Develop Rituals for Greetings and Goodbyes:** Use predictable phrases like "Hello, [Name]!" or "See you tomorrow, [Name]!" These phrases support children in understanding context and structure.

4. Clarity: Simplifying Language for Comprehension

Clear, concise language supports children at risk of language delay by making it easier for them to process information.

Strategies for Clarity:

- **Use Simple Sentences:** For instructions, keep language straightforward. "Time to clean up the blocks" is more accessible than a longer sentence with multiple instructions.
- **Break Down Complex Instructions:** If an activity requires multiple steps, guide them step-by-step. "First, get your paper. Next, choose a colour crayon".
- **Highlight Key Words:** When speaking, emphasise important words by pausing slightly before them or stressing their tone. For instance, "Today we are going to play with the *blocks*".

5. **Communication: Encouraging Engagement and Expression**

Active, supportive communication is fundamental to language growth. Encouraging expression and providing tools to help children convey their ideas enhances their communication skills.

Strategies for Enhancing Communication:

- **Use Visuals and Gestures Alongside Words:** Visual aids like pictures or gestures can reinforce spoken language. For instance, pointing to your mouth when saying "eat" or showing a picture of food can help clarify.
- **Facilitate Turn-Taking Games:** Engage children in games that involve turn-taking, like passing a ball or playing with toy animals. This practice lays the groundwork for conversational turn-taking.
- **Celebrate All Forms of Expression:** Recognise when children use gestures, sounds, or single words, showing them that their effort to communicate is valued.

PUTTING IT ALL TOGETHER: CASE SCENARIO FOR PRACTITIONERS

Imagine a child, **Sam**, who is hesitant to communicate verbally but expresses himself by pointing or making sounds. Here's how the *Can-Do* approach, airspace, and imitate-and-respond strategies might look in action:

1. **Connect:** At the start of the day, the practitioner sits beside Sam, greeting him warmly and making eye contact. During playtime, they join him, watching as he explores the blocks. Sam notices their presence and, feeling the connection, hands them a block.
2. **Confidence:** The practitioner nods and says, "block". They hand it back with a smile, prompting him to repeat the action. This exchange continues, reinforcing Sam's confidence in communicating through action.
3. **Airspace:** When Sam starts to reach for more blocks, the practitioner pauses and waits, giving him the chance to decide whether to engage further. This moment of airspace allows him to process without pressure.
4. **Imitate and Respond:** Sam makes a sound, perhaps a "vroom" for a car. The practitioner imitates with, "vroom!" and starts to roll the block along with a "vroom" sound, meeting him at his level of play and language.
5. **Consistency and Clarity:** During clean-up, the practitioner repeats familiar phrases: "Let's put the blocks in the bin" and reinforces with a song and an action, ensuring Sam understands the expectation. This predictable phrasing and visual support help Sam process the task clearly.
6. **Communication and Celebration:** When Sam gestures toward the door to indicate he's ready for outdoor play, the practitioner responds: "Outside! Let's go!" and celebrates by walking with him, affirming his choice and his non-verbal communication effort.

REFLECTION AND ONGOING PRACTICE

Supporting children with language needs requires a commitment to adapting communication strategies, remaining patient, and celebrating small victories. By consistently applying airspace, imitate and respond, and the 5Cs, early years practitioners can build a strong foundation, helping children not only to feel understood but also to engage meaningfully with the world around them. Each interaction, however small, reinforces their emerging skills, establishing a positive, proactive environment where all children can grow as confident communicators.

CHILDREN WITH AN IDENTIFIED NEED - SPECIALIST SUPPORT

Addressing the needs of children with significant, identified speech, language, and communication needs is a complex and nuanced task. Traditional approaches to speech and language therapy in educational settings often fall short of truly supporting these children. Reports, assessments, targets, and periodic reviews – although thorough on paper – rarely capture the child's lived experience or address their actual day-to-day communication needs. A rigid, target-focused approach risks overlooking the child's interests, confidence, and, ultimately, their motivation to connect. The *Can-Do* approach reframes this entirely, focusing on the child's strengths, current level, interests, and the environmental and interactive factors that can be transformative. Here's how we can rethink support for these children, moving from compliance-driven practices to those that truly enable communication success.

THE TRADITIONAL APPROACH: WHY IT FALLS SHORT

Most traditional methods begin with a cycle of assessment and reporting. A speech and language therapist (SLT) might assess the child, issue a report, and outline specific, measurable targets. While structured, this system has limitations:

1. **Time Constraints:** Traditional SLT sessions are often infrequent, with therapy sessions spaced out over weeks or even months. Between these sessions, progress is expected, but the lack of consistent, daily interaction and support can stall development. In a busy setting or classroom, there can be limited time, space or people to carry out the targets set. This means there is little consistency and the targets become "another thing" to do, or a watch and hope that the child achieves them on their own.

2. **Knowledge Gaps:** Educators and support staff may not receive adequate training to understand these goals, what they are trying to achieve and how they will impact the child in the long run. This makes implementing these SLT goals arbitrary to the team and this impacts the consistently, leaving children with little reinforcement outside of therapy sessions.
3. **Limited Child Participation:** Many of the reports, targets, and assessments are set without the child's interest and preferences taken into account which can result in targets that feel irrelevant or are not meaningful to them. For children, especially those with significant needs, participation can look like play or self-expression rather than standard assessments.
4. **What to do if it doesn't work:** Oftentimes the activities and strategies don't work for the child and the staff are left with no way to modify or change them to engage the child. This can leave huge gaps in support, while the teacher waits for the speech therapist to review the targets and adjust them.
5. **Sensory Considerations:** Often the targets are not set with sensory, regulation and the environment in mind, making them less effective than a joined-up approach.

Imagine a child, **Poppy**, who has difficulty with expressive language and often uses gestures rather than words. Her SLT report might list targets like "Poppy will use 2-word phrases". The staff are given activities to support this progress with flash card and animal games, but Poppy isn't interested in animals and the staff only have 15 minutes twice a week to do the activities. Poppy never pays attention and runs around the room. The staff have to wait for the speech therapist to return to make other suggestions.

Let's make *communication an all-day, every-day interaction*, woven into every moment rather than extracted from isolated "sessions". A more impactful approach focuses on everyday environments and interactions, not just periodic check-ins and technical targets.

RETHINKING THE ROLE OF THE ENVIRONMENT: COMMUNICATION AS AN ALL-DAY, EVERY-DAY PRACTICE

For children with significant needs, the classroom, playground, and even lunch table are central to their communication journey. These spaces provide the perfect context for natural communication practice, where interaction is meaningful, dynamic, and embedded in routine.

1. **Adapting the Physical Environment:** An interaction-friendly environment is one where children feel encouraged to engage. This could mean having visual aids, sensory supports, or communication boards accessible. Children with significant needs might feel overwhelmed in busy, cluttered spaces. A thoughtfully designed, calm area in the classroom, for example, invites them to communicate without sensory overload.

2. **Incorporating Familiar Faces:** Building a communication network around the child is crucial. If only the SLT or one teacher knows the child's communication strategies, then opportunities for growth are limited. Instead, everyone in the child's orbit - from teachers and peers to teaching assistants - needs to be involved in fostering communication.
3. **Seeing Communication in Every Interaction:** True communication growth happens when every adult sees themselves as a communication partner, not just an observer. Practitioners who see each exchange - whether verbal, gestural, or through AAC (augmentative and alternative communication)—as meaningful provide children with frequent, low-pressure opportunities to express themselves and refine their skills.

Take **Michael**, a child who uses a communication board. In traditional sessions, he's encouraged to practice naming objects. However, in a more immersive, environment-focused approach, his communication board might also feature phrases like "more", "help", or "finished", allowing him to use it in real-life scenarios across different settings. When he uses "help" to ask for assistance stacking blocks, he's engaging in meaningful communication, reinforcing his board skills naturally.

RE-EVALUATING EXPECTATIONS: FROM COMPLIANCE TO TRUE PARTICIPATION

Educational settings often impose expectations on children with significant communication needs, requiring compliance with classroom routines and norms. These expectations, however, can sometimes impede genuine communication and expression, especially when rigid.

1. **Reflecting on Compliance-Driven Practices:** For a child who processes language differently, compliance-based expectations can make them feel as though they're "getting it wrong" every day. If a child's response to a question is to look away or move, a compliance-based perspective might demand eye contact or sitting still - forcing a child into uncomfortable positions. Instead, understanding the intention behind the child's actions - such as needing more time or preferring non-verbal communication - leads to a more compassionate, effective approach.
2. **Helping the Child Be Successful, Not "Typical":** For children with unique needs, striving to become "typical" communicators may not be the most relevant or achievable goal. Instead, supporting their ability to communicate successfully - whatever that looks like for them - is far more meaningful. For example, a child with limited verbal skills may find great success and satisfaction in learning a few powerful words or using AAC devices confidently rather than mastering a standard conversation.
3. **Recognising the Irrelevance of Certain Educational Goals:** Some educational goals may not align with the child's personal growth needs. For instance, while a curriculum goal might be to "describe one's weekend in three sentences", for a child with complex needs, being able to indicate preference or ask for a specific toy may hold greater relevance to their daily life.

Take the example of **Danny**, a boy who loves trains but struggles with conventional sentence formation. An SLT report might target "answering open-ended questions", but Danny may be far more engaged – and successful – when he's asked specific questions about trains. By framing questions within his interest, Danny's participation and enthusiasm soar. In this way, success doesn't mean achieving arbitrary educational targets but engaging Danny in meaningful, relevant interaction.

MEETING THE CHILD WHERE THEY ARE: INTERESTS AS ENTRY POINTS

Many children with significant needs find it challenging to engage with conventional educational materials, adult-led activities or prompts. Meeting them where they are and using their interests as a starting point can make a world of difference.

1. **Harnessing Interests to Foster Engagement:** Whether a child loves trains, dinosaurs, or a particular song, using that as a bridge for communication opens the door to more meaningful exchanges. If Danny, from the example above, loves trains, a teacher might use this theme to build vocabulary ("fast train, slow train") and turn-taking ("your turn, my turn").
2. **Expanding Gradually from Familiar to New:** Starting from familiar topics, practitioners can then gently introduce new words, actions, or phrases. For instance, once Danny is comfortable talking about trains, his teacher might introduce "stops" and "starts", creating a pathway to talk about other things that "stop" and "start" in his world, building language from a place of confidence.
3. **Respecting the Child's Comfort Zone:** Children with complex needs often experience the world differently, and we can support them by honouring what brings them comfort. Rather than forcing them into unfamiliar social or sensory experiences, we can incorporate their interests as social bridges, letting them engage with peers in a comfortable way.

SEEING THE WORLD THROUGH THE CHILD'S EYES: PRIORITISING CONFIDENCE AND CONNECTION

A critical piece of supporting children with significant needs is understanding how they view their world and the confidence they gain when they feel connected to it. *Confidence and connection* – two pillars of the *Can-Do* approach – are key here.

1. **Building Confidence Through Predictable Interactions:** Children feel more confident in environments where the expectations are predictable, and they understand

the outcomes of their actions. Simple, consistent routines and familiar cues help them feel safe. When a child with language needs can predict the structure of an interaction, such as a turn-taking game, their confidence grows.
2. **Valuing Connection Over Correction:** Communication with these children should focus on connection, not correction. Rather than correcting "incorrect" communication attempts, practitioners should celebrate them as real efforts to connect. For instance, if a child signs "eat" to indicate they want water, responding with "You're thirsty! Let's get some water" validates the effort without correction, promoting confidence.
3. **Starting from a Place of Empathy:** Children with significant communication needs may express frustration, joy, or fear in unique ways. Seeing the world from their perspective helps adults create a space where children feel understood. When a child is distressed, instead of directing them to "calm down", an empathetic response might be, "I can see you're upset – would you like a quiet spot?" This response validates the child's experience, supporting emotional regulation and enhancing communication.

A STORY OF SUCCESS: THE CAN-DO APPROACH IN PRACTICE

Consider **Anna**, a non-verbal child who communicates using an AAC device. Traditional methods might focus on her achieving specific targets, like creating three-word sentences. However, Anna thrives in settings that respect her pace, interests, and need for predictable routines.

In her nursery, Anna loves the sensory table filled with textured items. Her practitioner, aware of Anna's interests, introduces words like "squeeze", "soft", and "smooth" on her AAC device and encourages her to use these words as she explores. There's no pressure for a complete sentence or specific structure; rather, Anna is given the freedom to explore language through touch and interaction.

Over time, Anna begins to use "squeeze" and "soft" independently, not because it's a target, but because it genuinely describes her experience and allows her to connect with her environment.

In essence, the *Can-Do* approach represents a shift from seeing specialist children as needing to reach certain standards or goals to seeing them as individuals who communicate uniquely and meaningfully. By prioritising confidence and connection, this approach creates a framework that's more in tune with each child's potential, valuing their voice in whatever form it takes. This child-focused perspective gives practitioners, caregivers, and educators a powerful lens through which to support these children, ensuring that their communication journey is not about compliance but about connection, expression, and success on their terms.

CONCLUSION

Creating an interaction-rich classroom isn't just about setting up communication-friendly spaces; it's about rethinking how we engage with children every day. By slowing down, following their lead, and building trust through small, meaningful moments, we create an environment where every child feels heard and valued. Whether it's adapting routines, embracing pauses, or fostering connection, each strategy strengthens children's ability to communicate confidently in their own

KEY TAKEAWAYS

- **Model Slow, Intentional Interactions:** Give children time to process and respond by incorporating pauses and simplifying language.
- **Adjust Your Perspective:** Get on the child's level - physically and emotionally - to foster trust and engagement.
- **Create Communication Opportunities:** Use small environmental tweaks, like offering choices or prompting requests, to encourage meaningful interactions.
- **Celebrate All Forms of Communication:** Validate gestures, facial expressions, and sounds as much as spoken words.
- **Focus on Connection:** At the heart of every interaction is the child's need to feel understood and valued.

REFERENCES AND RESOURCES

Bronfenbrenner, U. (1979). *The Ecology of Human Development: Experiments by Nature and Design*. Harvard University Press.

Bruner, J. S. (1983). *Child's Talk: Learning to Use Language*. Oxford University Press.

Gersten, R., Fuchs, L. S., Compton, D., Coyne, M., Greenwood, C., & Innocenti, M. S. (2005). Quality indicators for group experimental and quasi-experimental research in special education. *Exceptional Children, 71*(2), 149-164.

Greenspan, S. I. & Shanker, S. (2004). *The First Idea: How Symbols, Language, and Intelligence Evolved from Our Primate Ancestors to Modern Humans*. Da Capo Press.

Hart, B. & Risley, T. R. (1995). *Meaningful Differences in the Everyday Experience of Young American Children*. Paul H Brookes Publishing.

Landry, S. H., Smith, K. E., & Swank, P. R. (2006). Responsive parenting: Establishing early foundations for social, communication, and independent problem-solving skills. *Developmental Psychology, 42*(4), 627-642.

Light, J. & McNaughton, D. (2015). Designing AAC research and intervention to improve outcomes for individuals with complex communication needs. *Augmentative and Alternative Communication, 31*(2), 85-96.

Owens, R. E. (2008). *Language Development: An Introduction.* Pearson Education.

Suskind, D. (2015). *Thirty Million Words: Building a Child's Brain.* Dutton.

Parlakian, R. & Lerner, C. (2012). *Building Literacy with Love: A Guide for Teachers and Caregivers of Children from Birth through Age 5.* Zero to Three.

Pianta, R. C. (1999). *Enhancing Relationships between Children and Teachers.* American Psychological Association.

Schickedanz, J. A. (1999). *Much More than the ABCs: The Early Stages of Reading and Writing.* National Association for the Education of Young Children (NAEYC).

Shonkoff, J. P. & Phillips, D. A. (2000). *From Neurons to Neighborhoods: The Science of Early Childhood Development.* National Academy Press.

Snow, C. E. (1983). Literacy and language: Relationships during the preschool years. *Harvard Educational Review, 53*(2), 165-189.

Tannock, R. (2014). Educational practice and interventions for children with ADHD. *European Child & Adolescent Psychiatry, 23*(1), 35-45.

Tomasello, M. (2003). *Constructing a Language: A Usage-Based Theory of Language Acquisition.* Harvard University Press.

Tomlinson, C. A. (2001). *How to Differentiate Instruction in Mixed-Ability Classrooms.* Association for Supervision and Curriculum Development (ASCD).

Vygotsky, L. S. (1978). *Mind in Society: The Development of Higher Psychological Processes.* Harvard University Press.

CHAPTER 6
THE INTERPLAY OF SENSORY REGULATION AND COMMUNICATION IN THE CLASSROOM

UNDERSTANDING THE CONNECTION BETWEEN SENSORY PROCESSING AND COMMUNICATION CHALLENGES

The challenges of sensory regulation and communication are often deeply interconnected, impacting a child's ability to participate in both social and academic activities. Sensory regulation refers to how well a child can respond to and manage sensory input, while communication encompasses both expressive and receptive language skills. For children with sensory processing difficulties, these two domains do not function in isolation - issues in one area can directly affect the other, creating a cycle of challenge that educators must address comprehensively.

Children who experience sensory dysregulation may find it difficult to focus on verbal cues, understand social cues, or even express their own needs clearly. Likewise, communication difficulties - whether due to language deficits, social communication disorders, or other issues - can make it difficult for a child to ask for help when sensory overload occurs, leading to increased stress and dysregulation. This chapter explores how these two areas of challenge overlap and impact one another, providing educators with the tools to identify these needs in their students and apply integrated strategies that support both sensory and communication needs simultaneously.

UNDERSTANDING SENSORY REGULATION AND COMMUNICATION

Sensory Regulation

Sensory regulation refers to the ability of an individual to manage and respond to sensory stimuli from their environment. This includes processing sensory information – such as sights, sounds, textures, tastes, and smells – and modulating responses to that information in a way that is appropriate and functional. Sensory regulation is crucial for effective functioning in daily life, including learning, social interactions, and emotional well-being.

Children, especially those with sensory processing difficulties, may exhibit a range of behaviours based on their sensory needs. Some may be hypersensitive (over-responsive) to sensory input, leading to discomfort or distress in response to normal stimuli, such as loud noises, bright lights, or certain textures. Others may be hyposensitive (under-responsive), displaying a need for increased sensory input to feel grounded, often resulting in behaviours such as excessive movement, fidgeting, or seeking out physical sensations.

These sensory responses can significantly impact a child's ability to focus, engage with peers, and participate in classroom activities. For example, a child who is hypersensitive to noise may struggle to concentrate in a bustling classroom, leading to frustration or withdrawal. Conversely, a child who seeks sensory input may disrupt others while trying to self-regulate their needs.

Communication Challenges

Communication encompasses a broad range of skills, including the ability to understand language (receptive language), express thoughts and feelings (expressive language), and engage in social interactions (pragmatics). Communication challenges can arise from various developmental conditions, such as autism, specific language impairment, or other neurodevelopmental disorders.

These challenges can manifest in different ways. Some children may have difficulty articulating words, leading to speech delays, while others may struggle with understanding social cues or maintaining conversations. Additionally, children with communication difficulties may find it hard to express their sensory needs effectively. For instance, a child who feels overwhelmed by sensory input may struggle to communicate their discomfort verbally, leading to emotional outbursts or avoidance behaviours.

> **Reflective Prompt**
>
> Think about the children in your classroom. Are there any who may be struggling with sensory processing issues that are affecting their ability to communicate?

THE INTERRELATIONSHIP BETWEEN SENSORY REGULATION AND COMMUNICATION

The relationship between sensory regulation and communication is complex and reciprocal. Sensory regulation challenges can impede communication abilities, while communication difficulties can further complicate sensory regulation. Understanding this interdependence is essential for educators and caregivers who aim to support children's development holistically.

Impact of Sensory Regulation on Communication

Children with sensory regulation difficulties may experience challenges in communication due to the way their bodies react to sensory stimuli. For example, a child who is overstimulated by noise may find it challenging to focus on verbal instructions or engage in conversation. This difficulty can result in misunderstandings, frustration, and social withdrawal, creating barriers to effective communication. Moreover, sensory overload can lead to meltdowns or shutdowns, during which a child may become unresponsive or unable to articulate their feelings and needs. In such instances, the ability to communicate becomes compromised, reinforcing the notion that sensory regulation and communication are intertwined.

Research has shown that children with sensory processing disorders often exhibit co-occurring language difficulties, further emphasising the need to address both areas in a cohesive manner (Lane et al., 2010). Without appropriate sensory support, children may struggle to develop the communication skills necessary for social interaction and academic success.

Impact of Communication Challenges on Sensory Regulation

Conversely, communication challenges can exacerbate sensory regulation difficulties. When children lack the verbal skills to express their sensory needs, they may resort to maladaptive behaviours such as aggression, self-stimulatory behaviours, or withdrawal. For instance, a child who is feeling overwhelmed by their environment may not know how to ask for a break or communicate their discomfort. This inability to express their needs can lead to increased anxiety and sensory overload.

Furthermore, communication difficulties can hinder a child's capacity to understand social cues and expectations within the classroom. A child who struggles with pragmatic language may misinterpret a peer's actions or the teacher's instructions, leading to confusion and heightened stress levels. This stress can manifest as difficulties in self-regulation, further perpetuating the cycle of sensory and communication challenges.

The Role of the Environment

The classroom environment plays a significant role in influencing both sensory regulation and communication. A sensory-friendly environment can facilitate better communication by reducing sensory overload and creating a more conducive space for learning and interaction. Elements such as noise control, appropriate lighting, and comfortable seating arrangements can enhance a child's ability to focus and engage with their peers.

On the other hand, a chaotic or overstimulating environment can worsen both sensory regulation and communication challenges. For example, a loud classroom with bright lights and many distractions can overwhelm a child, making it difficult for them to concentrate on communication tasks. Teachers can mitigate these challenges by creating sensory-friendly classroom spaces that cater to diverse sensory needs, thus supporting effective communication.

Understanding the interplay between sensory regulation and communication is vital for fostering an inclusive and supportive learning environment. By recognising how these two areas influence each other, educators can implement strategies that address both sensory needs and communication challenges. This holistic approach will not only benefit children with identified difficulties but also enhance the overall classroom experience for all students.

Creating awareness of this interrelationship allows teachers to develop effective strategies that consider the sensory profiles of their students while also addressing their communication needs. In doing so, educators can empower children to navigate the complexities of the classroom environment, leading to improved outcomes in both learning and social interactions.

HOW SENSORY DYSREGULATION AFFECTS COMMUNICATION SKILLS

Attention and Focus

Sensory dysregulation often results in difficulties maintaining attention and focus. Children who are overwhelmed by sensory input may struggle to concentrate on verbal instructions or conversations. For example, in a noisy classroom, a child with auditory hypersensitivity may become distracted or anxious, making it challenging to listen to the teacher or engage with peers.

When attention is divided or compromised, children may miss critical verbal cues, social interactions, or instructions, leading to misunderstandings and communication breakdowns. For instance, a child who cannot hear a peer's request for help due to background noise may appear unresponsive or disengaged, further exacerbating feelings of frustration and isolation.

Understanding Language

Sensory dysregulation can impede a child's ability to comprehend language effectively. Children who are experiencing sensory overload may have difficulty processing spoken language, leading to misunderstandings or misinterpretations of information. For example, if a child is overwhelmed by visual stimuli in the classroom, they may struggle to follow verbal instructions or comprehend the context of a discussion.

Additionally, children with sensory processing difficulties may struggle with receptive language skills. They may have trouble understanding the nuances of language, such as idioms, metaphors, or nonverbal cues, which can hinder their ability to respond appropriately in social situations. This can lead to further communication difficulties, as children may not grasp the social expectations surrounding interactions.

Expressing Thoughts and Emotions

Sensory dysregulation can also affect a child's ability to express themselves verbally. When children are overwhelmed by sensory input, they may become anxious, frustrated, or withdrawn, making it challenging to articulate their thoughts and feelings. For instance, a child experiencing sensory overload may resort to nonverbal behaviours, such as crying or shutting down, rather than communicating their needs verbally.

Moreover, children with sensory processing difficulties may struggle to find the right words to express their emotions or thoughts. They may use simplified language or gestures instead of engaging in more complex verbal exchanges. This limitation can create barriers to effective communication, leading to misunderstandings and frustration for both the child and their peers or educators.

Social Interactions and Pragmatics

Sensory dysregulation can significantly impact a child's social interactions and pragmatic language skills. Children with sensory processing difficulties may find it challenging to navigate social cues, such as maintaining eye contact, understanding body language, or responding appropriately to others. This can lead to difficulties in forming and maintaining friendships, as well as participating in group activities.

For example, a child who struggles with sensory modulation may not recognise when a peer is feeling upset or overwhelmed, leading to inappropriate responses or behaviours. This lack of awareness can create social rifts and contribute to the child's sense of isolation or loneliness.

Additionally, children with sensory processing difficulties may struggle to engage in turn-taking during conversations, leading to interruptions or difficulties in group discussions. They may dominate conversations or fail to respond to others, further complicating social interactions and communication.

Reflective Prompt

How might sensory overload manifest in a child in your classroom? What strategies could you implement to help reduce sensory stimuli and support the child's communication needs during moments of dysregulation?

EXAMPLES OF COMMUNICATION DIFFICULTIES ARISING FROM SENSORY CHALLENGES

LET ME TELL YOU ABOUT JAMIE...

Jamie is a 7-year-old boy with auditory hypersensitivity. He often becomes overwhelmed in noisy environments, such as the school cafeteria or during group activities in the classroom. When the noise level rises, Jamie shuts down and is unable to focus on conversations. As a result, he struggles to engage with his peers, often missing out on important social interactions. His teachers notice that he frequently appears withdrawn and has difficulty responding to questions or participating in discussions.

LET ME TELL YOU ABOUT SOPHIA...

Sophia is a 6-year-old girl with sensory-seeking behaviours. She often fidgets with objects, moves around the classroom, or engages in loud vocalisations to self-soothe. While Sophia has a rich vocabulary and expressive language skills, her sensory-seeking behaviours often distract her from following conversations. During group activities, she may interrupt others or dominate discussions, making it difficult for her peers to engage with her effectively. Her teachers find it challenging to encourage appropriate social interactions in a structured environment.

LET ME TELL YOU ABOUT ETHAN...

Ethan is an 8-year-old autistic boy with sensory regulation challenges. He struggles with receptive language skills and often misinterprets verbal instructions. In a noisy classroom, Ethan may become anxious and disengaged, leading to meltdowns or shutdowns. His teachers notice that he has difficulty articulating his needs, often resorting to physical behaviours, such as pulling on his teacher's sleeve, instead of using words. This makes it challenging for educators to support Ethan effectively, as they cannot ascertain his needs without understanding his communication style.

Sensory dysregulation profoundly impacts a child's communication skills, creating barriers to effective interaction and social engagement. By understanding the interplay between sensory regulation and communication, educators and caregivers can implement strategies that support children in navigating these challenges. Addressing sensory needs in conjunction with communication difficulties allows for a more holistic approach to supporting children's development, ultimately leading to improved outcomes in both areas. By fostering an inclusive environment that recognises and accommodates diverse sensory profiles, we can empower children to communicate effectively and thrive in their social interactions.

THE ROLE OF COMMUNICATION CHALLENGES IN SENSORY REGULATION

Communication is a fundamental aspect of human interaction, serving as a bridge for expressing needs, emotions, and thoughts. For children, effective communication is crucial not only for social engagement but also for navigating their environments, including those filled with various sensory stimuli. When communication challenges arise, they can significantly exacerbate sensory regulation issues, leading to a cyclical relationship between communication difficulties and sensory overload. This chapter explores how these communication barriers impact sensory regulation and highlights the importance of addressing both areas to support children's overall development.

UNDERSTANDING COMMUNICATION CHALLENGES

Communication challenges can encompass a wide range of difficulties, including issues with expressive language (the ability to convey thoughts and needs), receptive language (understanding verbal input), pragmatics (social use of language), and nonverbal communication (such as body language and facial expressions). For children with sensory processing difficulties or neurodevelopmental disorders such as autism, these challenges may be pronounced, resulting in various barriers to effective communication.

Communication challenges can lead to frustration, anxiety, and social isolation, particularly when children struggle to express their needs or understand the cues of their environment. This lack of effective communication can exacerbate sensory regulation issues, creating a feedback loop where one problem intensifies the other.

HOW COMMUNICATION BARRIERS EXACERBATE SENSORY REGULATION ISSUES

Increased Anxiety and Frustration

Communication difficulties often lead to increased anxiety and frustration for children, particularly when they cannot express their feelings or needs effectively. For instance, a child who is overwhelmed by sensory input but cannot articulate this sensation may become agitated or distressed. This emotional turmoil can intensify their sensory dysregulation, leading to a cycle of escalating anxiety and sensory overload.

When children experience heightened anxiety, their ability to manage sensory input diminishes. They may become hyper-responsive to sensory stimuli, perceiving even mild inputs as overwhelming. This cyclical relationship can result in behavioural challenges, as the child may resort to maladaptive coping strategies, such as meltdowns or withdrawal.

Difficulty Seeking Support

Children with communication challenges may struggle to seek help when they experience sensory dysregulation. For example, if a child feels overwhelmed in a noisy classroom but cannot communicate their discomfort, they may not be able to ask for a break or support from their teacher. This inability to advocate for themselves can lead to prolonged exposure to distressing sensory stimuli, further exacerbating their dysregulation.

Moreover, teachers and peers may misinterpret a child's inability to communicate their needs as defiance or disengagement. This misunderstanding can create a cycle where the child feels increasingly isolated and unable to cope with their sensory environment. As a result, their sensory regulation continues to deteriorate, compounding the challenges they face.

Impaired Social Interactions

Communication barriers can hinder a child's ability to engage socially, further impacting their sensory regulation. For example, a child who struggles with pragmatic language may find it challenging to navigate social situations, such as group discussions or collaborative play. This social difficulty can lead to feelings of exclusion or frustration, causing the child to withdraw from interactions that might otherwise help them regulate their sensory experiences.

Additionally, children who experience social difficulties may have fewer opportunities to develop coping strategies through peer interactions. They may miss out on learning

THE INTERPLAY OF SENSORY REGULATION AND COMMUNICATION

how to communicate effectively in social contexts, which can contribute to their sensory dysregulation. The inability to share experiences, seek reassurance from peers, or engage in reciprocal conversations can deepen the sense of isolation and exacerbate sensory challenges.

THE CYCLICAL RELATIONSHIP BETWEEN COMMUNICATION DIFFICULTIES AND SENSORY OVERLOAD

Sensory Overload Leading to Communication Breakdown

Sensory overload can significantly impair a child's ability to communicate effectively. When children are exposed to overwhelming sensory input - such as loud noises, bright lights, or chaotic environments - their capacity to process information diminishes. This overload can lead to shutdowns, meltdowns, or withdrawal, further hindering their ability to communicate their needs or feelings.

In this state of overload, children may struggle to articulate their thoughts, resulting in a communication breakdown. For instance, during a sensory overload episode, a child may become mute or use nonverbal behaviours to express distress, such as crying or clinging to a familiar object. This reaction can further frustrate caregivers or teachers who may not understand the underlying cause of the child's behaviour, reinforcing the cycle of communication challenges and sensory dysregulation.

Communication Difficulties Leading to Sensory Overload

Conversely, persistent communication difficulties can create situations that heighten sensory overload. For instance, if a child cannot understand verbal instructions in a busy classroom, they may become anxious and overwhelmed by the sensory environment. The inability to process information can lead to confusion and distress, exacerbating their sensory regulation issues.

In social settings, communication barriers can also prevent children from accessing information that helps them navigate sensory challenges. For example, if a teacher fails to explain upcoming transitions or changes in routine, a child who struggles to communicate may become anxious and overwhelmed by the unexpected change. This lack of preparation can heighten their sensory dysregulation, leading to further communication challenges.

ADDRESSING THE INTERRELATIONSHIP BETWEEN SENSORY REGULATION AND COMMUNICATION

Given the cyclical relationship between sensory regulation and communication, it is vital for educators and caregivers to adopt an integrated approach when addressing these challenges. Here are some strategies to consider:

CREATING AN INCLUSIVE ENVIRONMENT

Teachers can create sensory-friendly classrooms that accommodate diverse sensory needs. This includes providing quiet spaces, sensory tools, and strategies for managing sensory input, such as movement breaks or calming techniques. By fostering an inclusive environment, children are better equipped to engage with their surroundings, ultimately enhancing their communication opportunities.

PROMOTING COMMUNICATION STRATEGIES

Implementing communication strategies that are accessible to all children is essential. Visual supports, such as pictorial schedules or visual cues, can help children understand routines and expectations, reducing anxiety and improving communication. Additionally, using alternative communication methods, such as sign language or augmentative and alternative communication (AAC) devices, can empower children to express their needs more effectively.

ENCOURAGING PEER INTERACTIONS

Facilitating opportunities for social interactions among peers can help children develop communication skills while providing a supportive environment for sensory regulation. Structured group activities, buddy systems, or peer mentoring can create a sense of belonging and encourage children to communicate and engage with their classmates.

FOSTERING EMOTIONAL REGULATION

Teaching emotional regulation strategies can help children manage their responses to sensory stimuli and improve their communication skills. Mindfulness techniques, breathing exercises, and self-soothing strategies can empower children to recognise their feelings and express them verbally. This self-awareness can reduce anxiety and enhance their ability to communicate their needs effectively.

The interplay between communication challenges and sensory regulation is a complex but crucial area of focus for educators and caregivers. By recognising the cyclical relationship between these two domains, we can develop comprehensive strategies to support children in overcoming their difficulties. Addressing sensory regulation alongside communication challenges creates a holistic approach that empowers children to thrive in their social interactions and navigate their sensory environments with greater ease. Ultimately, fostering effective communication and sensory regulation skills lays the groundwork for children's overall development and well-being.

COMMON CLASSROOM SCENARIOS WHERE SENSORY AND COMMUNICATION CHALLENGES INTERSECT

Group Activities and Collaborative Learning

Group activities are a staple in modern classrooms, promoting teamwork and social skills. However, for some children, the combined demands of sensory input and social communication can be overwhelming. A child who struggles with auditory processing may find it difficult to follow conversations in a noisy environment, leading to feelings of frustration and isolation.

Strategy: Teachers can implement structured group activities with clear expectations. Using visual aids to outline roles and tasks can help children understand their responsibilities, reducing anxiety. Providing options for quieter workspaces or allowing children to choose their group members can also facilitate a more comfortable environment.

Transitions Between Activities

Transitions can be particularly challenging for children with sensory and communication difficulties. The sudden shift from one activity to another can lead to sensory overload, especially if the change is unexpected or poorly communicated. A child who is nonverbal or struggles with receptive language may not understand what is happening, leading to confusion and distress.

Strategy: Teachers can use visual schedules to indicate upcoming transitions, allowing children to prepare mentally for changes. Additionally, providing sensory breaks before transitions can help children regulate their emotions and re-engage more effectively. This proactive approach supports both sensory regulation and communication by reducing the anxiety associated with transitions.

Classroom Noise Levels

Many children experience difficulties with sensory regulation in noisy environments. The clatter of chairs, voices, and other classroom sounds can create a chaotic atmosphere, which may lead to sensory overload. In turn, a child overwhelmed by noise may struggle to communicate their needs effectively, leading to frustration and potential behavioural issues.

Strategy: Implementing noise-reduction strategies, such as using soft furnishings, carpeted areas, or sound-absorbing panels, can create a more conducive learning environment. Teachers can also establish "quiet zones" in the classroom where children can retreat when feeling overwhelmed. Encouraging the use of nonverbal communication, such as hand signals, can help students express their needs without adding to the auditory chaos.

Unexpected Changes in Routine

Predictability is crucial for children with sensory and communication challenges. Unexpected changes in routine - whether due to a fire drill, a supply teacher, or a rescheduled activity - can trigger anxiety and dysregulation. Children who struggle to communicate may find it especially challenging to articulate their concerns or feelings during such transitions.

Strategy: Preparing students for potential changes through advance communication can help ease anxiety. Teachers can use social stories or visual supports to explain what to expect in the event of a routine change. Encouraging children to express their feelings about these changes - either verbally or through drawings - can help them process their emotions and feel more secure.

STRATEGIES FOR TEACHERS TO IDENTIFY AND ADDRESS CHALLENGES COLLECTIVELY

Observation and Assessment

Teachers play a crucial role in identifying sensory and communication challenges in their students. Regular observations can provide insight into how sensory input affects behaviour and communication. Implementing informal assessments, such as sensory checklists or communication logs, can help teachers track individual progress and identify specific areas of need.

Collaborative Planning

Collaboration among educators, speech and language therapists, and occupational therapists can enhance the effectiveness of interventions. By working together, professionals can create tailored strategies that address both sensory and communication needs. This collaborative approach ensures that interventions are cohesive and that all staff members are aware of individual students' challenges.

Professional Development and Training

Ongoing professional development can equip teachers with the skills and knowledge to support students with sensory and communication challenges effectively. Workshops on sensory processing, communication strategies, and inclusive practices can enhance teachers' understanding of how these areas intersect. Moreover, training in specific intervention strategies, such as the use of visual supports or sensory tools, can empower teachers to create a more inclusive classroom environment.

Involving Families

Engaging families in the process of addressing sensory and communication challenges is essential. Teachers can collaborate with parents to gather information about their child's needs and preferences, as well as to share strategies that can be implemented at home. This partnership fosters a consistent approach to supporting children and reinforces the importance of addressing both sensory regulation and communication together.

CASE STUDIES

Understanding the complex interplay between sensory regulation and communication challenges in students is crucial for educators seeking to create an inclusive classroom environment. The following case studies illustrate how these two areas interact and affect students' learning. Each example provides insight into specific challenges faced by the students, highlighting the importance of recognising and addressing both sensory and communication needs simultaneously.

CASE STUDY 1: MAX – SENSORY SEEKING WITH LANGUAGE DELAYS

Background

Max is an 8-year-old boy diagnosed with sensory processing disorder (SPD) and language delay. He exhibits sensory-seeking behaviours, such as climbing on furniture and jumping off objects. Max communicates verbally using single words or gestures to express his needs, which can lead to frustration.

Challenges

Max's sensory-seeking behaviours often result in disruptions during lessons and distract his peers. His language delays further complicate communication, as he struggles to express his needs and feelings effectively. When Max becomes overwhelmed by sensory input, such as loud noises or bright lights, his communication becomes unclear or he is not able to access it at all which leads to frustration.

Impact on Learning

Max's sensory needs often interfere with his ability to focus during lessons. For instance, when the classroom becomes noisy during group activities, Max struggles to concentrate, which hinders his ability to participate and communicate. His peers often misunderstand his communication, leading to social isolation and increased anxiety.

Interventions: The team implements strategies that focus on empowering Max and building his communication skills from a strengths-based perspective:

1. **Routine and Structure:** A consistent classroom routine helps Max anticipate transitions and reduce anxiety. Predictable structures in the day support his sensory and communication needs by offering clear cues and time to process information.
2. **Sensory Breaks:** Max is given sensory breaks that align with his sensory seeking needs. These breaks allow him to engage in structured movement activities, such as jumping or stretching, to help regulate his sensory system. These activities support his self-regulation and prepare him for further engagement in tasks.
3. **Communication Tools:** To support Max's verbal communication, the teacher introduces simple communication boards with visuals that allow Max to express his needs in real-time. This nonverbal approach builds on his strengths, helping him participate more fully in class activities.
4. **Peer Understanding and Support:** Educating Max's peers about his sensory needs fosters a supportive classroom environment. This helps to reduce misunderstandings and encourages Max's peers to offer support during activities, creating a more inclusive and empowering learning environment.

Through these strategies, Max is empowered to manage his sensory needs and express himself more effectively. By focusing on his strengths and building communication skills from his current abilities, Max gains confidence in his communication and participation.

THE INTERPLAY OF SENSORY REGULATION AND COMMUNICATION

> *Reflective Prompt*
>
> *How might Max's sensory sensitivities have been overlooked if his teacher hadn't considered both his sensory needs and communication abilities? What are some steps you could take to support students with similar sensory seeking and language delay challenges?*

CASE STUDY 2: EMMA – SENSORY OVER-RESPONSIVENESS AND NON-SPEAKING

Background

Emma, a 7-year-old autistic girl, experiences sensory over-responsiveness, often becoming overwhelmed by sensory stimuli like loud noises, bright lights, and crowded spaces. Emma communicates primarily through nonverbal means, such as gestures, eye contact, and her Picture Exchange Communication System (PECS) cards.

Challenges

Emma's sensitivity to sensory stimuli often causes her to withdraw from activities or areas in the classroom that overwhelm her. She may retreat to a quiet corner during group work, missing out on valuable social interactions. When Emma becomes overwhelmed, she may have meltdowns, which further escalate her sensory overload and disrupt her ability to communicate effectively.

Impact on Learning

Emma's heightened sensitivity makes it difficult for her to participate in group activities, and her nonverbal communication can sometimes make it harder for her to express her discomfort or needs. During a class project involving loud music and bright visuals, Emma struggles to use her PECS cards to express her feelings, leading to frustration and social isolation.

Interventions: The Team implements a strengths-based, empowerment-focused approach:

1. **Calming Environment:** The teacher modifies the classroom environment to include soft lighting, sound-absorbing materials, and designated quiet spaces. This provides Emma with a sensory-friendly retreat when she feels overwhelmed, allowing her to regain composure and engage more effectively in activities.
2. **Sensory Tools:** To address Emma's sensory needs, the teacher introduces sensory tools like noise-cancelling headphones and weighted blankets. These tools provide Emma with the means to self-regulate, helping her manage overwhelming sensory input and supporting her ability to participate in learning.

3. **Communication Tools:** In line with Emma's nonverbal communication, the teacher reinforces the use of her PECS cards and provides ample opportunities for Emma to use them throughout the day. Emma's teacher models the use of these communication tools to help her express her needs more effectively and confidently.
4. **Slowing Down:** The teacher slows down the language she uses with Emma, the number of transitions, and the expectations in the day, to reduce the stress for Emma.
5. **Choices:** The teacher offers Emma as many choices as possible throughout the day so she has her voice heard and can learn to meet her own needs

These strategies, based on Emma's sensory profile and communication abilities, help her engage more effectively with peers and participate in classroom activities. The focus on Emma's strengths and needs fosters greater inclusion, enabling her to feel more connected to her peers and classroom environment.

> *Reflective Prompt*
>
> Emma benefited from a calming space when she became overwhelmed. How could you integrate calming strategies into your classroom routine for children with sensory sensitivities?

CASE STUDY 3: LIAM – SENSORY UNDER-RESPONSIVENESS WITH EXPRESSIVE LANGUAGE DIFFICULTIES

Background

Liam is a 6-year-old boy with ADHD and sensory under-responsiveness. He tends to be less aware of sensory stimuli, often appearing uninterested or disengaged during activities. Liam also experiences expressive language difficulties, which impact his ability to articulate his thoughts and feelings clearly.

Challenges

In the classroom, Liam struggles to engage with tasks, often missing cues from teachers and peers. His under-responsiveness to sensory input leads him to overlook important cues, making it difficult for him to recognise when he's becoming overwhelmed. As a result, Liam's communication attempts can be vague or unclear, leading to misunderstandings and frustration among classmates.

Impact on Learning

Liam's under-responsiveness to sensory input affects his participation in group discussions and collaborative tasks. For example, during a reading session, Liam may not react to prompts or questions, which can lead to a perception that he is disinterested or disengaged. This lack of participation only exacerbates his communication difficulties, as his peers may not include him in discussions.

Interventions: The team focuses on empowering him by using strategies that build on his existing strengths:

1. **Interactive, Hands-On Activities:** To engage Liam's sensory system and enhance his communication skills, the teacher introduces interactive activities, such as hands-on learning games. These activities stimulate Liam's sensory awareness, help him stay alert, and encourage participation in group discussions.
2. **Verbal and Visual Cues:** The teacher uses both verbal prompts and visual cues to help draw Liam's attention during group activities. These cues provide him with clearer signals about when to engage, reinforcing his communication efforts and improving his confidence.
3. **Sensory Activities:** The classroom incorporates movement breaks and tactile experiences to stimulate Liam's sensory system and help him stay engaged. These activities are designed to increase his awareness of his environment, fostering greater focus and participation.
4. **Before|During|After:** The teacher uses a Before|During|After approach, by cuing Liam into the task on a 1:1 beforehand, helping him understand what is happening, the key points, and what is expected of him; during the activity she equips him with tools and visuals to help him succeed and then afterwards she spends a couple of minutes checking in with him that he understood. This approach scaffolds children to be successful in difficult moments.
5. **Peer Interaction and Support:** To address Liam's expressive language difficulties, the teacher encourages peer support during group work. This allows Liam to practice communication in a low-pressure setting, reinforcing his language development and social interaction skills.

Through these interventions, Liam is able to improve his engagement in classroom activities, develop his communication skills, and enhance his overall learning experience. The teacher's approach is rooted in Liam's strengths, providing him with opportunities to thrive both academically and socially.

> *Reflective Prompt*
>
> *Liam benefited from sensory integration activities and verbal cues to improve his engagement and communication. How could you incorporate sensory strategies, such as movement breaks or hands-on activities, to support students with similar sensory under-responsiveness and language challenges in your classroom?*

These case studies demonstrate the intricate relationship between sensory regulation and communication challenges in students. By recognising and addressing both areas simultaneously, educators can create a more inclusive and supportive classroom environment. The implementation of targeted strategies tailored to individual student needs not only enhances learning outcomes but also promotes social integration, empowering students to thrive in their educational journeys.

IMPLEMENTING INTEGRATED STRATEGIES IN THE CLASSROOM

Creating a supportive classroom environment that effectively addresses both sensory regulation and communication challenges is essential for fostering inclusive learning experiences. Educators can implement integrated strategies that promote sensory awareness and communication skills while ensuring that all students feel valued and supported. This approach not only enhances individual learning but also nurtures a cohesive classroom community. We've discussed many strategies in this chapter, but let's summarise ways in which teachers can support both sensory regulation and communication needs within the classroom without relying heavily on one-to-one support.

ESTABLISH A SENSORY-FRIENDLY CLASSROOM ENVIRONMENT

Creating a sensory-friendly classroom environment begins with optimising the physical space to cater to a variety of sensory needs. Teachers can:

- Minimise Sensory Overload by using soft lighting, such as lamps instead of harsh fluorescent lights, and consider the placement of windows to reduce glare. Acoustic panels or sound-absorbing materials can help manage noise levels, making the environment less distracting for students who are sensitive to sound.
- Establish specific areas within the classroom for sensory regulation, such as calming corners or sensory stations equipped with tools like stress balls, fidget toys, or calming visuals. These spaces provide students with opportunities to self-regulate when they feel overwhelmed or anxious.
- Arrange the classroom to allow for movement and flexible seating options. Encourage students to use wobble stools, standing desks, or cushions that promote active sitting. Providing opportunities for movement breaks throughout the day can help students release excess energy and enhance their focus during instructional periods.

IMPLEMENT STRUCTURED ROUTINES AND VISUAL SUPPORTS

Structure and routine play a crucial role in supporting sensory regulation and communication skills. Teachers can:

THE INTERPLAY OF SENSORY REGULATION AND COMMUNICATION

- Develop a daily schedule that is consistent and predictable, providing students with a clear understanding of what to expect. Visual schedules can enhance comprehension and assist students in transitioning between activities. This consistency reduces anxiety and enables students to focus on learning rather than uncertainty.
- Incorporate visual supports such as charts, pictures, and symbols to reinforce instructions and facilitate communication. Visuals help students who may struggle with verbal language to understand tasks, directions, and expectations, thereby enhancing their ability to engage with the lesson content.
- Provide students with checklists for tasks and use timers to signal transitions. This approach supports self-monitoring and encourages students to become more independent in managing their time and tasks.

FOSTER COLLABORATION AND PEER SUPPORT

Building a classroom culture that encourages collaboration and peer support is vital for addressing both sensory regulation and communication challenges. Teachers can:

- Implement cooperative learning strategies where students work in small groups to complete tasks. This format promotes communication, social interaction, and teamwork while allowing students to support one another in managing sensory needs and sharing ideas.
- Establish a peer buddy system where students can partner with classmates who model positive social behaviours and communication skills. This partnership encourages students to interact, share, and support each other, enhancing their social connections and fostering empathy within the classroom.
- Create a classroom culture that values open dialogue and encourages students to express their thoughts and feelings. Regular check-ins, group discussions, or circle time provide opportunities for students to share their experiences and support one another in navigating sensory and communication challenges.

INTEGRATE MOVEMENT AND SENSORY BREAKS

Integrating movement and sensory breaks throughout the school day can significantly improve sensory regulation and communication skills. Teachers can:

- Plan short movement breaks between lessons to allow students to stretch, engage in physical activity, or participate in calming exercises. These breaks can

help students release built-up energy, enabling them to refocus during instructional time.
- Incorporate movement into learning activities. For instance, using kinaesthetic learning strategies, such as acting out a story or using gestures to illustrate concepts, can make lessons more engaging and enhance communication skills.
- Introduce mindfulness activities, such as deep breathing exercises, yoga, or guided imagery, to help students regulate their sensory experiences and reduce stress. Mindfulness practices promote self-awareness and can enhance communication by enabling students to express their feelings and needs more effectively.

PROMOTE COMMUNICATION THROUGH CONTEXTUAL LEARNING

Effective communication can be nurtured by connecting learning to real-life situations. Teachers can:

- Design lessons that incorporate real-life scenarios or problem-solving activities. This approach encourages students to practice communication skills in meaningful contexts, promoting engagement and understanding.
- Invite students to share their experiences through storytelling, whether verbally or through visual means. Storytelling not only fosters communication skills but also encourages emotional expression and empathy among peers.
- Employ multi-sensory teaching strategies that engage students through various modalities (e.g., visual, auditory, tactile). By incorporating different senses into learning, teachers can support diverse communication styles and enhance overall engagement.

CONCLUSION

In this chapter, we have delved into the complex and multifaceted relationship between sensory regulation and communication challenges in the classroom. By understanding how these two areas are intertwined, educators can more effectively support students who face difficulties in both domains. Sensory regulation and communication are not isolated issues but are part of a continuous cycle that significantly influences a child's ability to engage, learn, and interact with their environment.

THE INTERPLAY OF SENSORY REGULATION AND COMMUNICATION

We began by recognising that sensory dysregulation can often hinder communication. For example, a child who is overwhelmed by sensory input may struggle to articulate their needs, leading to frustration, anxiety, or behavioural outbursts. Similarly, communication difficulties can exacerbate sensory regulation challenges. A child who cannot express discomfort or communicate effectively may become more dysregulated, leading to behavioural issues that disrupt both learning and social interaction. This cyclical relationship underscores the need for an integrated approach to addressing these challenges.

Throughout the chapter, we explored various classroom scenarios where sensory and communication difficulties intersect, such as during transitions, group activities, and in sensory-rich environments. Understanding how these challenges manifest in everyday classroom situations allows teachers to better identify when a student may be struggling with both sensory processing and communication, and to respond in a way that addresses both issues simultaneously.

Real-life examples and case studies have shown the importance of recognising the diverse ways in which sensory and communication needs can manifest in individual students. These case studies provided concrete examples of how a holistic approach can support children with a variety of sensory profiles and communication difficulties. By taking these examples into account, educators can implement practical strategies that promote inclusivity and ensure that all students, regardless of their sensory and communication challenges, are able to participate fully in the classroom environment.

The key takeaway from this chapter is the need for a holistic approach to education that acknowledges and addresses the interconnected nature of sensory regulation and communication. Traditional educational practices often treat sensory and communication needs in isolation, focusing on one area at a time. However, this compartmentalised approach can overlook the complex relationship between the two, potentially leading to missed opportunities for comprehensive support. An integrated approach, on the other hand, recognises the importance of addressing both areas simultaneously, fostering a more inclusive learning environment that promotes both academic achievement and social-emotional well-being.

To create truly inclusive classrooms, it is crucial for educators to not only implement individual strategies to address sensory or communication needs but to consider how these strategies can work together in a complementary manner. By doing so, teachers can build an environment where every child is supported in a holistic way, leading to more positive learning outcomes and better social engagement. This interconnected perspective benefits not only children with specific sensory and communication challenges but enriches the educational experience for all students. It promotes a culture of inclusivity and understanding, where every child's needs are recognised and met, fostering a sense of belonging and support that extends well beyond the classroom.

By adopting a holistic approach that integrates sensory regulation and communication strategies, educators can create classrooms that are not only responsive to the diverse needs of their students but also actively nurture their growth and development. The benefits of such an approach ripple out, impacting not just academic achievement but also the social and emotional well-being of students, enabling them to thrive in all aspects of their education and in life beyond the classroom.

KEY TAKEAWAYS

- Sensory regulation and communication are deeply interconnected and must be addressed together for effective support.
- Modifying the classroom environment to cater to sensory needs can enhance communication opportunities and improve engagement.
- Collaborative strategies involving teachers, therapists, and families ensure a cohesive approach to supporting students.
- A holistic approach that integrates both sensory regulation and communication strategies improves outcomes for students and promotes an inclusive, responsive classroom.

REFERENCE AND RESOURCE

Lane, A. E., Young, R. L., Baker, A. E. Z., & Angley, M. T. (2010). Sensory processing subtypes in autism: Association with adaptive behavior. *Journal of Autism and Developmental Disorders, 40*(1), 112-122.

CHAPTER 7
TAKING A FRESH LOOK AT SENSORY AND COMMUNICATION

LOOKING THROUGH THE CHILD'S EYES: UNDERSTANDING THEIR WORLD

To truly support children in their speech, language, and overall development, we must first learn to see the world from their perspective. Children, especially those with communication challenges, often navigate their environment in ways that can be easily misunderstood by adults. By endeavouring to understand how a child experiences their surroundings, we unlock the key to helping them thrive.

Seeing the world through the child's eyes means stepping back and observing how they interact with people, spaces, and objects. Are they overwhelmed by noise or busy environments? Do they struggle to process multiple instructions at once? Do they find comfort in specific routines or objects? Every child has unique preferences, sensory needs, and communication styles, and recognising these can transform how we support their development.

When adults approach children with curiosity and empathy, they can more easily identify barriers to communication and learning. For example, a child who is quiet or reluctant to speak might not be shy but could feel unheard in a busy classroom. Another child might struggle to concentrate because of overwhelming sensory input, such as bright lights or constant background noise. These factors can greatly influence how they express themselves.

Understanding the child's perspective also helps us reframe their behaviour. What adults might perceive as misbehaviour or a lack of engagement could be the child's way of coping with an environment that feels unpredictable or confusing. Instead of asking "Why won't they follow instructions?" we can ask: "What is it about this situation that makes it hard for them to respond?"

To help children thrive, we need to be responsive to their unique needs. This might involve adapting the physical environment to make it more predictable, creating opportunities for the child to take the lead in interactions, or simplifying language to match the child's level of comprehension. These changes foster connection and build the child's confidence, allowing them to communicate more freely and comfortably.

By seeing the world from the child's point of view, we are better equipped to provide the understanding and support they need to become their most fabulous, regulated, and confident selves. This approach is not about making the child fit into the world but about shaping the environment and our interactions to meet the child where they are. When children feel understood and appreciated, they thrive in every area of their development.

By fostering an environment where we look at supporting each child to be the best version of themselves, there are many benefits for all children, not just those with additional needs.

Adults who recognise this give permission to every child to be themselves, understand themselves, and understand others.

As an example, think of the traditional role of "social skills groups". These groups aim to teach social skills to neurodivergent children, so they can fit in better with their peers. But when we use the lens of "difference not deficit" it makes social skills groups feel irrelevant. It makes us realise that all children need to understand their own communication style and sensory needs and those of others, so we all have the skills to communicate with others.

5 TOP TIPS FOR SEEING THE WORLD THROUGH THE CHILD'S EYES

1. **Observe Without Judgement**
   Spend time simply watching how the child interacts with their environment. Notice what they are drawn to, what they avoid, and how they communicate non-verbally. This gives you insight into their needs and preferences without the filter of adult expectations. Think about the words you use to describe what they are doing: are you measuring them on how compliant they are or are you merely saying what you see?
2. **Create Predictable Routines**
   Children, especially those with communication challenges, thrive in environments that are predictable and consistent. Routines help reduce anxiety and allow children to focus on communication and interaction rather than figuring out what comes next.
3. **Simplify Language**
   Speak in short, clear sentences and allow the child time to process what you've said. Overloading children with too many words or instructions can overwhelm them. Give them the space to respond at their own pace.
4. **Provide Sensory Support**
   Be mindful of sensory sensitivities. Adjust the environment to reduce overwhelming stimuli, such as loud noises, bright lights, or clutter. Offer quiet, cosy spaces where the child can retreat if they need a break from sensory input.
5. **Let the Child Lead**
   Encourage the child to take the lead in activities. This builds confidence and gives them a sense of control. Follow their interests, and use these moments to engage in meaningful communication at their level. This helps the child feel seen and understood.

> **Reflective Prompt**
>
> *Take a moment to think about how the children you work with experience their environments. Are there sensory inputs or routines that might overwhelm them? How do they communicate their needs? Reflect on one child and note down three ways you could adapt your approach to better align with their perspective.*

FOCUSING ON STRENGTHS: CELEBRATING WHAT CHILDREN CAN DO

Too often, traditional assessments and educational systems focus on what children cannot do, measuring them against a narrow standard of "typical" development. This deficit-based approach can make children feel inadequate and overlook the unique abilities and potential they possess. Instead, by shifting the focus to what children *can* do, we unlock their confidence and enthusiasm for learning, and we create an environment where they can truly thrive.

Let's take carpet time as an example. Toby was a little boy who could sit on a chair for upwards of 15 minutes, as long as he had something to fiddle with and didn't have to look directly at the teacher. Afterwards he could recall what the teacher was saying. We could look at this in two ways. Toby is not sitting on the carpet facing the teacher and he is fiddling or for Toby to get the most from the teacher he needs to sit on a chair, fiddle and not look directly at the teacher. Do we want Toby to be able to listen, or do we want Toby to comply with what we think listening should look like?

Every child has strengths, whether it's in their ability to understand visual information, their capacity for empathy, their love of movement, or their deep interest in certain subjects. By recognising and celebrating these strengths, we validate the child's experiences and give them the foundation to grow in areas where they may struggle. Focusing on strengths doesn't mean ignoring challenges; it means using a child's natural abilities as a starting point for development.

Let's think about Tilly, she was a little girl, in reception, who showed no interest in numbers. Her love and special interest was dinosaurs and that is what she focused on mainly. When the teacher began to use dinosaurs to teach numbers, everything changed for Tilly, it was like it suddenly made sense to her and she was able to focus so much better.

When we celebrate what children can do, we're not only boosting their self-esteem, but also reinforcing positive behaviours and building their resilience. For example, a child with a strong visual memory but difficulty with verbal language might excel when given opportunities to learn through pictures, diagrams, or hands-on activities. Recognising and supporting this strength can, in turn, help the child build confidence in areas of challenge, like verbal expression or social interaction.

Shifting to a strength-based approach also changes how adults interact with children. Instead of focusing on deficits and setting goals based on what the child is lacking, we set goals based on how we can use their strengths to scaffold further learning. This could mean using a child's love of movement to build speech skills through physical games, or using a child's interest in a particular subject as a way to expand their vocabulary.

Additionally, when children feel that their strengths are recognised, they are more likely to engage in learning and communication. They begin to see themselves as capable and competent, which can be particularly important for children who may struggle with self-esteem due to speech or language challenges. When adults highlight what a child can do, rather than constantly pointing out what they cannot, it nurtures a sense of belonging and helps the child develop a positive self-image.

A strength-based approach not only benefits the child but also those around them. Parents, educators, and peers learn to appreciate the child's unique abilities, fostering an inclusive and supportive environment. When we focus on strengths, we create opportunities for everyone to understand and value each child's contribution, regardless of whether it fits into a "typical" developmental box.

5 TOP TIPS FOR FOCUSING ON STRENGTHS

1. **Highlight Individual Achievements**
   Celebrate even small successes, whether it's a new word, a moment of focus, or a creative solution. This helps children see that their efforts are valued and encourages further growth.
2. **Use Interests as a Bridge**
   Build on what the child loves, whether it's animals, cars, or drawing. Use these interests as a gateway to develop communication skills, encouraging the child to engage more fully in learning.
3. **Create Opportunities for Success**
   Design activities and tasks that play to the child's strengths, ensuring they can experience success regularly. This not only builds confidence but also motivates them to tackle more challenging areas.
4. **Incorporate Strengths into Goal Setting**
   When setting goals, think about how the child's strengths can support them in reaching new milestones. For example, if a child is good at puzzles, use this skill to enhance problem-solving or language skills.
5. **Encourage Peer Appreciation**
   Foster a classroom culture where children are encouraged to notice and appreciate each other's strengths. This builds a supportive environment where everyone's abilities are recognised and valued. Develop everyone's social skills by recognising their own sensory system and communication patterns and how they relate to others.

> **Reflective Prompt: What Does Success Look Like?**
>
> Take a moment to think about how you define success for the children in your care. Is it about meeting standardised expectations or nurturing their unique strengths? Consider Toby's example – does success mean that he sits on the carpet and looks at the teacher, or does it mean he absorbs and recalls the lesson while meeting his sensory needs? Reflect on a child you work with and ask yourself:
>
> ✦ What are their unique strengths or abilities?

- How could these strengths be harnessed to support areas of challenge?
- Are there ways your expectations might shift to better align with their individual needs?

THE FLAWS OF TRADITIONAL ASSESSMENTS: WHY "NORMAL" ISN'T ENOUGH

Traditional developmental assessments often measure children against a narrow set of standards, typically framed around what is considered "normal" or "typical" development. While these benchmarks may serve a purpose in tracking certain developmental milestones, they can be deeply flawed when used as the sole measure of a child's progress. For children who don't fit neatly into these boxes – whether due to speech delays, neurodiversity, or other individual differences – these assessments can not only misrepresent their abilities but also lead to feelings of inadequacy for both the children and their families.

One of the key issues with traditional assessments is that they are often deficit-focused. They zero in on what the child *cannot* do, rather than acknowledging the skills and strengths the child *does* have. This deficit-based approach can stigmatise children and label them as "behind" or "delayed", fostering a mindset that something is inherently wrong with them. Such assessments can put undue pressure on both children and their caregivers, creating a sense of failure for not meeting arbitrary developmental milestones.

These assessments also fail to account for the wide variety of developmental trajectories that exist. Development is not a linear process, and children – especially those with speech or language difficulties, or those who are neurodiverse – often develop skills in ways that don't follow traditional patterns. A child with autism, for instance, may take longer to develop verbal communication skills but might excel in visual problem-solving or emotional intelligence. By focusing solely on verbal communication milestones, traditional assessments can overlook the child's unique strengths and potential.

Moreover, these assessments are usually designed around a "one-size-fits-all" model, assuming that all children will eventually catch up to the same developmental markers. This approach ignores the fact that some children may never fit into the typical mould, nor should they have to. Children with conditions like developmental language disorder (DLD) or autism spectrum disorder (ASD) may develop language and social skills in entirely different ways, and expecting them to conform to a rigid, pre-defined path does a disservice to their individuality.

These assessments also frame how adults around the child describe or observe them. A child may be described as dysregulated or not engaging rather than a description of how the environment or others are impacting the child and how they are coping.

What is often missed in traditional assessments is the broader context of a child's environment and interactions. A child's progress is influenced not only by their individual abilities but also by the support they receive from adults, peers, and the environment around them. When assessments focus solely on what the child can or cannot do, they neglect the important role of these external factors in a child's development.

Another key flaw of traditional assessments is their failure to recognise the importance of emotional and sensory regulation in learning and communication. Children who are overwhelmed, anxious, or dysregulated are less likely to perform well in assessment situations. Yet, these underlying issues are often overlooked in favour of focusing on whether the child can achieve specific developmental targets, like counting or forming complete sentences. By not accounting for the emotional and sensory needs of children, traditional assessments provide an incomplete and sometimes misleading picture of their capabilities.

This deficit-based, one-size-fits-all approach is also disempowering for educators and caregivers. When we focus on what children *cannot* do, we lose sight of the important work of adapting the environment and our interactions to better support the child. Instead of placing all the responsibility on the child to "catch up", we should be focusing on how we can change the environment and provide the right support to help them thrive.

Finally, traditional assessments can perpetuate a culture of comparison and pressure. They encourage the notion that all children should develop in the same way and at the same pace, which not only creates unrealistic expectations but can also lead to unnecessary anxiety for parents and educators. Instead of helping children feel capable and celebrated for their unique progress, these assessments often lead to feelings of "not being enough" - both for the child and their family.

5 KEY CRITICISMS OF TRADITIONAL ASSESSMENTS

1. **Deficit-Focused Approach**
   Traditional assessments focus on what children *cannot* do, rather than celebrating their strengths and abilities. This can lead to negative labelling and stigma.
2. **Ignoring Diverse Developmental Paths**
   Many assessments fail to recognise that children, particularly those with speech or language difficulties or neurodiverse conditions, follow unique developmental trajectories.
3. **One-Size-Fits-All Mentality**
   The rigid nature of these assessments assumes that all children will eventually reach the same milestones, disregarding individuality and different ways of learning.
4. **Neglecting Environmental Factors**
   Traditional assessments often overlook the crucial role that the child's environment, including adult support and interaction, plays in their development.
5. **Emotional and Sensory Overload**
   Assessments that do not account for a child's emotional state or sensory needs provide an incomplete and sometimes unfair measure of their abilities.

REFLECTIVE POINT: REFRAMING THE ROLE OF ASSESSMENTS

- How do traditional assessments shape your expectations of a child's abilities? Reflect on an instance where an assessment focused on what a child *could not do*.

How might that perspective have changed if the assessment had celebrated their strengths instead?
- Consider a child you work with or know who doesn't fit into the "typical" developmental mould. How has the use of traditional assessments impacted your approach to supporting them, and what changes could you make?

A NEW PERSPECTIVE ON ASSESSMENT

Rather than relying on traditional assessments to determine what children lack, we need to adopt a holistic approach that focuses on their strengths, the environment, and how the people around them can better support their growth. By redefining success and progress in terms of individual development, not arbitrary norms, we give children the best chance to thrive on their terms.

BEYOND THE BOX: DISMANTLING THE PRESSURE TO CONFORM

Children are often expected to fit into pre-set developmental categories, with progress measured against rigid milestones and norms. This creates an undue pressure to conform, not only on children but also on parents and educators who are often tasked with ensuring that children "meet expectations" in terms of speech, language, social interaction, and academic skills. However, this approach can be harmful and limiting, particularly for children who develop in different ways or at different paces. Instead of nurturing a child's individuality and unique potential, the pressure to conform can suppress their natural strengths and create feelings of inadequacy.

One of the major problems with expecting children to fit into these developmental boxes is that it assumes there is only one correct way to grow and learn. Developmental milestones, such as speaking a certain number of words by a specific age, become rigid benchmarks against which children are judged. When a child doesn't meet these expectations, they may be labelled as delayed or "falling behind", even though their developmental trajectory may simply be different rather than deficient. This pressure to conform can negatively affect the child's self-esteem, leaving them feeling "less than" their peers.

This one-size-fits-all mentality also disregards the importance of neurodiversity and individual learning styles. Children with ASD, DLD, or other communication challenges often develop language, social interaction, and cognitive skills in unique ways. Expecting these children to follow the same path as their neurotypical peers not only misrepresents their potential but also ignores the richness that diversity brings to human development. A child who communicates non-verbally or takes longer to develop speech, for example, may excel in other areas like problem-solving or emotional intelligence, and these strengths can be overlooked when the focus is solely on "typical" development.

Furthermore, the pressure to conform can lead to interventions that are designed more to push children towards these arbitrary milestones rather than support their actual needs. In a system that prioritises conformity, children are often subjected to therapies or interventions that aim to "correct" their differences, rather than celebrate and support their unique abilities. This approach is not only frustrating for children but can also be disheartening for families, who may feel like their child is constantly being measured against an impossible standard. Instead of focusing on nurturing a child's strengths, this model tries to mould them into something they are not.

This pressure also trickles down to educators and caregivers, who may feel compelled to focus on getting children to meet these developmental boxes, rather than exploring more individualised approaches that honour a child's natural pace and abilities. Teachers may feel forced to adhere to rigid curriculums or expectations that don't reflect the diversity of needs within their classrooms, limiting their ability to foster a more inclusive, child-centred learning environment.

Moreover, this focus on conformity can have long-term consequences on children's self-perception and motivation. When children are repeatedly told, either explicitly or implicitly, that they are not meeting expectations, they can begin to internalise these messages, believing that they are not capable or good enough. This can lead to a reluctance to take risks, explore new skills, or engage in communication, as they fear falling short. Over time, this can stifle a child's natural curiosity and joy in learning.

Rejecting the pressure to conform means recognising that each child's developmental path is valid and valuable. It's about celebrating differences and creating environments where children feel supported and encouraged to be their true selves. It means shifting the focus away from "correcting" children who don't fit into typical developmental boxes and instead adapting our expectations and interventions to meet the child where they are.

When we dismantle the pressure to conform, we open the door to a more inclusive and understanding approach to development. Children are free to explore their interests, communicate in ways that are meaningful to them, and grow at their own pace, without the weight of external expectations. This creates a more empowering and supportive atmosphere where children can thrive, not because they fit into a box, but because they are valued for who they are.

We must not forget that the world needs people with a wide breadth of strengths and by aiming for a fixed tick box of "norms" we are doing the world a disservice. Take for example a neurodiverse child, with limited communication skills but a natural finesse for deep knowledge of a limited number of topics, or an incredible visual problem-solving brain: if we only focused on "social skills" or lack of language we may miss out what they have to offer the world.

LET ME TELL YOU ABOUT AMBER...

According to traditional assessments, Amber should have been working on building her vocabulary. She had been flagged as being behind her peers in this area, and there was significant pressure to focus on targeted interventions designed to increase the number of words she could use. However, Amber was an extremely shy and underconfident child who became resistant to any activity that felt like direct pressure. Traditional approaches only exacerbated her reluctance and made her withdraw further.

Instead of focusing solely on Amber's vocabulary deficit, her educators decided to take a step back and look at her strengths. One thing became clear: Amber had an incredible imagination. She loved storytelling, creating detailed worlds, and crafting intricate narratives for her play. This was her strength, and her teachers realised they could use it to build her confidence and support her vocabulary development.

They started small, introducing open-ended activities that encouraged Amber to use her imagination. For example, they provided a variety of props and asked her to create stories about them. They didn't push her to use new words but instead followed her lead, engaging with her narratives and gently expanding on her ideas with rich and descriptive language. Amber was in control of the interactions, which helped her feel safe and valued.

The staff then took it a step further. They began thinking about how they could intertwine the curriculum with Amber's natural love for imagination. When teaching topics like seasons or animals, they incorporated role-play scenarios and creative storytelling into lessons. For example, Amber was encouraged to imagine being an animal preparing for winter, which gave her opportunities to learn and use new words naturally, in a way that felt fun and engaging.

Another critical element was the role of the adults in Amber's environment. Instead of leading with instructions or directing the play, they acted as co-creators in Amber's imaginary worlds. They asked open-ended questions, mirrored her language, and provided subtle scaffolding to introduce new vocabulary without overwhelming her. They built on her ideas rather than redirecting them, which helped her feel more confident and encouraged her to take communication risks.

Over time, Amber began to thrive. Her vocabulary expanded significantly, not because of rigid drills or repetitive tasks, but because she was engaged in activities that played to her strengths. More importantly, Amber's confidence grew. She began participating more in group activities, volunteering to share her ideas, and even helping her peers develop their own stories.

Amber's journey is a powerful example of what happens when we look beyond developmental boxes and focus on the whole child. By celebrating her strengths and adapting their approach, her educators not only helped her develop her vocabulary but also nurtured her self-esteem and love of learning.

KEY POINTS TO REMEMBER

- **Developmental diversity is natural.** Expecting all children to meet the same milestones disregards the individuality of their growth patterns.
- **Neurodiversity is a strength, not a weakness.** Children with different developmental paths bring unique perspectives and talents that should be celebrated, not "corrected".

- **Interventions should support, not conform.** The goal of support should be to nurture a child's strengths and help them thrive, rather than forcing them to fit into rigid developmental categories.
- **The pressure to conform affects confidence.** Constantly measuring children against arbitrary standards can harm their self-esteem and motivation to learn.
- **Educators and caregivers play a key role.** By resisting the pressure to conform, they can create environments where children feel understood, appreciated, and empowered to reach their true potential.

This more inclusive and accepting approach ultimately leads to healthier, more confident children who are equipped to communicate, learn, and grow on their terms.

Take a moment to reflect on how you currently approach supporting children who may not fit into typical developmental expectations. Are there moments where focusing on what a child *cannot do* might have overshadowed their strengths or unique abilities? Consider Amber's story and ask yourself:

- Can you think of a child in your care whose strengths may be hidden under their reluctance or shyness?
- How might shifting your focus to their strengths – like imagination, problem-solving, or creativity – open up new opportunities for connection and growth?
- What role do you play in creating an environment where those strengths can flourish?
- Are there ways you could integrate the curriculum or goals into activities that align with a child's natural interests and abilities?

Challenge Yourself

Choose one child you work with and identify three specific strengths they have. Reflect on how you could use these strengths to support areas they find more challenging. What small, practical changes could you make today to adapt your approach and celebrate what they *can* do?

NEURO-AFFIRMING PRACTICES: EMBRACING DIFFERENT DEVELOPMENTAL PATHS

Neuro-affirming practices acknowledge and celebrate the diverse ways in which children learn, grow, and communicate. This approach is rooted in the understanding that not all children will follow the same developmental trajectory as we discussed above, and knowing that that is okay. It is about appreciating differences without imposing typical expectations or trying to "normalise" those who do not fit into conventional frameworks. Instead, neuro-affirming practices focus on creating environments and interactions that support each child's unique developmental path, allowing them to thrive as their authentic selves.

Neuro-affirming practices reject this deficit-based model and instead embrace the notion that development is not a linear, one-size-fits-all process of communicating.

By adopting a neuro-affirming approach, educators and caregivers shift their focus from fixing or correcting children to helping them flourish within their unique abilities. This means adapting the environment, adjusting interactions, and providing resources that align with the child's needs. It also involves working with the child's strengths, fostering their interests, and celebrating their achievements – no matter how different they may look from traditional standards of success.

For children with different developmental paths, communication can take many forms beyond spoken language. Non-verbal communication, gestures, or alternative communication methods like sign language or picture systems can be just as valid and meaningful as verbal speech. Neuro-affirming practices embrace these different forms of communication without pushing children to develop speech or social behaviours that feel unnatural or challenging for them.

At the heart of neuro-affirming practices is the belief that it is the responsibility of the adults around the child to adapt and understand their needs, rather than expecting the child to adapt to fit a standard model. This perspective empowers educators and caregivers to take a more compassionate and flexible approach to supporting children. It also alleviates pressure on the child, allowing them to develop at their own pace and in their own way.

KEY POINTS TO REMEMBER

For neuro-affirming practices to be effective, it's essential that educators and caregivers:

- **Respect developmental differences.** Each child has their own rhythm and way of learning. A neuro-affirming approach respects these differences rather than trying to force conformity.
- **Create supportive environments.** The classroom, home, or care environment should be designed to meet the child where they are, with tools, materials, and setups that support their needs.
- **Celebrate diverse forms of communication.** Not all children will use verbal language, and that's okay. Alternative communication methods should be encouraged and embraced.
- **Build trust and connection.** A strong, trusting relationship with the child is the foundation of any neuro-affirming approach. Children need to feel safe, valued, and understood.
- **Be flexible in goal setting.** Goals should focus on supporting the child's individual strengths and needs, rather than pushing them to meet arbitrary developmental milestones.

Neuro-affirming practices ultimately lead to more empowered and confident children, who are better able to explore their world, communicate in ways that work for them, and develop their skills at their own pace. This approach benefits not only the child but also the adults around them, fostering a more compassionate, inclusive, and understanding learning environment.

By embracing different developmental paths, we allow children to become their fullest, most authentic selves, free from the constraints of typical expectations. It's not about making every child the same - it's about celebrating the richness that diversity brings to human development.

> **Reflective Prompt**
>
> Embracing a Neuro-Affirming Mindset: Take a moment to reflect on the ways you currently support neurodiverse children. Are there moments where traditional expectations have shaped how you view a child's progress? Consider the following questions:
>
> - How do you respond when a child communicates in a way that differs from what is typically expected? Do you instinctively try to guide them toward spoken language, or do you embrace their unique ways of expressing themselves?
> - Have you ever felt pressure - either personally or from external systems - to push a child towards conventional milestones? How did that influence your approach?
> - Think of a child you work with who learns or communicates in a way that falls outside of typical developmental norms. How can you further adapt their environment, interactions, and learning experiences to be more in tune with their natural way of being?
> - In what ways could you shift your focus from "fixing" or "correcting" differences to celebrating and nurturing a child's strengths and individuality?

Challenge Yourself

Identify one practice in your current setting that may unintentionally reinforce the idea that children should conform to typical developmental paths. How could you adapt or reframe this practice to make it more neuro-affirming? What small changes could you make today that would help a child feel more understood, valued, and free to be their authentic self?

BEHAVIOUR AS COMMUNICATION: LISTENING TO WHAT CHILDREN ARE TELLING US

Children, especially those with speech and language challenges, often use behaviour as their primary form of communication. When words are difficult to find or express, actions, gestures, and even challenging behaviours can convey their thoughts, emotions, and needs.

Understanding that behaviour is communication is crucial for educators and caregivers, as it shifts the focus from managing behaviour to interpreting and responding to it with empathy.

For children who struggle to express themselves verbally, frustration can easily build. This frustration may manifest in behaviours such as tantrums, withdrawal, or refusal to participate. Rather than seeing these behaviours as disruptions or signs of defiance, it's important to recognise them as the child's way of saying, "I need something", "I don't understand", or "I'm overwhelmed". The key to supporting these children lies in interpreting what their behaviour is communicating and responding in ways that help meet their needs.

Every behaviour, whether it's positive or challenging, has a reason behind it. It could be that the child is trying to gain attention, avoid a difficult task, or communicate discomfort or confusion. When adults take the time to understand the root cause of a behaviour, they can better support the child in finding healthier, more effective ways to communicate.

For example, a child who throws toys or becomes physically aggressive during playtime may be overwhelmed by sensory input, struggling to understand the social dynamics of the play situation, or simply unable to express their desire for a break. A child who avoids engaging in group activities may not be disinterested or lazy but may feel anxious, overstimulated, or unsure how to participate. In both cases, the behaviour is communicating a deeper need that verbal language cannot express in the moment.

One of the most powerful things an educator or caregiver can do is listen - to the behaviour, the environment, and the child's non-verbal cues. This includes watching for patterns in behaviour, paying attention to what situations trigger certain responses, and being attuned to the child's emotional state. Often, children with speech and language difficulties rely heavily on non-verbal communication, such as facial expressions, body language, and tone of voice. By tuning into these subtle cues, adults can gain valuable insight into what the child is trying to express.

When behaviour is understood as communication, the approach to helping children changes. Instead of focusing solely on stopping or correcting the behaviour, the goal becomes understanding it and providing the child with tools and strategies to communicate more effectively. This may include teaching them simple phrases, using visual supports, or offering them a quiet space to regulate their emotions.

KEY TAKEAWAYS FOR INTERPRETING BEHAVIOUR AS COMMUNICATION

1. **Observe and Reflect:** Take a step back and observe the child's behaviour in different contexts. Consider what might be causing the behaviour - are they hungry, tired, frustrated, or overwhelmed? Reflect on what the child might be trying to communicate through their actions.
2. **Look for Patterns:** Notice if certain behaviours occur at specific times or in specific situations. Understanding patterns can provide clues about triggers and underlying needs. For instance, does the child become anxious during transitions or act out in noisy environments?

3. **Acknowledge the Child's Emotions:** Validate the child's feelings, even if their behaviour is challenging. Acknowledging their emotions – "I can see you're upset" – can help them feel heard and understood, which can de-escalate situations.
4. **Provide Visual Supports:** Many children with speech and language difficulties benefit from visual aids, such as picture cards, schedules, or communication boards. These tools give them an alternative way to express their needs and reduce the likelihood of frustration-driven behaviour.
5. **Teach Emotional Regulation:** Helping children learn how to manage their emotions is key to reducing challenging behaviours. Techniques like deep breathing, sensory breaks, or simple mindfulness exercises can empower children to regulate their emotions more effectively.

By shifting our perspective and understanding that behaviour is simply another form of communication, we can approach children with more patience, empathy, and insight. This allows us to respond in ways that help them feel heard and supported, ultimately improving their ability to communicate both verbally and non-verbally. When children feel understood and safe, their behaviour often improves, and their confidence in expressing themselves grows.

In this way, behaviour becomes an invaluable tool for deeper connection, fostering communication and emotional development in children who might struggle with speech and language challenges.

CHECKLIST: UNDERSTANDING AND RESPONDING TO BEHAVIOUR AS COMMUNICATION

Use this checklist to guide your observations and responses when working with children who use behaviour as a primary means of communication.

Step 1: Observe and Identify

- ☑ Have I taken a step back to observe the child's behaviour in different contexts?
- ☑ Am I considering what might be causing the behaviour – hunger, tiredness, frustration, or sensory overload?
- ☑ Have I noticed if this behaviour happens at specific times, in certain settings, or with particular people?

Step 2: Look for Patterns and Triggers

- ☑ Does this behaviour frequently occur during transitions, after a certain instruction, or in busy environments?
- ☑ Have I identified sensory factors that might be influencing the behaviour (e.g., noise levels, lighting, physical contact)?
- ☑ Have I kept a record or journal of behaviours to track patterns over time?

Step 3: Interpret the Communication Behind the Behaviour

- ☑ Have I considered what the child might be trying to tell me?
- ☑ Could the behaviour be expressing a need for help, independence, connection, or a break?
- ☑ Have I explored whether the child's behaviour is a response to difficulty understanding language or expectations?

Step 4: Acknowledge and Validate

- ☑ Have I acknowledged the child's emotions – e.g., "I can see you're frustrated" or "That must feel tricky"?
- ☑ Am I responding with empathy rather than trying to stop the behaviour immediately?
- ☑ Have I provided reassurance that their feelings are valid and that I am here to support them?

Step 5: Offer Alternative Communication and Support

- ☑ Have I provided visual supports like schedules, picture cards, or a communication board?
- ☑ Have I modelled simple phrases or gestures that the child could use instead?
- ☑ Am I using a calm, clear voice and body language that communicates safety and understanding?

Step 6: Adjust the Environment

- ☑ Have I reduced potential triggers, such as noise, visual clutter, or unexpected changes?
- ☑ Am I offering a quiet or sensory-friendly space for the child to regulate?
- ☑ Have I adapted my language, giving clear, simple instructions to make expectations easier to follow?

Step 7: Teach Self-Regulation and Coping Strategies

- ☑ Have I introduced tools like deep breathing, fidget toys, movement breaks, or mindfulness exercises?
- ☑ Have I supported the child in developing emotional awareness by naming emotions and modelling strategies?
- ☑ Am I reinforcing positive behaviour by acknowledging and celebrating when they use alternative communication strategies?

Step 8: Reflect and Adapt

- ☑ Have I reflected on whether my response to the behaviour was effective?
- ☑ Am I open to adapting my approach if something isn't working for the child?

- ☑ Have I shared observations and strategies with colleagues, therapists, or families to ensure a consistent approach?

By using this checklist, we can move from managing behaviour to truly understanding it, ensuring that our responses empower children and help them develop confidence in their communication.

MEASURING SUCCESS: REDEFINING OUTCOMES FOR EVERY CHILD

Measuring success should extend far beyond traditional academic achievements. Instead, a holistic approach to assessing progress emphasises emotional regulation, a sense of belonging, and the cultivation of individual strengths. By shifting the focus away from conventional metrics, we can create an environment that values each child's unique journey and fosters their overall well-being.

Emotional Regulation

Emotional regulation is a critical outcome that impacts all areas of a child's life, including communication, social interactions, and learning. Success in this area means helping children understand and manage their emotions effectively. Educators and caregivers can implement strategies that teach children to recognise their feelings, develop coping mechanisms, and express their emotions appropriately. This understanding creates a foundation for confident communication and enhances their ability to connect with others.

Sense of Belonging

A child's sense of belonging plays a crucial role in their development and overall happiness. Children who feel accepted and valued in their environment are more likely to engage in learning and take risks in their communication. Success should be measured by how well *we* foster inclusive environments where every child feels like they are an integral part of the community. This can be achieved through collaborative activities, peer support, and promoting positive relationships among children. A strong sense of belonging contributes to children's confidence and willingness to express themselves.

Development of Strengths

Recognising and nurturing each child's strengths is fundamental to fostering their potential. Rather than focusing solely on areas of difficulty, we should celebrate what children can do and support them in developing these abilities further. Success can be measured by how well we help children identify their interests and talents, encouraging them to explore and excel in these areas. This approach not only boosts confidence but also provides children with a sense of purpose and motivation.

Individualised Goals

Instead of applying a one-size-fits-all approach to assessment, it is essential to establish individualised goals that align with each child's unique needs and aspirations. By setting goals that focus on emotional regulation, social skills, and strengths development, we create a framework that respects the individual developmental trajectory of every child. These personalised outcomes ensure that children feel supported and valued in their progress, reinforcing the idea that their journey is as important as the destination.

Continuous Reflection and Adaptation

Measuring success also requires a commitment to continuous reflection and adaptation. Educators and caregivers should regularly assess the effectiveness of their strategies and interventions, making adjustments as needed to better support each child's growth. This ongoing process not only helps children achieve their goals but also fosters an environment of responsiveness and flexibility, where their changing needs are acknowledged and met.

KEY TAKEAWAYS FOR REDEFINING SUCCESS

1. **Prioritise Emotional Well-Being**: Assess success by evaluating children's emotional regulation and their ability to express and manage their feelings.
2. **Cultivate a Sense of Belonging**: Measure the inclusivity of the environment and the relationships children build with peers and adults to ensure they feel valued and connected.
3. **Celebrate Individual Strengths**: Focus on identifying and nurturing each child's strengths, encouraging exploration and growth in areas where they excel.

4. **Set Individualised Goals**: Develop personalised outcomes that align with each child's unique journey, rather than relying solely on traditional benchmarks.
5. **Commit to Ongoing Reflection**: Engage in regular assessment and adaptation of strategies to ensure they meet the evolving needs of each child.

By redefining success in this manner, we create a more comprehensive understanding of child development that values emotional well-being, community connection, and individual strengths. This approach not only enhances communication skills but also empowers children to thrive as their authentic selves, ensuring that they have the tools and confidence needed for lifelong success.

Action Step:

Write down one small change you could make to better acknowledge and celebrate the diverse ways children succeed. This could be a shift in mindset, a new way of tracking progress, or a simple adjustment to how you provide feedback and encouragement.

By embracing a broader view of success, we ensure that every child feels valued, understood, and empowered in their journey.

EARLY INTERVENTION THAT COUNTS: ACTING BEFORE THE CRISIS

Early intervention is a vital component in the journey of children who experience speech and language challenges. The sooner we identify and address these difficulties, the better the outcomes for the child. Waiting for formal diagnoses can lead to missed opportunities for growth, increased frustration for the child, and a widening gap in their communication skills. This section emphasises the necessity of early detection and proactive support, illustrating how immediate action can significantly impact a child's development.

The Critical Window for Language Development

Research shows that the early years of a child's life are crucial for language acquisition and overall development. During this period, children's brains are highly receptive to learning, making it the optimal time to intervene. Delaying support can exacerbate difficulties, leading to increased challenges in communication, social interaction, self-esteem and emotional regulation. Recognising and acting upon signs of speech and language difficulties early on allows educators and caregivers to provide timely support that aligns with the child's developmental needs.

Proactive Identification Strategies

To facilitate early intervention, it is essential to implement proactive identification strategies within educational settings. This includes regular observations and assessments that focus on communication milestones rather than waiting for a formal diagnosis. Educators should be trained to recognise signs of potential language delays, such as difficulty following instructions, limited vocabulary, or challenges in social communication. By identifying these signs early, educators can initiate appropriate support measures without waiting for external evaluations.

Creating a Supportive Network

Early intervention is most effective when it involves collaboration among educators, parents, and specialists. Building a supportive network ensures that children receive consistent messaging and strategies across different environments. Educators should actively engage parents in discussions about their child's communication development, offering guidance and resources to help reinforce learning at home. This collaboration fosters a holistic approach to intervention, maximising the potential for success.

Implementing Targeted Strategies

In the absence of formal diagnoses, educators can implement targeted strategies that support language development for children displaying early signs of difficulty. These strategies may include:

1. **Creating Opportunities for Communication:** Create time and space for children to express themselves through play, structured activities, and daily routines.
2. **Utilising Visual Supports:** Incorporate visual aids, such as pictures or symbols, to enhance understanding and encourage expressive language.
3. **Modelling Language Use:** Imagine the language you use is a gift to the child. Give the children the words they need in the moment. Move away from questioning and testing with questions and directions and instead give the child the words they need in the moment without expectation.
4. **Encouraging Peer Interactions:** Foster opportunities for children to engage with their peers, facilitating natural communication practice and social skills development for all children to understand each other.
5. **Implementing Sensory and Movement Activities:** Recognise the connection between movement, sensory experiences, and language development, incorporating activities that promote physical engagement to support communication skills.

Preventing Escalation of Challenges

One of the most significant advantages of early intervention is its potential to prevent the escalation of challenges. When children receive timely support, they are more likely to develop effective communication skills, reducing the likelihood of behavioural issues stemming from frustration or misunderstanding. By addressing speech and language difficulties proactively, we not only support the child's current needs but also set the foundation for their future success.

KEY TAKEAWAYS FOR EFFECTIVE EARLY INTERVENTION

1. **Act Quickly:** Identify and address speech and language difficulties as soon as they arise, rather than waiting for formal diagnoses.
2. **Focus on Critical Windows:** Recognise the importance of the early years as a crucial time for language development and intervene accordingly.
3. **Collaborate with Parents and Specialists:** Build a supportive network to ensure consistent strategies and messaging across home and educational environments.
4. **Implement Targeted Strategies:** Use proactive and targeted interventions tailored to the child's individual needs to support their language development.
5. **Prevent Future Challenges:** Early intervention can mitigate the risk of more significant challenges arising later on, promoting overall success in communication and social skills.

By prioritising early intervention and taking immediate action, we can create a positive impact on children's speech and language development. This proactive approach not only empowers children to communicate effectively but also lays the groundwork for their emotional, social, and academic success in the years to come.

Reflective Prompt

Consider one small change you could implement this week to improve early intervention in your setting. It could be:

- Taking 10 minutes each day to **observe a child** and identify areas where they may need communication support.
- Sharing your observations with a **colleague or parent** to begin a discussion about early intervention strategies.
- Introducing **one new strategy** (e.g., reducing questioning, using more visual supports, or incorporating movement into language learning).
- Keeping a **reflection journal** to track small wins and adjustments in your approach.

THE ROLE OF EDUCATORS AND CAREGIVERS: BEING THE KEY TO A CHILD'S SUCCESS

Educators and caregivers play a pivotal role in shaping the speech and language development of children. Their influence extends far beyond mere instruction; they are essential in fostering communication skills, building confidence, and nurturing a positive sense of self in each child. This section explores the significant impact that adults have in a child's life and emphasises the importance of their supportive presence in the journey of communication development.

Creating a Nurturing Environment

One of the fundamental ways educators and caregivers contribute to a child's success is by creating a nurturing and supportive environment. As discussed in earlier chapters a safe space where children feel heard and valued encourages them to express themselves freely. This environment is characterised by warmth, patience, and understanding, allowing children to explore their thoughts and feelings without fear of judgement. When children sense that they are in a supportive setting, they are more likely to engage in communication, take risks, and develop confidence in their abilities.

Modelling Positive Interactions

Educators and caregivers serve as role models for communication. By demonstrating effective communication skills – such as active listening, clear articulation, emotional language articulated, and empathetic engagement – they provide children with valuable examples to copy. These interactions can help children learn how to express their own thoughts and emotions, fostering language growth. When adults model respectful and engaging communication, they set the tone for how children interact with others, instilling essential social skills that will serve them throughout their lives.

Be mindful of how much language happens in the classroom, are adults talking to each other, is there a lot of background chatter? How do the adults address the children? Do they use positive supportive language that focuses on developing the language skills of the children or are the children mainly hearing questions and directions.

Encouraging Exploration and Curiosity

Children are naturally curious, and educators and caregivers can harness this curiosity to promote communication development. By encouraging exploration and open-ended questions, adults can stimulate children's thinking and language use. Providing opportunities for children to express their ideas, share their interests, and ask questions helps them practice language in a meaningful context. When children feel encouraged to explore their environment and share their thoughts, their communication skills flourish.

Building Trust and Rapport

Establishing strong, trusting relationships with children is crucial for their emotional and social development. Educators and caregivers can build rapport by showing genuine interest in each child's experiences and feelings. When children know they can trust the adults in their lives, they are more likely to communicate openly and seek support when needed. This trust fosters a sense of belonging, which is essential for children to thrive both socially and emotionally.

LET'S TALK ABOUT LUCAS...

A recent example of this is when Lucas moved from Nursery to Reception. In nursery Lucas was described as disruptive, having limited language and play skills and rarely co-operating. The adults in reception took a trust-based approach to communication. They spent time one to one with Lucas, following his interests, limiting their language and connecting through non-verbal strategies. Lucas began to gain confidence, he started to make more attempts to communicate with the adults, sought them out to show them things he had done and was less anxious in the room. As his confidence and trust in the adults grew, his skills developed and he was able to co-operate more fully within the routine. The extra time and strategies used by the staff at the outset allowed Lucas to have a much more productive time in school and start to open up and show staff what he was capable of.

Recognising Individual Needs

Every child is unique, with their own set of strengths and challenges. Educators and caregivers play a vital role in recognising and addressing these individual needs. By observing children closely and understanding their communication styles, adults can tailor their approaches to support each child effectively. This individualised attention ensures that all children feel seen and valued, which is fundamental for building their confidence and promoting their success.

Facilitating Collaboration

The partnership between educators, caregivers, and families is essential for supporting a child's development. By collaborating with parents and specialists, educators can create a cohesive support system that reinforces communication strategies both at home and in the classroom. Regular communication with families about their child's progress and needs fosters a united front, allowing for more comprehensive support. Sharing day to day information such as the books that were read, songs sung, themes covered and friends engaged with, can help families reinforce words and concepts that may have been new to the children,

Empowering Children to Find Their Voice

Ultimately, the role of educators and caregivers is to empower children to find their own voice. By providing space encouragement, support, and the tools necessary for effective communication, adults can help children express their thoughts, feelings, and ideas confidently. This empowerment not only enhances children's communication skills but also contributes to their overall self-esteem and sense of identity.

KEY TAKEAWAYS FOR EDUCATORS AND CAREGIVERS

1. **Create a Nurturing Environment:** Foster a safe and supportive space where children feel comfortable expressing themselves.
2. **Model Positive Interactions:** Demonstrate effective communication skills to serve as role models for children.
3. **Encourage Exploration:** Stimulate curiosity by providing opportunities for open-ended questions and exploration.
4. **Build Trust and Rapport:** Establish strong relationships with children to promote openness and communication.
5. **Recognise Individual Needs:** Pay attention to each child's unique strengths and challenges, tailoring support accordingly.
6. **Facilitate Collaboration:** Work closely with families and specialists to create a comprehensive support network.
7. **Empower Communication:** Encourage children to find their voice and express themselves confidently.

By acknowledging the powerful influence of educators and caregivers, we can better understand how their support shapes children's communication skills and overall development. This emphasis on nurturing relationships, positive interactions, and individualised support is crucial for fostering a generation of confident, expressive, and thriving individuals.

> **Reflective Prompt**
>
> *Your Role in a Child's Success: Take a moment to reflect on the way you interact with the children in your care. Your words, actions, and responsiveness have a*

profound impact on their communication confidence and emotional well-being. Consider the following questions:

- How do you create a nurturing environment where children feel safe and valued?
- Think about a recent interaction with a child – did you provide more instructions and questions, or did you follow their lead and model language in a meaningful way?
- Are there children in your setting who may need more trust-building and connection before they feel comfortable communicating? How can you adjust your approach to meet them where they are?
- Do you actively encourage exploration and curiosity, allowing children to initiate conversations and share their ideas?

Action Step

Over the next few days, make a conscious effort to slow down and observe how you communicate with children. Choose one child who may need additional support and focus on building rapport by following their interests, modelling language, and responding to their non-verbal cues.

By being intentional about our role in a child's communication journey, we create spaces where they feel empowered to express themselves confidently and authentically.

REWRITING GOALS: SHIFTING FOCUS TO THE ENVIRONMENT AND INTERACTION

In traditional approaches to goal setting it often revolves around what children need to achieve, typically framed in terms of academic skills or behavioural milestones. However, a more effective and compassionate method is to shift this focus from the child to the surrounding environment and the interactions they experience. By prioritising the context in which children learn and the quality of adult interactions, we can create a more supportive framework that fosters growth, development, and true communication.

Understanding the Impact of Environment

The environment plays a pivotal role in shaping a child's experiences and outcomes. A supportive, engaging, and inclusive setting can significantly enhance a child's ability to communicate and thrive. Goals should be directed toward making changes in the classroom or home environment that promote interaction, engagement, and accessibility. This might include:

- **Creating Interaction-Friendly Spaces:** Design areas that encourage dialogue and exploration, such as cosy reading corners or interactive play zones.
- **Minimising Distractions:** Reducing sensory overload can help children focus better and engage more fully in communication.
- **Providing Resources:** Ensuring that children have access to materials that facilitate communication, such as visual aids, manipulative, or interactive technology.

Fostering Meaningful Adult Interactions

The quality of interactions between adults and children is fundamental to effective communication development. By setting goals that emphasise the importance of these interactions, educators and caregivers can create more meaningful and impactful communication opportunities. Strategies may include:

- **Active Listening:** Training adults to listen attentively and respond to children's verbal and non-verbal cues can enhance understanding and trust.
- **Responsive Engagement:** Encouraging adults to engage with children's interests, leading to more authentic conversations and connections.
- **Matching Language:** Adults can set goals to model language in context, providing examples of vocabulary and communication strategies that children can adopt. Getting the right level of language at the right time can have far reaching impact on the children.

Encouraging Collaborative Goal Setting

Involving children in the goal-setting process can empower them and provide a sense of ownership over their learning journey. This practice can encourage children to express their own ideas and preferences regarding their environment and interactions. This can be done actively by verbal children, or by close observation and observation of children who are not yet communicating their ideas and thoughts. Goals could include:

Redefining Success

When we shift our focus to the environment and adult interactions, we also need to redefine what success looks like. Rather than aiming for specific behavioural or academic outcomes, success can be measured by:

- **Increased Engagement:** Observing higher levels of participation and enthusiasm in communication activities.
- **Improved Relationships:** Noting the development of trusting relationships between children and adults, leading to more open communication.

- **Enhanced Confidence:** Recognising the growth in a child's willingness to express themselves and take risks in their communication.

Creating a Culture of Support

Ultimately, rewriting goals to focus on the environment and interactions fosters a culture of support that prioritises understanding and appreciation for each child's unique path. By shifting the lens away from what children lack and toward what they need to thrive, we can create more inclusive, affirming, and effective educational practices. This approach aligns with our ethos of celebrating individuality, fostering growth, and supporting children in becoming the best versions of themselves.

In conclusion, by setting goals that emphasise modifying the environment and enhancing adult interactions, we empower children to thrive in ways that resonate with their individual needs and strengths. This shift not only fosters communication development but also nurtures a sense of belonging and self-worth in every child.

GROUP AND COLOUR PROFILING: A STRENGTH-BASED APPROACH TO ASSESSMENT

In the journey of supporting children's speech and language development, assessment plays a crucial role. As we have discussed, traditional assessment methods often focus on deficits, measuring children against a narrow standard of "typical" development. This approach can inadvertently label children as lacking or insufficient, leading to feelings of inadequacy for both them and their families. To counter this, a strength-based approach through group and colour profiling provides a more holistic and empowering way to assess children, emphasising their abilities and unique needs.

What Is Group and Colour Profiling?

Group and colour profiling is an alternative assessment strategy that categorises children based on their strengths and developmental needs rather than deficits. This method involves grouping children into clusters based on shared their communication abilities and sensory systems, allowing educators to identify patterns and tailor their support accordingly. The use of group and colour profiling can add a visual element to this process, helping to highlight specific traits or strengths.

- **Group Profiling:** By screening children's communication against the five Can-Do groups it is easy to see where their strengths lie and which areas to focus on. This quick overview gives adults a starting point of how to help the children's language reach the next level.

- **Colour Profiling:** This approach uses colours to represent different sensory profiles so adults quickly understand what sensory needs the child has and are able to match the approach to the specific children.

Tailoring Support to Individual Needs

Group and colour profiling also enables educators to tailor their support to each child's unique strengths and developmental trajectory. This method allows for:

- **Individualised Strategies:** By understanding a child's profile, educators can implement strategies that align with their strengths. For example, a child who thrives in a visual learning environment may benefit from more visual aids and interactive materials.
- **Focused Interventions:** Educators can design targeted interventions that build on children's existing strengths, helping them to develop in areas where they may need additional support without making them feel inadequate.

Celebrating Diversity in Development

This assessment approach recognises and celebrates the diverse ways in which children develop and learn. By adopting a strengths-based perspective, we validate each child's unique path and acknowledge that there is no singular way to achieve success. This is particularly important for children with speech and language difficulties and/or sensory, as it allows them to be seen for their capabilities rather than their challenges.

Moving Toward Inclusive Practices

Group and colour profiling not only benefits individual children but also promotes inclusive practices within the classroom. By creating a culture of strength-based assessment, educators can foster an environment where all children feel valued and supported. This approach encourages collaboration among educators, as they can share insights and strategies for supporting each child's growth based on their profiles.

Understanding the Importance of Strengths and Interests

Every child possesses unique strengths and interests that can be harnessed to facilitate learning and communication. When we pay attention to what excites and motivates children, we can tailor our support in a way that resonates with them. This not only fosters a love for learning but also encourages children to take ownership of their development. Here are some key benefits of embracing strengths and interests:

- **Increased Motivation:** When children engage in activities aligned with their interests, they are more likely to participate actively and enthusiastically. This intrinsic motivation is crucial for developing language skills, as children are more inclined to express themselves when they feel passionate about a topic.
- **Enhanced Learning:** By incorporating children's interests into learning activities, educators can create relevant and meaningful experiences. For instance, if a child is fascinated by dinosaurs, using dinosaur-themed stories or games can enhance their vocabulary and storytelling abilities.
- **Confidence Building:** Celebrating a child's strengths reinforces their self-esteem and sense of identity. When children see their abilities recognised, they feel valued and more willing to take risks in their communication, ultimately leading to greater success in expressing themselves.

Strategies for Identifying Strengths and Interests

Educators and caregivers play a pivotal role in discovering and nurturing children's strengths and interests. Here are several strategies to effectively identify and support them:

1. **Observation:** Spend time observing children during free play and structured activities. Note what captures their attention and how they engage with different materials. Observations can reveal a child's natural inclinations and preferences.
2. **Conversations:** Engage children in conversations about their interests. Ask open-ended questions to encourage them to share what they love doing, their favourite books, or hobbies. This dialogue not only provides insights into their passions but also helps build their communication skills.
3. **Play-Based Assessment:** Utilise play-based assessments to gauge children's strengths. Play is a natural way for children to express themselves and can highlight areas where they excel or feel comfortable, providing valuable information about their abilities.
4. **Encourage Exploration:** Create opportunities for children to explore various activities and subjects. This could involve introducing them to different arts, sports, or nature experiences. Providing diverse options allows children to discover new interests and talents.
5. **Parental Involvement:** Collaborate with parents to gain insights into their child's interests and strengths. Parents often have valuable knowledge about their child's behaviours and passions at home, which can inform educators' approaches in the classroom.

Nurturing Strengths and Interests in the Classroom

Once strengths and interests have been identified, educators can implement strategies to nurture them effectively:

- **Tailored Learning Experiences:** Design learning activities that align with children's interests. For example, if a child enjoys animals, use animal-themed vocabulary games or storytelling sessions that allow them to engage and express themselves.
- **Flexible Grouping:** Create opportunities for children to work in groups based on shared interests. Collaborative projects can help children learn from one another and develop their communication skills in a supportive environment.
- **Celebrate Achievements:** Recognise and celebrate children's successes, no matter how small. This positive reinforcement can motivate them to continue exploring their interests and developing their skills.
- **Incorporate Choice:** Provide children with choices in their learning activities. Allowing them to select topics or materials that resonate with them fosters a sense of ownership and autonomy, which can enhance their engagement and communication.

Embracing strengths and interests is a powerful way to unlock a child's true potential. By focusing on what children can do and what excites them, we can create enriching learning experiences that support their speech and language development. This approach not only helps children build confidence and communication skills but also fosters a lifelong love of learning. As educators and caregivers, our role is to recognise, celebrate, and nurture these strengths, allowing children to thrive and become the best versions of themselves. When we empower children to explore their interests, we open doors to new possibilities and help them discover their unique paths to success.

Reflective Prompts

Rewriting Goals – Shifting Focus to the Environment and Interaction: Take a moment to reflect on how goal setting is approached in your setting. Consider the following questions:

- When setting goals for children, do you focus more on what the child *must* achieve or on how the environment and adult interactions can support their progress?
- Think about a child who has struggled to meet traditional developmental goals. How might adjusting the **environment** (e.g., minimising distractions, providing communication-friendly spaces) change their experience?

- Reflect on the role of **adult interactions**. Are the children in your setting hearing more instructions and questions than meaningful language modelling? How could you shift towards providing more responsive, engaging communication?
- How do you currently involve children in shaping their own learning experience? Are their interests, strengths, and needs guiding the way you set expectations and goals?
- What does success look like when we measure **engagement, relationships, and confidence** rather than just outcomes?

BELONGING AND APPRECIATION: THE FOUNDATIONS OF A THRIVING CHILD

Creating an environment where every child feels heard, appreciated, and a sense of belonging is fundamental to their overall development and well-being. When children feel valued and connected to those around them, they are more likely to thrive emotionally, socially, and academically. This sense of belonging not only fosters positive self-esteem but also enhances their communication skills and willingness to engage with others.

The Importance of Belonging

Belonging is a crucial psychological need that influences a child's sense of self-worth and confidence. When children feel they belong, they are more likely to express themselves freely and engage in meaningful interactions with peers and adults. Here are some key reasons why fostering a sense of belonging is essential:

1. **Emotional Security:** Children who feel they belong in their environment experience emotional security, which allows them to explore, take risks, and express themselves without fear of judgement. This security is vital for healthy emotional regulation and resilience.
2. **Social Skills Development:** A sense of belonging encourages children to engage in social interactions, practice communication skills, and build friendships. When they feel accepted, they are more likely to initiate conversations, collaborate with peers, and develop empathy.
3. **Motivation to Learn:** When children feel appreciated and included, their motivation to learn increases. They are more willing to participate in activities, contribute to discussions, and take on challenges, which positively impacts their academic progress.
4. **Fostering Identity:** Belonging helps children develop a positive sense of identity. When they see themselves reflected in their environment and feel accepted for who they are, it nurtures their self-esteem and encourages them to embrace their unique qualities.

Strategies to Foster Belonging and Appreciation

Creating a sense of belonging requires intentional effort from educators and caregivers. Here are several strategies to help ensure every child feels heard, appreciated, and valued:

1. **Active Listening:** Take the time to listen actively to children's thoughts, feelings, and ideas. Acknowledge their contributions by responding thoughtfully and encouraging further dialogue. This demonstrates that their voices matter and fosters a culture of respect.
2. **Celebrating Individuality:** Recognise and celebrate the unique qualities and talents of each child. This could involve highlighting their achievements, showcasing their work, or creating opportunities for them to share their interests with others.
3. **Inclusive Practices:** Implement inclusive practices that embrace diversity and respect individual differences. Create a classroom environment where children feel safe to express themselves and where their varied backgrounds and experiences are acknowledged and valued.
4. **Encourage Collaboration:** Foster opportunities for collaboration among children, allowing them to work together on projects, share ideas, and support one another. Group activities can help build a sense of community and strengthen social bonds.
5. **Create Routines and Traditions:** Establish routines and traditions that promote connection and belonging within the group. This could include circle time, sharing sessions, or special celebrations that bring everyone together and reinforce their sense of community.
6. **Provide Supportive Feedback:** Offer constructive and positive feedback that emphasises effort and growth rather than solely focusing on outcomes. This helps children understand that their contributions are valued, promoting a growth mindset.

The Role of Educators and Caregivers

Educators and caregivers play a pivotal role in cultivating a sense of belonging among children. Here's how they can create an inclusive and supportive environment:

- **Model Inclusive Behaviour:** Demonstrate inclusive behaviour by treating all children with respect and kindness. Show them how to appreciate differences and foster a sense of community.
- **Be Approachable and Available:** Create an atmosphere where children feel comfortable approaching you with their thoughts and concerns. Being accessible allows children to express their feelings and seek support when needed.
- **Engage Families:** Involve families in the process of fostering belonging. Communicate regularly with parents and caregivers, invite them to participate in classroom activities, and celebrate their contributions to the learning environment.
- **Reflect on Practices:** Regularly reflect on your own practices to ensure they promote belonging and appreciation. Be open to feedback and make adjustments to create a more inclusive and supportive atmosphere for all children.

Belonging and appreciation are essential foundations for a thriving child. By ensuring that every child feels heard, valued, and connected to their environment, we create a nurturing space where they can develop their communication skills, build confidence, and engage meaningfully with others. As educators and caregivers, our commitment to fostering belonging is a powerful investment in each child's future, helping them to flourish as individuals who feel secure, understood, and empowered to reach their full potential. When we prioritise belonging and appreciation, we cultivate an environment where children can truly thrive, fostering a sense of community that enhances their learning and emotional well-being.

THE RIPPLE EFFECT: HOW UNDERSTANDING AND SUPPORT LEAD TO GROWTH

The concept of the ripple effect underscores the profound impact that understanding and support can have on a child's development. When caregivers and educators commit to fostering an environment that prioritises emotional connection, communication, and recognition of individual strengths, they lay the groundwork for significant growth in various areas of a child's life.

Holistic Development

When children feel understood and supported, their emotional well-being flourishes. This holistic approach enhances not only their communication skills but also their ability to regulate their emotions effectively. For example, when educators take the time to understand a child's unique communication style and needs, they create opportunities for that child to express themselves in ways that resonate with them. This process fosters confidence, enabling children to communicate more freely and assertively. As their communication skills improve, they also become more adept at managing their emotions and social interactions, leading to greater overall development.

The Importance of Relationships

Understanding that each child is a unique individual helps educators and caregivers build strong, trusting relationships with them. These relationships are the foundation upon which children feel secure enough to explore their world. A supportive environment encourages children to take risks, whether in learning new skills or forming social connections. As children engage in these experiences, they grow emotionally, socially, and cognitively. The more they are listened to and appreciated, the more they develop a sense of belonging, which further enhances their willingness to engage with peers and adults alike.

Fostering Resilience

The right support also cultivates resilience in children. When they encounter challenges - whether related to communication, emotional regulation, or social interactions - children who feel understood and appreciated are better equipped to navigate these difficulties. They learn that setbacks are a natural part of growth and development, and they develop coping strategies to overcome obstacles. This resilience will serve them well throughout their lives, helping them adapt to new situations and build positive relationships.

Promoting a Positive Cycle

The ripple effect extends beyond individual children; it influences the entire learning environment. When educators and caregivers model understanding and supportive practices, they create a culture of empathy and collaboration. This culture fosters mutual respect among children, encouraging them to support one another and develop their communication skills in a peer-based setting. As children learn to appreciate each other's strengths and differences, they contribute to a positive cycle of growth that benefits the entire community.

CONCLUSION

In conclusion, the ripple effect of understanding and support in a child's development cannot be overstated. By prioritising emotional connection, recognising individual strengths, and creating a nurturing environment, caregivers and educators can facilitate significant growth in communication skills, emotional regulation, and social interactions. This holistic approach fosters resilience and cultivates a sense of belonging, empowering children to thrive both inside and outside the classroom. Ultimately, the commitment to understanding and supporting each child lays the foundation for a brighter future, not just for the individual, but for the entire community. When we invest in understanding and supporting children, we create ripples of positive change that extend far beyond the classroom, nurturing the next generation of confident, capable individuals.

KEY TAKEAWAYS

- Sensory and communication challenges are interconnected and need to be addressed together to support children effectively.
- Adjusting the sensory environment can reduce overload and enhance communication opportunities.

- Tailored, strengths-based strategies promote better engagement and communication development.
- Collaboration between teachers, therapists, and families ensures consistency and cohesion in supporting children's needs.
- A holistic, integrated approach improves outcomes and fosters an inclusive classroom environment for all students.

REFERENCES AND RESOURCES

Baker, D. L. & Manfredi-Petitt, L. A. (2018). *Inclusion in Schools: A Collaborative Approach to Educating Students with Disabilities*. Pearson Education.

Brown, B. (2020). *The Gifts of Imperfection: Let Go of Who You Think You're Supposed to Be and Embrace Who You Are*. Hazelden Publishing.

Case-Smith, J., & O'Brien, J. C. (2014). *Occupational Therapy for Children and Adolescents*. Mosby.

Dunn, W. (2007). *Living Sensationally: Understanding Your Senses*. Jessica Kingsley Publishers.

Gray, C. & White, A. L. (2002). *My Social Stories Book*. Jessica Kingsley Publishers.

Greenspan, S. I. & Wieder, S. (2006). *Engaging Autism: Using the Floortime Approach to Help Children Relate, Communicate, and Think*. Da Capo Lifelong Books.

Kranowitz, C. S. (2005). *The Out-of-Sync Child: Recognizing and Coping with Sensory Processing Disorder*. Perigee Books.

MacMillan, L. & Crowe, T. (2016). *Strengths-Based Approaches in Social Work*. Sage Publications.

Miller, L. J. & Fuller, D. A. (2007). *Sensational Kids: Hope and Help for Children with Sensory Processing Disorder (SPD)*. Penguin Group.

Murray, A. E. & Goldbart, J. (2009). Emerging Issues in Functional Communication Assessment for Children with Learning Disabilities, *Communication Disorders Quarterly*, 30(4), 233-241.

Prizant, B. M., Wetherby, A. M., Rubin, E., Laurent, A. C., & Rydell, P. J. (2006). *The SCERTS Model: A Comprehensive Educational Approach for Children with Autism Spectrum Disorders*. Brookes Publishing.

Rogers, S. J., & Dawson, G. (2009). *Early Start Denver Model for Young Children with Autism: Promoting Language, Learning, and Engagement*. Guilford Press.

Schneider, N., & Wedgewood, E. (2015). The Role of a Strengths-Based Framework in Educational Practices for Children with Developmental Delays, *Early Child Development and Care*, 185(8), 1245-1261.

Sicile-Kira, C. (2014). *Autism Spectrum Disorder: The Complete Guide to Understanding Autism*. Penguin Random House.

Shapiro, B. K. & Accardo, P. J. (2010). *Neurodevelopmental Disabilities: Clinical Principles and Practice*. Brookes Publishing.

Silberman, S. (2015). *Neurotribes: The Legacy of Autism and the Future of Neurodiversity*. Avery.

Sherratt, D. & Peter, M. (2002). *Developing Play and Communication Skills in Children with Autism Spectrum Disorders*. Routledge.

Sullivan, A. & Siegel, D. J. (2015). *Brainstorm: The Power and Purpose of the Teenage Brain*. Scribe Publications.

Turnbull, A., Turnbull, R., & Wehmeyer, M. L. (2010). *Exceptional Lives: Special Education in Today's Schools*. Pearson.

Vygotsky, L. S. (1978). *Mind in Society: The Development of Higher Psychological Processes*. Harvard University Press.

Williamson, G. & Anzalone, M. (2001). *Sensory Integration and Self-Regulation in Infants and Toddlers: Helping Very Young Children Interact with Their Environment*. Zero to Three.

Woolfson, L. & Thomas, C. (2015). Understanding Parental Engagement in Educational and Therapeutic Settings: The Role of Strengths-Based Approaches, *Journal of Child Psychology and Psychiatry*, 56(5), 487-495.

CHAPTER 8
COLLABORATING WITH PROFESSIONALS AND FAMILIES

INTRODUCTION TO COLLABORATION

Collaboration among educators, therapists, and families is essential to support children with sensory and communication needs effectively. When all parties work together, they form a robust support network that helps children thrive academically, socially, and emotionally. This chapter explores the importance of collaboration, the roles of each professional involved, and how clear communication and shared responsibility lead to better outcomes for children.

We will cover how educators, speech and language therapists (SLTs), occupational therapists (OTs), and parents can work together to meet the unique needs of each child, the risks of poor collaboration, and practical strategies to build strong, effective partnerships.

WHY COLLABORATION MATTERS

Children today face a range of challenges in and out of the classroom. Each child has a unique combination of strengths and needs, which requires a tailored approach. When professionals work in isolation, they may not fully understand the child's needs or the context in which those needs arise. Collaboration helps bridge these gaps, ensuring that the child receives a well-rounded, comprehensive support plan.

A collaborative approach fosters an environment where educators, therapists, and parents contribute their unique expertise. For example, a teacher who understands a child's sensory processing difficulties can work with an OT to implement strategies that create a more conducive learning environment, allowing the child to engage more effectively in lessons.

The benefits of collaboration extend beyond individual interventions. Research shows that children who receive coordinated support from a team of professionals demonstrate improved outcomes. A unified approach ensures that children's sensory and communication needs are met in ways that promote their overall growth and inclusion in the classroom.

> **Reflective Prompt**
>
> Think about a student in your class who may be struggling with sensory or communication challenges. How might collaboration with therapists and parents help you identify their unique needs and create a more supportive environment?

UNDERSTANDING ROLES AND RESPONSIBILITIES

Effective collaboration starts with understanding the distinct roles and responsibilities of each team member involved in the child's support.

The Role of Educators

Teachers play a pivotal role in recognising and responding to a child's sensory and communication challenges. They observe children in the classroom setting and provide critical insights into how children engage with lessons, interact with peers, and respond to environmental stimuli. Educators also implement strategies, such as sensory breaks or communication supports, to meet the child's needs.

The Role of Therapists

Both OTs and SLTs offer specialised expertise to address sensory processing and communication difficulties. OTs focus on helping children manage sensory input, develop self-regulation strategies, and adapt their environments. SLTs, on the other hand, help children develop essential communication skills, whether verbal or non-verbal, and provide strategies to enhance their social interaction and understanding of language.

The Role of Parents and Caregivers as Experts

Parents and caregivers are often the first and most knowledgeable advocates for their children. They understand their child's behaviours, preferences, and challenges better than anyone. By recognising parents and caregivers as experts in their child's needs, educators and therapists can gain valuable insights into the child's sensory profile and communication style, ensuring that strategies are truly tailored to their individual needs.

> **Reflective Prompt**
>
> Consider the professionals involved in supporting a child with sensory and communication needs. How can you ensure each professional's role is respected and that they are actively involved in the child's progress?

BUILDING EFFECTIVE COMMUNICATION

Effective communication is the cornerstone of successful collaboration. Without it, professionals and families can miss key information, leading to fragmented support. Here are strategies for establishing open, clear, and constructive communication channels:

Open Communication Channels

Regular meetings and check-ins are essential for keeping everyone aligned. This ensures that professionals and families can share updates, concerns, and progress on a child's development. Technology can also enhance communication by providing a shared space for notes, progress updates, and resources - tools like Google Docs or dedicated messaging apps help ensure that everyone stays informed and connected.

Active Listening and Constructive Feedback

Collaboration thrives when all parties listen actively and offer feedback in a constructive manner. Teachers, OTs, SLTs, and parents should be willing to engage in open dialogue, respecting each other's perspectives. Feedback sessions should focus on what's working, what isn't, and what can be adjusted, ensuring that the child's needs are met in a responsive way.

Establishing Clear Communication Goals

It's important to set expectations for how and when communication will take place. What information needs to be shared? How often should updates be given? What are the best methods for communicating with each participant? By clarifying these goals upfront, the team can reduce misunderstandings and keep the child's support plan on track.

> **Reflective Prompt**
>
> What communication strategies have worked well in your practice? How can you improve communication with other professionals and families to enhance the support for students with sensory and communication needs?

THE RISKS OF POOR COLLABORATION

Collaboration is not just a beneficial approach in the context of education and child development; it is essential for achieving successful outcomes. Effective collaboration between educators, therapists, and families creates a unified support system, which helps children overcome the challenges they face in the classroom and at home. However, when collaboration breaks down, there are several risks that can undermine the progress of children with sensory and communication difficulties. These risks can negatively affect the child's development, self-esteem, and overall educational experience.

In this section, we will explore the key risks of poor collaboration, focusing on inconsistent support and fragmentation, labelling and misunderstanding of needs, and how the lack of a coordinated approach can hinder the success of children with sensory and communication difficulties.

Inconsistent Support and Fragmentation

One of the most significant risks of poor collaboration is inconsistent support. When communication between professionals is fragmented or absent, children may experience a lack of consistency in the strategies and interventions implemented to support them. Inconsistent support can arise when teachers and therapists are not aligned in their approach, leading to mixed messages for the child. This inconsistency can confuse the child, leaving them unsure about what is expected of them and making it harder for them to make progress.

For example, imagine a child who struggles with sensory processing issues in the classroom. If their teacher is unaware of their sensory needs or does not receive adequate support from an OT or SLT, they may use disciplinary measures to address behaviours that are actually responses to sensory overload, such as fidgeting or becoming withdrawn. Meanwhile, the therapist might be working on strategies to address these sensory needs, but if there is no communication between the two, the child might find themselves receiving conflicting instructions or expectations. The teacher may view the behaviour as disruptive, while the therapist may see it as a sign of sensory overwhelm. This lack of alignment creates confusion for the child, who might not understand why their behaviour is being addressed in such different ways across different environments.

The consequences of this inconsistency are profound. The child may start to feel frustrated, unsupported, and misunderstood, which can lead to an increase in challenging behaviours. The breakdown in communication between professionals also reduces the child's chances of receiving the help they need in a timely manner. Without a cohesive strategy, children are less likely to thrive in their learning environment, making it harder for them to progress academically or socially.

Example: A child who is unable to focus in class due to sensory overload might be sent out of the classroom for "disruptive" behaviour. Meanwhile, the therapist working with the child may suggest providing the child with regular sensory breaks. If the teacher and therapist are not communicating, the teacher may continue to see the child's behaviour as disruptive and act accordingly, while the therapist's approach may never reach the classroom environment. This lack of collaboration can lead to missed opportunities for meaningful intervention and improvement in the child's focus and behaviour.

Labelling and Misunderstanding Needs

Another serious risk of poor collaboration is labelling and the misunderstanding of a child's needs. When professionals are not collaborating effectively, children may be mislabelled based on their behaviours, rather than on a full understanding of the underlying sensory or communication difficulties they are experiencing. Mislabelling occurs when behaviours are seen in isolation, without considering the child's broader sensory, social, or emotional context. For example, a child who struggles to sit still in class may be labelled as "difficult" or "unmotivated", when in reality, their behaviour might be a response to sensory needs, anxiety, or difficulty processing verbal instructions.

Such labels can have a long-term impact on the child's self-esteem and sense of identity. If a child is constantly labelled as "disruptive", they may internalise this perception and begin to believe that they are difficult or unworthy of support. Over time, this negative self-image can hinder their motivation to engage in the classroom and make it even harder for them to ask for help when they need it.

Example: Consider a child who struggles with social communication due to a language delay. When this child struggles to make friends or engage in group activities, their peers and even their teacher might perceive them as shy or unwilling to interact. However, without clear collaboration between the teacher, SLT, and parents, the child's language delay may not be understood as the root cause of the social challenges. Instead, the child might be labelled as "antisocial" or "rude", which exacerbates their sense of isolation. If the child's communication difficulties are not addressed appropriately, their social struggles will persist, and they will continue to be misunderstood.

The damage caused by these labels can be long-lasting. A child who is labelled as "difficult" may not receive the appropriate interventions or support they need to develop social or communication skills. The child may then begin to act in ways that reinforce the label, creating a vicious cycle that is hard to break.

> **Reflective Prompt**
>
> Inconsistent support and mislabelling of children are common risks of poor collaboration. Can you think of a situation in your practice where these risks might have occurred? How could collaboration have helped prevent these issues?

> **LET ME TELL YOU ABOUT CHARLIE...**
>
> Charlie is an 8-year-old boy in Year 3. Charlie has significant sensory processing difficulties and experiences high levels of anxiety in social situations, which often leads to him becoming withdrawn or acting out. However, his teacher, Ms Roberts, does not understand that Charlie's withdrawal is a coping mechanism for sensory overload and does not receive clear guidance from the OT. As a result, Ms. Roberts labels Charlie as "unmotivated" and "difficult to engage", especially during group work.
>
> Charlie's behaviour worsens as he is repeatedly sent out of class or asked to leave the group, further exacerbating his feelings of isolation. He becomes labelled as "the disruptive child" by his peers, and his self-esteem begins to plummet. Meanwhile, his therapist, who is aware of his sensory needs, has been recommending strategies such as allowing Charlie to have a quiet space for breaks, using noise-cancelling headphones, and providing structured social opportunities. However, these strategies were never communicated effectively to Ms. Roberts.
>
> Had the teacher, therapist, and parents collaborated more effectively, they could have recognised the sensory overload as the source of Charlie's behaviour. By developing a shared understanding of Charlie's needs and implementing consistent strategies both at home and school, his behaviour could have been better managed, and his self-esteem could have been protected.

THE ROLE OF COLLABORATION IN PREVENTING THESE RISKS

The key to preventing these risks is consistent, effective collaboration. When professionals work together, they can identify the root causes of children's behaviours and ensure that these issues are addressed in a way that is both sensitive and effective. A shared understanding of the child's needs, coupled with regular communication and check-ins, helps to prevent misunderstandings and labels from taking root.

By collaborating, professionals can ensure that the strategies and interventions used in different environments are aligned. Teachers, therapists, and parents can exchange valuable insights that help identify the most effective ways to support the child. Furthermore, a unified approach ensures that the child receives consistent messages and expectations, which is crucial for building trust and reducing anxiety.

Proactive Steps

- Frequent check-ins between teachers, therapists, and parents allow for the continuous exchange of information. This helps everyone stay aligned on the child's progress and the strategies that are working.
- Transparent communication about the child's needs and behaviours helps avoid confusion and ensures that everyone involved has the same understanding of the child's difficulties.
- A collaborative approach allows professionals to view a child's behaviour within the broader context of their needs. By considering sensory, emotional, and communication factors, professionals can avoid placing blame or making assumptions based on incomplete information.
- By using similar strategies at home and in school, children experience a sense of continuity and predictability, which fosters better engagement and reduces behavioural issues.

STRATEGIES FOR EFFECTIVE COLLABORATION

Building a culture of collaboration within educational settings requires effort, but it is fundamental to creating an inclusive, supportive environment that meets the needs of all children, especially those with sensory and communication challenges. When educators, therapists, and parents collaborate effectively, children receive consistent support, which enhances their ability to thrive in both academic and social settings. Below are key strategies for fostering effective collaboration among all involved parties.

Regular Check-ins

One of the most important strategies for effective collaboration is regular check-ins. These meetings allow professionals and parents to review a child's progress, discuss successes and challenges, and adjust strategies as needed. Regular check-ins can take various forms, from formal meetings to informal discussions, but they all serve the same purpose: to ensure that everyone involved in the child's support plan is on the same page.

These meetings provide an opportunity to share observations, discuss what's working, and identify areas that may need modification. For instance, a teacher might highlight that a child is succeeding with a visual schedule but is struggling with group work. The OT might suggest incorporating sensory breaks or a quiet space during group activities to help the child stay regulated. By meeting regularly, professionals can adapt strategies to better support the child's evolving needs, ensuring they are continually providing the most effective interventions.

For parents, regular check-ins provide a space to ask questions, share feedback, and stay informed about their child's progress. This collaborative exchange helps to build trust and keep everyone aligned, ensuring that the support provided at school is mirrored at home.

> **Reflective Prompt**
>
> What steps can you take to create a more collaborative and supportive environment in your school or practice? How can regular check-ins and shared goals improve your team's effectiveness?

Use of Technology

In today's digital age, technology plays a crucial role in enhancing communication and streamlining collaboration. By using shared documents, messaging apps, and online progress trackers, all team members – teachers, therapists, and parents – can access the same up-to-date information about the child's needs, strategies, and progress.

For example, shared Google Docs or online platforms like Microsoft Teams or Google Classroom can serve as central hubs where professionals can record observations, make notes on strategies, and track the child's progress. This ensures that everyone involved is working with the same data, reducing the risk of miscommunication or missed opportunities.

Messaging apps like WhatsApp or Slack can be used for more informal communication between team members, facilitating quick discussions about any immediate concerns. Parents can also be included in these conversations, allowing them to stay engaged in real time. Moreover, online progress trackers can visually map out the child's growth, making it easier for everyone to see the effects of interventions and adjust their approach when necessary.

Using technology to keep communication open and accessible is not only time-saving but also ensures that no one is left out of the loop, which is critical for providing consistent and coordinated support.

Collaborative Planning

Collaborative planning involves all relevant professionals – teachers, therapists, and parents – working together to create and implement intervention plans. This process ensures that the child's support is comprehensive and aligned with their unique strengths and needs. When planning interventions, it is crucial to involve all key stakeholders.

For example, when developing an Individual Education Plan (IEP) for a child, teachers, therapists, and parents should all contribute their insights. Teachers can provide information on how the child interacts with peers and engages with the curriculum, while therapists can offer strategies for sensory or communication support. Parents can share valuable insights into how the child behaves at home, helping to identify triggers or challenges that may not be as visible in the school setting.

By collaborating during the planning phase, the team can ensure that interventions are well-rounded and address the child's needs holistically. Moreover, involving parents in the planning process empowers them to take an active role in their child's education and ensures that everyone is working towards shared goals. This helps to create a sense of unity and consistency across home and school environments.

Fostering a Positive, Inclusive School Culture

An inclusive school culture is essential for successful collaboration. To foster this, schools must promote a collaborative mindset among staff and create an environment where every child's needs are valued and addressed. This requires providing training and professional development on the importance of teamwork, inclusion, and working with external specialists like OTs and SLTs.

Schools should regularly offer opportunities for professionals to engage with one another, whether through cross-disciplinary team meetings, collaborative teaching planning sessions, or joint professional development activities. These opportunities allow staff to share expertise, learn from one another, and build a more cohesive support system for students. When teachers and therapists understand each other's roles and approaches, they can collaborate more effectively, ultimately benefiting the child.

Additionally, creating an inclusive school environment goes beyond just the teachers and therapists. Schools should also work to create an atmosphere where parents feel welcomed and valued as partners in their child's education. This can be achieved by regularly inviting parents to school events, providing resources and training for families, and maintaining open communication channels.

In an inclusive school culture, every member of the school community – staff, parents, and students – feels a sense of belonging. This strengthens the collaboration between all parties and helps to ensure that every child's unique needs are met.

Engaging Parents and Caregivers Effectively

Parents and caregivers are often the most knowledgeable and passionate advocates for their children. Their involvement in the collaboration process is crucial, as they bring unique insights into their child's needs, preferences, and behaviours that professionals may not be fully aware of. When educators and therapists actively engage parents and recognise their expertise, they can work together to create more effective and holistic support strategies. Here are key strategies for engaging them effectively in the collaboration process.

Recognising Parents and Caregivers as Experts

Parents and caregivers are, without a doubt, the foremost experts on their child. They spend the most time with the child, observing their behaviours in a variety of settings, and have a deep understanding of their child's likes, dislikes, strengths, and challenges. It's important for educators and therapists to recognise this expertise and make a concerted effort to listen to parents' insights.

By actively involving parents in the decision-making process, such as during IEP meetings or reviews of support strategies, professionals can ensure that the child's support plan is comprehensive and well-rounded. Parents can share essential information about the child's sensory preferences, social interactions, and emotional responses, which may not be evident in a classroom or therapy setting.

For example, a child who struggles with social interactions at school may be perceived as shy or antisocial by teachers, but a parent might reveal that the child's struggles stem from a sensory processing issue, such as becoming overwhelmed in noisy environments. This vital information allows professionals to adjust their strategies – perhaps introducing quieter spaces for breaks or more structured, predictable routines – which may not have been considered without input from the parents.

When professionals actively seek and incorporate parent feedback, it fosters a sense of partnership and collaboration, which ultimately benefits the child. It also helps build trust and respect between parents and professionals, ensuring that the child's best interests are at the forefront of the decision-making process.

Creating a Welcoming Environment

A welcoming, inclusive atmosphere is essential for parents to feel comfortable and respected when engaging with the school or therapy services. If parents feel that their input is valued and that they are integral members of the team, they will be more likely to actively participate in the child's educational and therapeutic journey.

Schools and therapists should create physical and emotional spaces that make parents feel invited and respected. This can start with meeting spaces that are welcoming and conducive to open conversations. For example, a comfortable, private room with seating that fosters dialogue can make a big difference in how parents feel about the process. Additionally, professionals should greet parents warmly and provide an atmosphere of trust where parents can share concerns, ask questions, and offer feedback without fear of judgement or dismissal.

Incorporating inclusivity into all aspects of school and therapy services is equally important. Schools can create opportunities for parents to get involved in activities, events, and even volunteer roles, which helps them feel more connected to the school community. Offering workshops or information sessions on topics like sensory processing, supporting communication needs, or emotional regulation can provide parents with tools to better understand and support their child's needs at home. This builds an open relationship between parents and educators, making it easier for parents to approach the school with questions, concerns, or insights about their child.

Additionally, fostering an inclusive culture where parents of all backgrounds are encouraged to participate strengthens the partnership between the home and the school. Schools can make a concerted effort to consider the diverse needs of families, such as offering materials in different languages, providing childcare during meetings, or making meetings flexible in terms of timing. This ensures that all families have the opportunity to engage meaningfully in their child's education.

STRATEGIES FOR PARENT LEADERSHIP AND PARTICIPATION

In order to deepen parental involvement, schools can implement strategies that encourage parent leadership and active participation. One way to do this is by creating committees or advisory boards where parents can contribute to decisions about school policies or educational strategies. These committees can focus on various aspects, such as creating more inclusive school practices, improving sensory support for children, or even shaping the curriculum to be more adaptable to students with special needs.

By inviting parents to take on leadership roles, schools help parents feel a greater sense of ownership over their child's learning environment. This involvement empowers parents to voice their perspectives, share their unique experiences, and advocate for their child and others in the school community. It also strengthens the collaboration between home and school, as parents become partners in decision-making rather than just recipients of information.

Another example of encouraging parent leadership is by organising parent-teacher conferences that allow parents to play an active role in shaping their child's educational journey. In these conferences, parents are not only briefed on their child's progress but also have the opportunity to suggest strategies or support mechanisms that have been successful at home. This creates a two-way flow of information, where both professionals and parents bring their expertise to the table, resulting in more effective and personalised plans for the child.

Finally, schools can promote parent participation by creating a school-parent network, where parents can connect, share experiences, and offer each other support. These networks can provide emotional support for parents and help them feel more empowered in their roles. For example, parents who have children with similar needs can share strategies that have worked for them or provide advice on navigating educational systems. These networks not only benefit the children but also build a strong sense of community among families and the school.

Engaging parents effectively in the collaboration process is essential for ensuring that children receive the best possible support. Recognising parents as experts, creating a welcoming and inclusive environment, and offering opportunities for parent leadership and participation all play vital roles in fostering a strong home-school partnership. When parents are actively involved, they can contribute valuable insights, strengthen strategies, and ensure that their child's needs are consistently met. By creating a culture of collaboration and valuing the perspectives of parents, educators and therapists can work together more effectively to support every child's development, both at home and in the classroom.

THE STRENGTHS-BASED APPROACH

Let's build on Chapter 7 and explore how a strength-based approach can support collaboration. In educational settings, there is often a tendency to focus on a child's compliance with rules and expectations, such as "Sit still during class" or "Follow instructions without hesitation". While these compliance-based goals may seem essential for classroom management, they can inadvertently neglect the child's intrinsic abilities, interests, and personal strengths. A strengths-based approach, on the other hand, places emphasis on the child's capabilities and builds upon them to encourage positive growth, engagement, and self-motivation. By shifting the focus from compliance to strengths, educators can create a more supportive, empowering, and motivating environment for children, especially those who may struggle with traditional behavioural expectations. This section will delve into the benefits of a strengths-based approach, highlighting how focusing on a child's strengths rather than compliance fosters motivation, engagement, and development.

SHIFTING FROM COMPLIANCE-BASED GOALS TO STRENGTHS-BASED GOALS

Compliance-based goals often focus on what a child *should* do, such as adhering to rules or following specific instructions without deviation. These goals can create a rigid framework where children are expected to conform to predefined expectations, regardless of their unique abilities, interests, or challenges. While these goals are important in maintaining structure and discipline, they can unintentionally alienate children whose strengths do not align with traditional classroom expectations. For example, a child who struggles with attention may find it challenging to sit still during a lecture, leading to frustration or disengagement.

In contrast, strengths-based goals focus on what a child *can* do and aim to build on these inherent abilities to promote learning and development. Rather than expecting a child to meet generic behavioural standards, strengths-based goals are tailored to the child's individual profile, considering their strengths, interests, and unique ways of engaging with the world. This approach celebrates the child's natural abilities and encourages educators to create learning experiences that resonate with the child's strengths.

Examples of Compliance-Based vs. Strengths-Based Goals:

- **Compliance-Based Goal:** "Sit still for 20 minutes during a lesson".
  This goal assumes that all children are capable of sitting still for extended periods, which may not be realistic for children who need movement to regulate their sensory input or attention.
- **Strengths-Based Goal:** "Engage in a hands-on learning activity for 15 minutes, with movement breaks every 5 minutes".

This goal recognises that a child may learn better through active participation and provides a solution that accommodates the child's sensory and learning needs while still promoting engagement.

Another example might be:

- **Compliance-Based Goal:** "Complete all assigned homework without assistance".
- **Strengths-Based Goal:** "Use visual aids and hands-on tools to support completion of homework tasks, with a teacher or peer providing assistance as needed".
 This shift acknowledges that some children may need additional support or alternative strategies to access and complete tasks, and it creates a plan that builds on available resources to support the child's success.

By focusing on strengths, children are not merely trying to fit into a predefined mould but are encouraged to work with the tools that best suit their individual needs. This helps to build confidence and promotes long-term engagement in learning.

PROMOTING POSITIVE, CHILD-CENTRED GOALS

A strengths-based approach is inherently child-centred, focusing on the child's capabilities rather than deficiencies. This framework empowers children by recognising their unique qualities and personal strengths. Children who are encouraged to work within their areas of strength feel more capable, confident, and motivated to succeed. Instead of feeling like they are constantly failing to meet externally imposed standards, children are given the opportunity to excel in areas where they naturally shine.

Strengths-based goals create an environment where children are actively involved in setting their own objectives. This process is empowering because it involves the child in decision-making, allowing them to identify their interests, areas of strength, and personal goals. By incorporating the child's voice in the goal-setting process, educators can foster a sense of ownership and agency in the child's learning journey.

For example, a child who has a strong interest in art but struggles with reading and writing could set a goal like: "Express ideas through drawing and visual projects, and work towards improving written communication with support from visual aids". This goal centres the child's strengths – creativity and visual communication – while also providing a clear path for developing other skills, such as writing, with the right support.

By promoting intrinsic motivation, strengths-based goals encourage children to take responsibility for their own learning. When a child is engaged in an activity that aligns with their strengths, they are more likely to put in the effort, persist through challenges, and feel a sense of accomplishment when they meet their goals. This is a far more sustainable approach to learning than relying solely on external rewards or the need to conform to behavioural expectations. Instead of focusing on what the child *cannot* do, a strengths-based approach nurtures what the child *can* do, creating a more positive and motivating learning environment.

CELEBRATING ACHIEVEMENTS

A key component of the strengths-based approach is the celebration of small wins and milestones. Recognising and celebrating achievements – whether big or small – reinforces a child's self-confidence and encourages continued progress. Celebrating achievements is not about providing superficial praise but about acknowledging the child's efforts, improvements, and successes, no matter how incremental.

For example, if a child has been working on improving their focus in class and has managed to stay engaged for 15 minutes during a lesson, this is a significant achievement and should be celebrated.

Celebrating small victories helps to reinforce the child's belief in their ability to succeed and encourages them to keep pushing forward, even when faced with challenges. This approach shifts the focus from merely completing tasks to valuing the effort and progress that the child makes along the way.

Examples of celebrating achievements:

- A child who is learning to use a communication aid for the first time might be celebrated with a simple, heartfelt recognition: "I noticed how you used your new communication board to share your thoughts today. That's a fantastic way to express yourself!" This recognition acknowledges the effort involved in learning a new skill and encourages the child to continue using it.
- If a child has successfully navigated a challenging situation, a teacher or therapist can celebrate by saying, "I see how you used your strategies to feel more comfortable today. You're showing such great self-awareness and problem-solving!"

Celebrating achievements also extends beyond academic success. Positive reinforcement for social or emotional achievements – such as building relationships with peers, self-advocating, or exploring new activities – fosters a sense of self-worth and pride. Children who see their efforts being recognised are more likely to feel motivated to continue learning and growing.

Sharing these moments of achievement with parents and caregivers is an essential part of reinforcing progress and fostering a collaborative support system for the child. Whether it's a brief note home, a quick conversation at the end of the day, or a message through a communication app, keeping parents informed of their child's progress – no matter how small – can help them celebrate these achievements at home as well. For instance, a teacher might say, "Today, your child showed incredible focus and curiosity during the group activity. They brought their own unique perspective, and it was wonderful to see!" or "They used their sensory toolkit independently when they felt overwhelmed, which shows how well they understand their needs".

When parents are aware of these successes, they can continue to reinforce and celebrate them in familiar environments, providing additional encouragement and consistency. This strengthens the child's sense of accomplishment and helps them see that their efforts are valued across different settings. Encouraging parents to celebrate these moments also empowers them to adopt a strengths-based mindset, focusing on their child's capabilities and progress rather than perceived challenges.

WHY STRENGTHS-BASED GOALS ARE MORE EFFECTIVE THAN COMPLIANCE-BASED GOALS

Strengths-based goals are far more effective than compliance-based goals because they tap into the child's intrinsic motivation and provide meaningful, personalised learning experiences. Rather than forcing a child to conform to rigid behavioural expectations, strengths-based goals enable children to work within their natural abilities, which boosts their self-esteem and increases their chances of success.

When children are encouraged to work within their areas of strength, they are more likely to experience positive learning outcomes, as the process is engaging and aligned with their interests. In contrast, compliance-based goals often lead to frustration, disengagement, and a lack of motivation, especially for children who may struggle to meet traditional behavioural expectations.

Moreover, strengths-based goals contribute to a child's overall development by providing opportunities for growth in a way that is empowering and affirming. These goals build the foundation for a positive self-image, foster a growth mindset, and help children see themselves as capable learners.

A strengths-based approach shifts the focus from compliance to celebration, empowering children to thrive by building on their strengths. By setting goals that are centred around the child's abilities, educators can foster intrinsic motivation, boost self-confidence, and encourage sustained progress. Recognising and celebrating small achievements reinforces positive behaviour and creates a learning environment where children feel valued for who they are. This approach ultimately leads to more engaged, motivated, and confident learners, and provides them with the tools to succeed both academically and socially. The power of strengths-based goals lies in their ability to honour each child's unique potential, paving the way for a more inclusive and supportive learning experience.

SUPPORTING FAMILIES THROUGH TRAUMA

Families of children with special needs often experience unique emotional challenges, which can significantly impact their overall well-being. These challenges include heightened levels of stress, isolation, and stigma, which can be overwhelming and difficult to navigate. The emotional toll of raising a child with additional needs is compounded by the complexities of seeking and accessing appropriate care, dealing with educational challenges, and facing societal misconceptions about disabilities. Educators and therapists have a crucial role in acknowledging these struggles and offering support. By recognising family trauma and addressing it with sensitivity, professionals can help mitigate some of the challenges families face and provide them with the tools and resources to cope with the emotional weight of their situation.

Understanding Family Trauma

Family trauma, in the context of children with special needs, refers to the emotional, psychological, and social strain that parents and caregivers endure as they navigate various systems of care and support. This trauma often begins with the *diagnosis-related stress*, which can be an overwhelming experience. Many parents may feel a sense of grief, loss, and confusion after receiving a diagnosis of a developmental, language delay, or sensory processing disorder, especially if the child's needs are not immediately understood or addressed. In these cases, parents may experience a *trauma of uncertainty* - the stress of not knowing what their child's future will look like, or whether the child will receive the appropriate support to thrive.

Once the diagnosis is made, parents often find themselves facing multiple barriers, such as limited access to resources, a lack of adequate support services, or challenges in understanding complex medical and educational systems. Navigating these systems can feel like a constant struggle, leaving parents feeling fatigued, defeated, and isolated. For many families, these challenges are made even more difficult by *stigma* - the negative societal attitudes or misconceptions about disabilities. Families may feel judged by others, or experience feelings of shame when their child's behaviours or needs are misunderstood or criticised. This stigma can prevent families from seeking help or sharing their struggles with others, leading to a sense of social isolation.

In addition to stigma, parents of children with special needs often experience an emotional toll that comes from the *everyday demands* of caregiving. The relentless nature of managing medical appointments, therapy sessions, school-related issues, and emotional needs can result in *caregiver burnout*. This exhaustion can affect both the physical and mental health of the family, especially when there is no emotional or practical support system in place.

The challenges of raising a child with special needs can often lead to profound *emotional trauma* for the parents and caregivers. This trauma is not only about the stress they face on a daily basis but also about the emotional strain of advocating for their child, protecting them from discrimination, and trying to secure the best opportunities for their development.

Acknowledging Family Trauma

The first and most important step in supporting families through trauma is **acknowledging** the emotional toll that raising a child with special needs can take on parents. Educators and therapists should approach families with deep empathy, recognising the unique challenges they face, and validate their experiences. Acknowledgement helps to create a sense of safety and trust, allowing families to feel heard and understood.

When educators and therapists acknowledge the trauma that families experience, it helps to reduce feelings of isolation and shame. Parents often feel that they must "keep it together" or hide their struggles to avoid being judged. By opening the door for honest conversations and showing empathy, professionals can encourage parents to express their feelings and share their challenges. This can help parents feel less alone, knowing that their struggles are recognised and that they are not the only ones facing such difficulties.

Empathetic communication involves listening attentively to the family's concerns without judgement or immediate solutions. Sometimes, the best way to help a family is simply to provide a space where they can talk about their experiences. For example, an educator might say, "I can see that this is really difficult for you, and I want to make sure we are supporting both you and your child in the best way possible". This simple acknowledgement can go a long way in helping families feel validated and understood.

In addition, professionals should recognise the complexity of the family's trauma. The emotional strain of managing a child's special needs is often compounded by financial stress, relationship strain, and the pressure of juggling multiple roles. It is important for educators and therapists to recognise the full extent of what families are dealing with and offer holistic support.

Addressing Trauma with Sensitivity

Once family trauma is acknowledged, the next step is to **address it with sensitivity**. This involves offering support in ways that respect the family's emotional needs and provide practical solutions to help them cope with the stress they face.

Emotional Support: Professionals should offer a compassionate approach, ensuring that families feel supported both emotionally and practically. This can be done through regular check-ins, where educators and therapists ask parents how they are coping and whether there are any specific areas where they need help. Parents may appreciate having someone to talk to who truly understands the emotional complexities of their situation. For example, a teacher might say, "I know this has been an emotionally draining time for you. Please let me know how I can support you further".

Educators and therapists can also play a vital role in connecting families with appropriate resources. This might include referring parents to mental health professionals, support groups, or community organisations that specialise in helping families of children with special needs. These resources can provide parents with the tools to manage stress, improve coping mechanisms, and connect with others who understand their experiences. Support groups, for example, allow parents to share their stories, exchange coping strategies, and find solidarity with others in similar situations.

Parents may also benefit from *family therapy* or *individual counselling* to address emotional challenges such as depression, anxiety, or trauma-related stress. By offering referrals to these services, professionals can help parents manage their mental health and improve their ability to care for their child.

Teaching parents about self-care and stress management is also essential. Educators and therapists can share techniques that help reduce the emotional toll of caregiving, such as mindfulness practices, relaxation techniques, or time management strategies. Encouraging parents to prioritise their own well-being is vital for preventing burnout and ensuring they can be the best advocates and caregivers for their children.

Providing Resources and Emotional Support

In addition to referring families to formal resources, educators and therapists can also provide informal resources and support. This can include **educational workshops** designed to help parents better understand their child's needs, learn strategies for managing difficult behaviours, and access information on navigating systems of care. Workshops or seminars on topics such as sensory processing, communication strategies, and special education rights can empower parents and give them the knowledge they need to advocate for their child effectively.

Many families of children with special needs face financial strain due to the costs associated with therapy, medical care, and educational support. Educators and therapists can help families identify financial resources or grants that may be available to assist with these costs. In some cases, professionals may be able to connect families with local charities or government programmes that can provide financial assistance or help with accessing medical equipment and therapies.

Additionally, educators and therapists can provide families with resources on managing the logistics of caregiving. For example, information on respite care services, which allow parents to take a break while their child is cared for by trained professionals, can be crucial for preventing caregiver burnout.

Supporting families through trauma is a vital part of helping children with special needs thrive. By acknowledging the emotional toll that caregiving can take, addressing trauma with sensitivity, and providing families with resources and emotional support, educators and therapists can make a meaningful difference in the lives of families. A trauma-informed approach that includes empathy, validation, and practical support enables families to cope with the stresses they face and empowers them to become more effective advocates for their children. In turn, this holistic support helps children receive the care and attention they need to succeed academically, socially, and emotionally. Recognising and addressing family trauma in a compassionate and sensitive way ensures that the child's overall development is supported not only at school or therapy but within the family unit as well.

SUCCESS STORIES: THE IMPACT OF COLLABORATION

Here are a two case studies that demonstrate the transformative impact of effective collaboration:

CASE STUDY 1: SARAH

Background

Sarah is a 10-year-old autistic girl. She has struggled with communication, social interaction, and sensory regulation throughout her life. Sarah finds it difficult to engage in classroom activities and often experiences high levels of anxiety. This anxiety manifests through meltdowns, withdrawal, and difficulty following class routines, which creates challenges for her teachers and peers. As Sarah's challenges intensified, her teachers, SLT, OT, and parents were all involved in developing a tailored support plan to address Sarah's sensory processing needs, social communication challenges, and emotional regulation.

Interventions

At the outset, Sarah's teacher, Ms. Thompson, was aware of her struggles but felt unsure about how to best support Sarah's sensory and communication needs. Ms. Thompson, recognising the importance of collaboration, initiated regular meetings with Sarah's OT, SLT, and her parents to establish shared goals and strategies. The team's focus was to understand Sarah's unique needs and to find a way to implement a consistent approach both at home and at school. Ms. Thompson was keen to learn more about sensory processing issues and how they could impact Sarah's ability to engage in classroom activities.

In the first meeting, Sarah's OT provided valuable insights into how Sarah's sensory needs affected her behaviour. Sarah had difficulty processing sounds in the classroom, which often led to overstimulation and anxiety. The SLT noted that Sarah struggled with verbal communication, and her social withdrawal seemed to be a way of avoiding anxiety-inducing interactions. Her parents contributed by sharing their observations of Sarah's responses to sensory inputs at home, noting that Sarah became overwhelmed by noise, crowds, and even the texture of certain clothes. This information was vital in understanding the root causes of her anxiety and meltdowns.

Through this collaborative approach, the team worked to develop a set of shared strategies, including sensory-friendly classroom adjustments, visual supports, and a sensory break routine to help Sarah regulate her sensory input. The goals were aligned across all professionals and family members, with a strong emphasis on reducing anxiety and improving Sarah's engagement in class activities.

Communication Strategies

Effective communication was key in ensuring the success of Sarah's plan. Regular check-ins were scheduled every two weeks to review Sarah's progress. During these check-ins, the team discussed what strategies were working, identified areas that needed further adjustment, and shared new insights from the classroom and home environments. This open communication helped the team stay aligned and made it easier to adjust strategies as needed.

Ms. Thompson worked closely with Sarah's OT to implement changes in the classroom. They agreed to introduce sensory breaks, where Sarah could step away from the classroom environment, engage in calming activities, and return to class feeling more regulated. Visual schedules were created to provide Sarah with a predictable routine, helping to reduce anxiety about transitions. The SLT, on the other hand, worked with Sarah to develop alternative communication strategies. Sarah began using communication cards to express her needs when she felt overwhelmed, allowing her to communicate without resorting to withdrawal or meltdowns.

The school also worked in partnership with Sarah's parents. The team encouraged Sarah's parents to incorporate similar strategies at home, such as creating a sensory-friendly space where Sarah could retreat when feeling overstimulated. They also established a shared communication journal, where her parents could log Sarah's behaviours and emotional responses, which was reviewed by the professionals during their check-ins. This enabled the team to maintain a consistent approach across environments, ensuring that Sarah's sensory needs were being met in a coordinated way.

Impact of Collaboration

As a result of these collaborative efforts, Sarah's anxiety levels began to decrease significantly. The sensory breaks provided her with the necessary time and space to regulate, reducing the frequency and intensity of meltdowns. The visual schedule helped Sarah understand and anticipate transitions, which had previously been a major source of anxiety. With the support of the SLT, Sarah's communication skills also improved. She began using her communication cards more frequently, expressing her needs more effectively and participating more in class activities.

Sarah's teachers noticed a marked improvement in her engagement. While she still preferred quieter, individual tasks, she became more willing to join group activities, especially when she had her sensory breaks and the structure provided by the visual schedule. Her social interactions also improved, as she started to feel more comfortable in one-on-one exchanges, reducing her anxiety around group work.

Sarah's parents observed similar improvements at home. The sensory-friendly space created in their home gave Sarah a place to retreat when she became overwhelmed. Additionally, her parents were able to use the communication cards at home, reinforcing the new communication strategies. Sarah's emotional regulation improved as she felt more in control of her environment, both at school and at home.

The case of Sarah highlights the profound impact that collaboration, clear communication, and shared goals can have on a child's success. The regular check-ins, involvement of all professionals, and consistent strategies across school and home environments led to tangible improvements in Sarah's emotional regulation, communication, and classroom participation.

TAKEAWAY MESSAGE

As seen with Sarah, the joint efforts of her teachers, therapists, and parents led to improved outcomes due to regular check-ins, shared strategies, and a consistent approach. This case demonstrates the power of collaboration and communication in addressing complex sensory and communication needs, allowing Sarah to thrive both at school and at home.

COLLABORATING WITH PROFESSIONALS AND FAMILIES

> **Reflective Prompt**
>
> Sarah's case shows the importance of clear communication and shared goals. What strategies can you implement in your own practice to ensure collaboration with families and professionals is effective for children with similar challenges?

CASE STUDY 2: JAMIE

Background:

Jamie is an 8-year-old boy with a diagnosis of attention deficit hyperactivity disorder (ADHD) and language delays. Jamie has always struggled to focus in class and often finds it difficult to engage in social interactions. His impulsivity, paired with his language difficulties, has led to challenges in both academic performance and peer relationships. Jamie's teacher, Mr. Anderson, had observed his difficulty staying on task and his impulsive behaviour but felt unsure about how best to support him in the classroom.

Jamie's language delays also made it harder for him to communicate effectively, often leading to frustration and difficulty building peer relationships. His parents had expressed concern that Jamie's impulsivity was affecting his ability to develop meaningful friendships and succeed in school. Given the complexity of Jamie's needs, the school team, including his teacher, SLT, OT, and parents, began collaborating to develop a comprehensive support plan.

Interventions

At the first meeting, Jamie's teacher and therapists discussed the impact of ADHD on his ability to stay focused and follow instructions. The SLT explained that Jamie's language delays were exacerbating his difficulties with social communication. His impulsivity, paired with his struggle to understand language and social cues, was causing frustration in peer interactions. The OT identified that Jamie had difficulty with self-regulation, which contributed to his impulsive behaviour.

Together, the team developed a series of shared goals aimed at improving Jamie's ability to focus in class, regulate his behaviour, and develop better communication skills. These goals included providing Jamie with clear visual cues to help him stay on task, implementing movement breaks to help him regulate, and using social stories and opportunities for interest-based group activities with his peers to enhance his social interaction skills.

Jamie's parents were crucial in this process. They provided insights into how Jamie's impulsivity manifested at home and the strategies they had been using to support him, such as offering clear, concise instructions and creating structured routines. Jamie's parents were keen to work closely with the school to ensure that the strategies used at school were aligned with those used at home.

Communication Strategies

Effective communication between Jamie's school team and his parents was a priority throughout this process. Regular meetings were scheduled to monitor Jamie's progress and adapt strategies as necessary. The team also established a shared communication system with Jamie's parents to ensure they were kept informed of any new strategies or changes in his support plan.

Mr. Anderson and the SLT worked together to implement strategies in the classroom that aligned with Jamie's needs. Visual cues and timers were introduced to help Jamie stay on task, and movement breaks were incorporated into his daily routine to help him manage his energy levels and impulsivity. The OT provided advice on strategies for self-regulation, including breathing exercises and sensory tools to help Jamie calm down when he became overwhelmed.

The SLT worked with Jamie to develop his social communication skills through interest-based activities that were engaging and motivating for him. Instead of traditional role-playing, the focus was on using Jamie's personal interests to create meaningful interactions. For example, they used his favourite games or topics to practice taking turns, understanding non-verbal cues, and expressing emotions in a way that felt natural and enjoyable for him. At home, Jamie's parents supported these skills by incorporating his interests into daily interactions, creating opportunities for communication that were relaxed, supportive, and focused on his strengths, making learning feel more like play.

Impact of Collaboration

The collaborative approach had a significant impact on Jamie's behaviour and academic performance. Mr. Anderson reported that Jamie was able to stay on task for longer periods of time, thanks to the visual cues and movement breaks that helped regulate his attention. His impulsivity decreased as he began to recognise when he needed a break and how to manage his energy levels.

Jamie's language skills improved as he began using strategies that aligned with his interests and strengths. By incorporating his favourite activities into communication opportunities, he became more confident in initiating and maintaining conversations with peers. The focus on real-life, interest-based interactions helped him better understand social cues in a natural context, leading to improved connections with others and stronger friendships. This approach allowed Jamie to feel more engaged and motivated, making social interactions feel more meaningful and enjoyable.

Jamie's parents also saw progress at home. The structure provided by the school's visual cues and routines was mirrored at home, helping Jamie stay focused during homework and daily tasks. The shared communication system allowed Jamie's parents to stay informed about his progress and ensure consistency between home and school strategies.

TAKEAWAY MESSAGE

As seen with Jamie, the joint efforts of his teacher, therapists, and parents led to positive changes in his behaviour and communication. Regular check-ins, shared goals, and consistent strategies across both home and school environments helped Jamie improve his focus, self-regulation, and social interactions. This case reinforces the importance of collaboration and communication in supporting children with ADHD and language delays.

> **Reflective Prompt**
>
> Jamie's success highlights the importance of using strengths-based approaches. How can you incorporate strengths-based strategies into your approach to supporting children with sensory and communication difficulties?

CONCLUSION

In conclusion, collaboration is the key to supporting children with sensory and communication challenges. By working together, educators, therapists, and families can create a unified approach that maximises the child's potential. It's essential to value each team member's expertise, communicate effectively, and remain committed to ongoing collaboration. When all parties are aligned, children can thrive in an inclusive, supportive environment that promotes their academic, social, and emotional growth.

KEY TAKEAWAYS

- Effective collaboration between teachers, therapists, and families is essential for supporting children with sensory and communication challenges.
- Regular communication and shared goals ensure that strategies are aligned and consistently applied across environments.
- Recognising each professional's unique role fosters a holistic approach that addresses the child's full range of needs.
- A strengths-based approach promotes engagement, self-esteem, and long-term success in children with sensory and communication difficulties.
- Ongoing collaboration and regular check-ins allow for adjustments to be made, ensuring continuous support for the child's evolving needs.

REFERENCES AND RESOURCES

Ainscow, M., Booth, T., & Dyson, A. (2006). *Improving Schools, Developing Inclusion*. Routledge.

Brown, S. & McDonald, S. (2016). *Collaborative Working in a Multi-Agency Environment*. Springer.

Dunn, W. (2001). The sensory profile: A tool for measuring sensory processing in children. In *Sensory Processing Disorders: From Assessment to Intervention* (pp. 35-58). Therapy Skill Builders.

Dyson, A. & Gallannaugh, F. (2008). Exploring the complexities of school collaboration and co-ordination. *Journal of Education Policy, 23*(4), 385-404.

Guralnick, M. J. (2011). Early intervention for children with intellectual disabilities: An overview. In B. Reichow, B. A. Boyd, E. E. Barton, & S. L. Odom (Eds.), *Handbook of Early Childhood Special Education* (pp. 235-252). Springer.

King, G. & Law, M. (2011). *Collaborative Practice in Occupational Therapy and Speech Therapy*. Routledge.

Odom, S. L. & Strain, P. S. (2002). The benefits of early intervention for young children with autism spectrum disorders. *The Journal of Early Intervention, 25*(3), 87-104.

Stein, P. M. & Bridges, D. (2014). *Strengths-Based Approaches in Education: Evidence and Impact*. Springer.

Winzer, M. A. & Mazurek, K. (2015). *Inclusive Education: An International Agenda*. Routledge.

CHAPTER 9
LOOKING AHEAD
FUTURE DIRECTIONS AND RESOURCES

INTRODUCTION: A CALL TO ACTION

As we come to the end of this book, the journey of supporting children's communication and sensory development is just beginning. The work does not stop here. Now is the time to take what we've explored and put it into action – whether that means changing how we support a child in the classroom, advocating for better communication resources, or simply reflecting on how we interact with children each day. Small, intentional changes lead to significant transformations.

This chapter provides an overview of emerging trends, practical strategies, and resources to keep learning and evolving. By staying informed and engaged, we can ensure that children receive the support they need to thrive in a world that values their unique communication styles and strengths.

EMERGING TRENDS IN SPEECH AND LANGUAGE DEVELOPMENT

The way we think about speech and language development is shifting, with an increasing recognition that there is no single "correct" way for children to learn and communicate. Instead, approaches that honour neurodiversity and individual learning styles are proving to be far more effective in fostering meaningful communication. As research continues to evolve, we are moving towards more personalised, child-centred strategies that support children holistically, acknowledging that communication is deeply intertwined with emotional well-being, social connections, and cognitive growth.

One of the most significant changes is the move towards **play-based learning** as a key method for developing language. Children naturally engage in communication when playing, and structuring opportunities for meaningful interactions through play allows them to develop language in a relaxed, engaging way. Additionally, the **role of the environment** is being recognised as a crucial factor in communication success – settings that reduce sensory overload, offer visual supports, and provide predictable routines help children feel more comfortable expressing themselves.

It is also becoming increasingly clear that **adult interactions** play a crucial role in language development. When adults model effective communication, scaffold conversations, and respond to children's communication attempts with warmth and encouragement, they create the foundation for language growth. Peer interactions also provide natural communication opportunities, helping children build their confidence in real-world settings. Finally, an increasing focus on **emotional regulation strategies** is showing how closely linked communication development is to a child's ability to manage emotions. When children feel calm and supported, they are more likely to engage in meaningful communication.

These approaches are not just theories – they are practical, research-backed methods that can be applied in real-world settings to make a tangible difference. By embracing these strategies, we are aligning with the latest research and innovations in speech and language development and taking an active role in shaping a more inclusive and responsive approach to communication support.

Putting This into Action: 5 Key Steps

- **Prioritise Play-based Learning** – Encourage language development through interactive and engaging play opportunities.
- **Optimise the Environment** – Reduce sensory overload, offer visual supports, and create predictable routines to support communication.
- **Model Effective Communication** – Use clear, positive language and scaffold conversations to build confidence and skills.
- **Support Peer Interactions** – Facilitate opportunities for children to communicate with each other in natural settings.
- **Integrate Emotional Regulation Strategies** – Help children manage emotions to support their ability to engage in meaningful communication.

By embedding these practices into our daily interactions, we create environments that nurture every child's potential and provide them with the support they need to thrive.

ADVANCEMENTS IN SENSORY PROCESSING SUPPORT

Sensory processing challenges are often linked to speech and language difficulties, and our understanding of this relationship has grown tremendously in recent years. Sensory regulation is the foundation for engagement, learning, and communication, and when children struggle with sensory input, it can significantly impact their ability to process information and interact with others.

Advancements in sensory integration strategies have led to more effective classroom and therapeutic approaches. **Sensory-friendly classrooms** are now being designed with flexible seating, calming areas, movement breaks, and access to tools like fidget aids and noise-reducing headphones. These adaptations not only help children with sensory challenges but also support overall classroom engagement and emotional well-being.

Additionally, **sensory modulation strategies** have become more refined, allowing educators and therapists to better support children who are over-responsive, under-responsive, or sensory-seeking. Providing opportunities for movement, offering sensory breaks, and incorporating structured activities tailored to sensory profiles are now standard practices in many inclusive settings.

Future developments in this field will continue to focus on **individualised sensory interventions**, with greater collaboration between occupational therapists, speech therapists, and educators to create tailored sensory plans that support both communication and self-regulation. The goal is to ensure that every child has access to an environment that allows them to feel regulated, comfortable, and ready to communicate.

Taking Action: 5 Practical Steps

- **Assess the Environment** - Observe the learning space and make small changes to reduce sensory overwhelm and increase accessibility.
- **Incorporate Sensory Breaks** - Ensure children have opportunities for movement, quiet time, or hands-on sensory activities throughout the day.
- **Use Visual and Physical Supports** - Provide visual schedules, fidget tools, and alternative seating options to help children self-regulate.
- **Engage in Multidisciplinary Collaboration** - Work with other professionals, such as occupational therapists and speech therapists, to create comprehensive support plans.
- **Advocate for Sensory-Friendly Practices** - Encourage schools, nurseries, and workplaces to adopt sensory-aware approaches that benefit all children.

By making these small but powerful changes, we can create environments where children feel safe, regulated, and empowered to communicate in ways that work best for them. The future of sensory processing support is one of inclusion, understanding, and proactive adaptation - ensuring that every child is given the best chance to thrive in their learning and communication journey.

INTEGRATING TECHNOLOGY IN COMMUNICATION SUPPORT

Technology is playing an increasingly vital role in supporting speech and language development. From communication apps to interactive speech therapy games, digital tools are becoming valuable resources for both educators and therapists. Augmentative and Alternative Communication (AAC) devices are helping children with complex communication needs express themselves more effectively. Similarly, speech-to-text programmes, language development apps, and video modelling techniques are providing children with new ways to engage and practise communication. Technology not only enhances access to communication but also empowers children to participate in conversations, learn new vocabulary, and build their confidence. As digital solutions evolve, they offer exciting possibilities for expanding the ways children learn and communicate.

COLLABORATIVE APPROACHES: THE IMPORTANCE OF MULTIDISCIPLINARY TEAMS

A child's speech and language development is not the responsibility of a single person; it requires a collective effort from educators, speech therapists, occupational therapists, parents, caregivers, and other professionals. When these individuals work together, they bring diverse perspectives and areas of expertise, ensuring a holistic and well-rounded approach to communication support.

The Power of a Multidisciplinary Team

Multidisciplinary teams allow for a **comprehensive understanding** of a child's strengths, challenges, and needs. Speech and language development is closely linked to sensory processing, motor skills, emotional regulation, and social interaction. A team-based approach ensures that all these elements are considered, rather than addressing speech in isolation.

Each professional plays a vital role:

- **Speech and Language Therapists:** Focus on assessing and developing communication skills, supporting language comprehension, expression, and alternative communication methods.
- **Occupational Therapists:** Address sensory processing and motor coordination challenges that may impact a child's ability to engage in communication activities.
- **Educators:** Provide the learning environment where communication happens daily and implement strategies to support children in classroom settings.
- **Parents and Caregivers:** Reinforce communication strategies at home, ensuring consistency and real-life application.
- **Psychologists and Behavioural Specialists:** Support emotional regulation and social interactions that play a key role in communication success.

Benefits of Collaboration

By working together, professionals can:

- **Share insights** to create a complete picture of the child's needs.
- **Develop unified goals** that align across home, school, and therapy settings.
- **Ensure consistency** in strategies, making it easier for children to apply skills across different environments.
- **Provide tailored interventions** that address multiple aspects of development simultaneously.

The Future of Multidisciplinary Collaboration

As we move towards more inclusive and child-centred approaches, **integrated care models** will become even more crucial. Schools and early years settings are increasingly adopting **team-based interventions**, where professionals work collaboratively rather than in isolation. Technology is also enhancing collaboration, with digital platforms allowing teams to share progress, strategies, and insights in real-time.

Taking Action: How to Foster Strong Multidisciplinary Collaboration

- **Encourage Open Communication** – Ensure regular meetings and shared documentation between all professionals involved.
- **Create a Shared Plan** – Develop individualised strategies that align across home, school, and therapy environments.
- **Involve Parents and Caregivers** – They know the child best and should be actively involved in planning and decision-making.
- **Utilise Technology** – Digital tracking tools and shared online spaces can improve coordination and ensure everyone is on the same page.
- **Commit to Continuous Learning** – Professionals can benefit from cross-training to understand different perspectives and best practices.

When professionals, families, and educators come together, the result is a **fully supported child** who has the tools, strategies, and confidence to develop their communication skills. The future of communication support lies in **shared responsibility, teamwork, and a commitment to seeing the whole child – not just their challenges, but their full potential.**

A child's speech and language development is not the responsibility of a single person; it requires collaboration among educators, speech therapists, occupational therapists, parents, and caregivers. Multidisciplinary teams bring together diverse expertise to address all aspects of a child's communication journey. By working together, these professionals can create tailored strategies that meet the child's needs across different environments – school, home, and therapy settings. A collaborative approach ensures that no aspect of the child's communication challenges is overlooked. In the future, integrated care models that emphasise teamwork and shared responsibility will become even more critical for ensuring the best outcomes for children.

ONGOING PROFESSIONAL DEVELOPMENT: STAYING INFORMED AND ENGAGED

For educators and caregivers, staying updated on the latest research and methods in speech, language, and sensory support is essential. Ongoing professional development through workshops, seminars, and specialised training allows them to stay at the forefront of best practices. Many programmes now offer courses that focus on neurodiverse communication strategies, sensory processing, and inclusive education. Attending conferences or joining professional organisations, such as The Royal College of Speech and Language Therapists (RCSLT) or local special education networks, can provide access to cutting-edge information. Continuing education ensures that professionals are equipped with the knowledge and skills to provide the best support for children with communication and sensory challenges.

Key Areas for Professional Learning in Communication

- **Supporting Neurodiverse Communication** – Training in alternative communication methods, including AAC and visual supports.
- **Developing Interaction-Based Strategies** – Learning how to foster communication through meaningful interactions, play, and engagement rather than focusing solely on speech output.
- **Building Strength-Based Approaches** – Understanding how to recognise and nurture children's communication strengths rather than focusing on deficits.
- **Enhancing Emotional Regulation and Language Development** – Exploring the connection between self-regulation and communication success, with strategies to support both areas simultaneously.
- **Adapting Language Environments** – Learning how to create communication-friendly environments that reduce pressure, increase accessibility, and encourage spontaneous language use.

Integrating Sensory Learning into Professional Development

Given the close relationship between sensory processing and communication, professional development opportunities should include training in sensory integration techniques. Understanding how a child's sensory profile affects their communication and behaviour allows educators and caregivers to create more effective interventions. Key areas for professional learning include:

- **Sensory Modulation and Regulation Strategies:** Understanding how children process sensory input and how this impacts attention, engagement, and interaction.
- **Creating Sensory-Supportive Environments:** Learning how to adapt classrooms, therapy rooms, and home environments to better support sensory regulation and communication.
- **Recognising Sensory Triggers:** Training in how sensory overload can manifest as communication breakdowns or behavioural responses and how to provide proactive support.
- **Collaborating with Occupational Therapists:** Learning how to work alongside sensory professionals to create a more holistic approach to supporting children's development.

The Future of Professional Learning

The future of professional development lies in interdisciplinary learning - bringing together speech therapists, occupational therapists, teachers, and parents to create a shared understanding of communication and sensory needs. More training programmes are focusing on hands-on, practical strategies that professionals can implement immediately.

Additionally, **technology is playing a larger role** in professional education. Online courses, virtual conferences, and digital mentorship programmes allow educators and caregivers to access high-quality learning from anywhere. New developments in AI-driven learning and virtual reality (VR) training could soon provide professionals with interactive, immersive experiences to better understand the sensory and communication challenges children face.

By committing to continuous learning and collaboration, professionals can ensure they are providing the most effective, inclusive, and responsive support to children. Whether through formal training, peer collaboration, or self-directed study, staying informed empowers those working with children to create environments where every child can thrive.

For educators and caregivers, staying updated on the latest research and methods in speech and language support is essential. Ongoing professional development through workshops, seminars, and specialised training allows them to stay at the forefront of best practices. Many programmes now offer courses that focus on neurodiverse communication strategies, sensory processing, and inclusive education. Attending conferences or joining professional organisations, such as The RCSLT or local special education networks, can provide access to cutting-edge information. Continuing education ensures that professionals are equipped with the knowledge and skills to provide the best support for children with communication challenges.

RESOURCE HUB: TOOLS AND MATERIALS FOR SUPPORTING CHILDREN

There is a wealth of resources available to educators, therapists, and parents to support children with communication needs. Websites like the American Speech-Language-Hearing Association (ASHA) and Communication Matters offer guidance, research, and practical tools. Books like *The Out-of-Sync Child* by Carol Stock Kranowitz provide valuable insights into sensory processing issues. Additionally, apps like Proloquo2Go and Voice4U are instrumental in helping non-verbal or minimally verbal children communicate effectively. Schools and families should also be aware of local support groups and professional organisations that offer training, advice, and community support. By accessing these resources, educators and caregivers can build an informed and supportive environment for every child.

YOUR NEXT STEPS: PUTTING KNOWLEDGE INTO ACTION

Now that you have explored new perspectives, strategies, and resources, it's time to take action. Here are some practical steps to ensure this knowledge leads to meaningful change:

- **Observe and Adapt:** Spend a week observing how communication happens in your setting. What works well? What could change?
- **Create a More Inclusive Space:** Adjust the environment to support sensory and communication needs (e.g., visuals, sensory-friendly spaces, reduced language load).
- **Engage with a Community:** Join a professional group, attend a webinar, or read a new book to continue growing your knowledge.
- **Support Strengths, Not Deficits:** Shift your language and expectations from "What's missing?" to "What can this child do?"
- **Advocate for Change:** Speak up for more inclusive policies, better training, and greater recognition of neurodiversity in educational and healthcare settings.

LOOKING AHEAD

REFLECTION: MOVING FORWARD WITH CONFIDENCE

Before closing this book, take a moment to reflect on your journey:

- What is one key insight from this book that challenged your previous thinking?
- What small change can you make today to create a more communication-friendly environment?
- How will you commit to ongoing learning and improvement?

By reflecting on these questions, you reinforce your role as an active participant in creating more inclusive, supportive environments for all children.

LOOKING FORWARD: ENVISIONING FUTURE SUCCESS FOR ALL CHILDREN

The way we approach communication, learning, and development is changing for the better. We are moving towards a world that sees children for their abilities, not their deficits. A world that values connection, not correction. A world where every child is supported to communicate in their own way. And **you** are a vital part of that change.

You now hold the tools, the understanding, and the mindset to make a real difference. What will you do next?

Let this be the beginning of a continued journey - one that embraces flexibility, curiosity, and the belief that **every child deserves to be heard, valued, and supported**. By taking even small steps today, you are shaping a future where children grow into confident communicators, ready to navigate the world in their own unique way.

The future starts with us. Let's make it one where every child thrives.

KEY TAKEAWAYS

- Understanding the intersection of sensory regulation and communication is essential for developing effective strategies to support children's growth.
- Sensory-friendly environments, including sensory breaks and structured routines, help children engage more fully in their learning and communication.
- Technology, such as AAC devices and language-learning apps, plays an increasingly important role in supporting children with communication challenges.

- A collaborative approach involving teachers, therapists, families, and caregivers ensures a holistic and unified plan for supporting children's needs across different settings.
- Professional development and continued learning help educators stay informed about the latest strategies, resources, and trends to support children with communication and sensory needs.
- Advocacy for inclusive, neurodiverse practices promotes systemic change and ensures every child has access to the support they need to thrive.

REFERENCES AND RESOURCES

American Speech-Language-Hearing Association (ASHA) (2023) *Augmentative and Alternative Communication (AAC)*. Available at: https://www.asha.org

Bishop, D. V. M. (2017) *Uncommon Understanding: Development and Disorders of Language Comprehension in Children*. Psychology Press.

Botting, N., Marshall, C., & Morgan, G. (2022) Neurodiversity and language development: Rethinking typical pathways, *Journal of Child Language*, 49(2), 235-258.

Dunn, W. (2014) *Sensory Profile 2 Manual*. Pearson.

Gascoigne, M. (2019) *Supporting Children with Speech and Language Difficulties*. 2nd edn. Routledge.

Kranowitz, C. S. (2005) *The Out-of-Sync Child: Recognizing and Coping with Sensory Processing Disorder*. Penguin Books.

National Institute for Health and Care Excellence (NICE) (2021) Autism spectrum disorder in under 19s: Support and management (CG170). Available at: https://www.nice.org.uk

Royal College of Speech and Language Therapists (RCSLT) (2023) Guidelines for inclusive communication practices. Available at: https://www.rcslt.org

Scheiner, K. & Bogdashina, O. (2020) *Neurodiversity and Sensory Processing: A Paradigm Shift in Autism Research*. Jessica Kingsley Publishers.

Shanahan, T. & Lonigan, C. (2017) The role of early oral language in literacy development, *Educational Psychologist*, 52(4), 225-238.

Tomblin, J. B., Zhang, X., Buckwalter, P. & O'Brien, M. (2020) The stability of primary language disorder: Four years after kindergarten diagnosis, *Journal of Speech, Language, and Hearing Research*, 63(1), 1-14.

World Health Organization (WHO) (2022) International Classification of Functioning, Disability and Health (ICF) for children and youth. Available at: https://www.who.int

Ziviani, J., Feeney, R., & Khan, A. (2019) *Children, Sensory Processing, and Learning: A Comprehensive Guide for Educators and Clinicians*. Routledge.

INDEX

achievements: celebration of 155, 176; highlighting 130
active listening 76, 151, 157, 165
adaptation 194
ADHD (attention deficit hyperactivity disorder) 62, 77, 120, 183-5
adult conversation overload 93
adult interaction 156, 188; adult talk, impact of 82
advocacy 194
agency 46
agitation 23
airspace 94, 96; importance of 93-4
alerting zones 60-1
American Speech-Language-Hearing Association (ASHA) 194
anxiety 65, 70, 112; making mistakes 44; performance 83; reducing 114-15, 118, 123, 168, 181-2; routine and 116; see also selective mutism
appreciation: belonging and 156-8; strategies to foster 157
approachability 157
artificial intelligence (AI) 193
assessment: perspectives on 133; play-based 154; role of 132-3; traditional, criticisms of 131-2
attention 18-19, 69, 92-3, 108; busy settings 84; as currency 84
attention deficit hyperactivity disorder see ADHD (attention deficit hyperactivity disorder)
auditory modifications 67
auditory over-responsiveness 53
auditory sense see hearing
auditory sensitivities 14
auditory under-registration 16
augmentative and alternative communication (AAC) 99, 101, 114, 190, 192, 195

autism spectrum disorder (ASD) 1, 60, 77, 106, 110-11, 131, 133, 180-1
availability 157
avoidance 23

balance see vestibular sense
Before/During/After approach 121
behaviour: 'bad' 29, 31; communication as 37; sensory needs and learning 55-6; specialists 190
belonging: appreciation and 156-8; importance of 156; sense of 142, 143; strategies to foster 157
body awareness 17; see also proprioception
body language 91, 111, 139
break cards 32
breaks see movement breaks; sensory breaks
breathing exercises 43, 71, 73, 124, 140
burnout 178-9

calm environment 119; strategies 44; zones 60-1
Can-Do Approach 2, 27-52; 5Cs approach 94-6; perspectives 33-4, 102; in practice 101
caregivers: as experts 172; burnout 178; engagement 171; involvement 191; role of 147-9, 157-8, 164-5, 190
challenge 94; escalation of 146
check-ins: regular 123, 169-70, 185
chewable necklaces 66
chewing gum 66
child-centred goals 175
child-led communication 87, 128
child-level positioning 83
child's perspective 127-61
choice 155
clarity 95-6; strategies for 95

197

classroom design: activities, tailoring of 66-8; adjustment of 73-5; class norms and values 77; clear pathways 60; environment for communication 86; evaluation 73-4; flexible seating options 60, 66; furniture choices 62; inclusive culture 58, 75-7; inclusive environment 53-79; layout and physical environment 60; natural lighting 61; noise control 62; observations 74-5; physical layout 86; sensory-friendly 23-4, 56-7, 59, 70, 122, 189; visual organisation 60
co-regulation 42-3
cognitive skills 12-13
collaboration: benefits of 191; effective 169-73; impact of 180-2, 184; interventions 181, 183, 191, multidisciplinary 189, 191-2; multidisciplinary 191-2; proactive steps 169; risk prevention 168-9; role and responsibilities 164-5; significance of 163-4; see also collaborative approach
collaborative approach 5-6, 74, 123, 148-9, 157; families and professionals 7, 39, 46, 163-86; goal setting 151-2; learning 115; occupational therapists 71-2; parents and specialists 146; planning 117, 170-1; speech therapists 71-2
colour: classroom design 60; profiling 152-3; visual aids 61
comfort zones 100
commenting 89
communication: alternative, offer of 141; behaviour as 31-3, 37, 138-42; beyond the classroom 36; boards 140; breakdown 58-9; can-do approach to 29; celebration and 96; challenges 4; choices 35, 45-6; clear goals 165-6; co-regulation and 42-3; confidence and 31, 90; connection and 42, 90; continuous 29-30; effective 165-6, 188; empathy and 36; empowerment through 33, 45-6; everyday routines 30, 34, 98-9; facilitation strategies 89-90; home and school, between 46; importance of 27-8; individual journeys 38, 48; interests, through 30-1; journey, as a 48; joy, through 44; lifelong skills 39, 47-8; modes of 28-9, 49, 102, 137; multi-faceted nature of 38; natural flow 40; neurodiverse 192; non-verbal see non-verbal communication; open channels 165, 191; opportunities 102; passport 39; patience and 36; play and 44; poor 166-8; positive 85; self-awareness and 82; sensory regulation and 58, 68-70; sensory support and 6-7; skills beyond the classroom 43; slowing of 88; speech and language skills 81; strategies 70-2, 85, 90, 96, 114, 181-2, 184; tools 118, 120; as an umbrella 28; value of 35; zones 86; see also sensory overload; sensory regulation
Communication Matters (website) 194
community engagement 194
compliance 99-100; compliance-based goals 174-5, 177; compliance-driven practices 99
confidence 94-6, 100-1, 152, 156, 195; building 48, 90, 154; predictable interactions 100-1
conformity: challenges to 78-9, 133-6
connection 90, 94, 96, 100-2; correction and 101; strategies for 94; trust and 137
consistency 94-6, 191; environment 46
consolidation 94
contextual learning 124
continuous learning 191
control: choice and 45-6; lack of 45
coping strategies 141
counselling 179
'count-to-five' strategy 92
critical windows 144, 146
curiosity 147-8
curriculum integration 77-8

daily check-ins 94
dancing 72
deep pressure 15, 61; see also weighted objects
deficit-focused approach 132
delivery: speed of 88
developmental diversity 132, 135, 136-7
developmental language disorder (DLD) 131, 133
diagnosis: waiting times 5
direct teaching 88-9
disruptions 23; disruptive behaviour 166-7
distractions 151, 155; reduction in 57
diversity 77; in development 153
dysregulation see regulation

early intervention 5, 144-6; effective strategies 146
early screening 90-1
earplugs 66; see also noise-cancelling headphones
echolalia 41
educational goals: irrelevance of 99
educational workshops 179-80
educators: role of 147-9, 157-8, 164, 190

INDEX

emotion 94, 109, 140
emotional overload 132
emotional regulation 13, 114-15, 140, 142, 192; social interaction and 69-70; strategies 188
emotional security 156
emotional support 44
emotional well-being 24, 56-7, 106, 125, 143-4, 158
empathy 7, 36, 43-4, 76, 94, 101, 123; in action 76; empathy-building activities 76; open dialogue 76
empowerment 149
engagement 151, 156
enhanced learning 154
environment 150-2, 155; adjustment 141; assessment of 189; for growth 5; ignoring factors 132; impact of 150-1; language 192; role of 187-8
evaluation 73-4; importance of 74
executive functions 19
exploration 147-9, 154
expression: forms of 96
expressive language 106, 111
eye contact 33
eye pointing 91

face-to-face interaction 82-4; participation 83-4
facial expressions 111, 139
facilitation 88-9; conversations 89
familiar faces 99
familiarity 100
families 117; engagement with 157; therapy 179
feedback 172; constructive 165; supportive 157
feelings circle 76
fidget tools/toys 16, 57, 61, 65, 122
fidgeting 20, 53-55, 64, 74, 106
'fight, flight, or freeze' response 58
flexibility 75, 86-7; goal-setting 137
flexible grouping 155
focus 18-19, 69, 108; promotion of 57
focused interventions 153
fragmentation 166-7
freedom 44
frustration 18, 19, 32, 108, 112, 140
furniture 60-2
future challenges 7-8, 146, 187-96

games 129, 154-5; turn-taking 96
gestalt language processors 40-1
gestures 38, 96
goodbyes 95
Google: Classroom 170; Docs 165

greetings 95
gross motor skills 17
group activities 115
group profiling 152
gustatory sensitivities 14-15; see also taste

'hands-on' activities 66, 121, 174
handwriting 17
headphones see noise cancellation headphones
hearing 11
holistic approach 125-6, 142, 185
holistic development 5-6, 158
hypersensitivity (over-responsiveness) 106, 110
hyposensitivity (under-responsiveness) 106

identification strategies 145
identity 156
idioms 109
imitation 96
inclusion: definition of 2-3
inclusive behaviour 157
inclusive culture 171
inclusive environment 7, 53-79, 114; importance of 56
inclusive practices 153, 157
inclusive spaces 194
Individual Education Plans (IEPs) 170-2
individual needs 148-9, 153
individualised goals 143-4; sensory interventions 189; strategies 153
individuality 157
inner voice 85
instructions: simplification of 32, 95
integrated strategies 122
interaction 150-2; intentional 102; interaction-based strategies 192; interaction-friendly environments 35, 151; meaningful 151
interactive activities 121
interests 30-1, 34-5; as a bridge 130; as entry points 100; engagement 100; identifying 154; importance of 153-4; nurturing 155-6
internal sensations see interoception
interoception 12, 21

joy 44
jumping 71, 72

key words 95
knowledge gaps 98

Lane, A. E. 107
language demands 27

INDEX

language development 192; apps 190; critical window for 144
language processing 69
language simplification 128
late talkers 91-2; strategies for 93-4
lighting 14, 19, 54, 57, 58, 66, 119, 122; natural 61-3
limited child participation 98
listening: empathy and 43-4; importance of 39
low-pressure interaction opportunities 83
lunchtime 30

magic moments 30-1, 34-5, 93
mainstream school: special school vs 1
matching language 151
meaningful interaction 84-5
meltdowns 22-3, 110, 112-13
memory: formation and retrieval 19
messaging apps 165, 170
metaphor 109
Microsoft Teams 170
mindfulness 124, 140; activities 73
mirroring 83, 94
motivation 154; to learn 156
motor skills 12
movement areas 66
movement breaks 15-16, 57-8, 64-6, 122-4; classroom movement 72; implementation of 72; sensory circuits 72; structured 72
movement see vestibular sense
movement-based activities 61, 174
multi-sensory teaching strategies 124
multidisciplinary teams: collaboration 189; future of 191; importance of 190-2; power of 190
multiple learning modalities 68

natural lighting see lighting
needs: labelling 167; misunderstanding 167; see also individual needs
neuro-affirming practices 136-7
neurodiverse communication 76-8, 135, 192, 194, 196
NHS (National Health Service) 1
noise control 62, 116
noise-cancelling headphones 14-15, 20, 54, 57-8, 66, 119
noisy environments 14-15
non-verbal communication 1, 69, 94, 109, 111, 116, 119-20, 139, 194
nurturing environment 147, 149

observation 146, 154, 194; identification and 140; reflection and 139; without judgement 128

Occupational Therapists (OTs) 6, 163, 165-9, 171, 181-5, 190, 193
olfactory sensitivities 14-15; see also smell
'one-size-fits-all' model 38, 131-3, 137, 143
online progress trackers 170
overload see sensory overload

pace of interaction 28, 81
parents: as experts 172; engagement 171; involvement 154, 191; leadership and participation 173; role of 164-5, 190
patience 36, 40-1
patterns 139, 140
pauses 88, 93
peer interaction 188; appreciation 130-1; encouragement of 114, 121; positive 32; sensory supports 71; support and understanding 118, 123
personalised interaction 92-3
physical environment: adaptations 98; proximity 94
physical support 189
physiotherapists 6
picture cards 140
Picture Exchange Communication System (PECS) cards 119-20
play: airspace and 94; language through 85; playtime 30; power of 44
play-based approaches: assessment 154; communication strategies 44; learning 187-8
positive cycle 159
positive goals 175
positive interaction 147, 149
positive responses 83
practical strategies 49, 65-7
pragmatics 106, 109, 111
predictability 87, 116, 128; confidence-building 100-1; consistency and 95; see also routine
pressure: reducing 48; physical see deep pressure
problem-solving 19
processing time 92
professional development 75, 117, 192-4; future of 193-4; key areas 192; sensory learning, integration of 193
Proloquo2Go (app) 194
proprioception 12, 20, 53; chewing aids 66; proprioceptive seeking 15; proprioceptive under-registration 17
psychologists 190
puzzles 32, 61, 130

qualitative data 74
quantitative data 74

INDEX

questioning 89
quick action 146
quiet: activities 61; children 89; corners 73; spaces 44; times 93; zones 66-7, 116

rapport 148-9
receptive language 106, 111
reflection 97; adaptation and 141-3; journals 146; ongoing 143-4; on practices 157
regulation: classrooms 53; communication development 68; dysregulation and 22, 109-11; impact on communication 68-70; sensory *see* sensory regulation; strategies 193; *see also* co-regulation; emotional regulation; self-regulation
relationships 151, 156; importance of 158
resilience 57, 159
resistance bands 71
resources 151, 194
respect for differences 78
response 96; time 88, 92
responsive engagement 151
review meetings 75, 172
'Ripple effect' concept 158-9
role models 147
routine 60, 118, 122-3, 157; language 95; power of 34; predictable 65, 87, 128; unexpected changes to 116
Royal College of Speech and Language Therapists (RCSLT) 192, 194

scaffolding 45
seating arrangements 57, 58, 66, 122; flexibility of 66
security: sense of 87
selective mutism 41
self-awareness 82
self-regulation 57, 141
senses 11-12
sensitivities *see* sensory sensitivities
sensory activities 121
sensory breaks 57, 65, 70-1, 73, 118, 123-4, 140, 189
sensory circuits 72
sensory considerations 98
sensory difficulties: challenging behaviours 22-3; individualised support strategies 23; student support for 23-4
sensory dysregulation 109-11
sensory experiences affecting learning 19-21
Sensory Modulation Disorder (SMD) 65
sensory modulation strategies 189, 193
sensory needs: behaviour and learning 55-6; common 54-5; diversity of 62-3

Sensory Over-Responsive (SOR) 54, 63, 119-20; low-stimulus alternatives 67-8
sensory overload 58-9, 105, 132; communication breakdown 113; communication difficulties 113
sensory processing: behaviour and 21-2; classroom support 7; common difficulties 13-18; communication challenges 105; definition of 11; disorder *see* sensory processing disorder (SPD); impact on learning 18-24; significance of 11; support 188-9; understanding 7, 11-25
sensory processing disorder (SPD) 56, 62, 78, 111, 118
sensory profiles 63-5, 71
sensory regulation 105-26; activities, transitions between 115; case studies 117-21; classroom scenarios 115-16; collaborative planning 117; communication and 114; communication barriers 112-13; communication challenges 106-8, 111; communication difficulties 110-11; definition 106; difficulty seeking support 112; dysregulation and communication skills 108-10; environmental role 108; families, input from 117; impact on communication 107; observation and assessment 116; professional development and training 117; teaching strategies 116-17; thoughts and emotions 109; understanding language 109; *see also* regulation
Sensory Seeking (SS). 53, 55, 60, 64-5, 110, 118-19; behaviours 15-16, 22; impact on language development 59; sensory enrichment for 67
sensory sensitivities 14-15
sensory support 128; communication support and 6-7
sensory tools 65-6, 119
sensory under-registration behaviours 16-18
Sensory Under-Responsive (SUR) 54-5, 63-4, 120-1
sensory-avoidant behaviours 22
sensory-friendly: classroom design 23-4; practices 189
sensory-supportive environments 193
sentences: simplicity of 95
shared insights 191
shared responsibility 191
shutdowns 22-3, 111, 113
sight 11, 19, 38
Slack (app) 170
slow interaction 102, 120
smell 12, 20

social interaction: emotional regulation and 69-70; impairment in 112-13; pragmatics and 109
social scripts 43
social skills 13, 134; development of 156; groups 128
soft furnishings 60-2, 66, 122
sound 20
specialist support 97
speech: content *vs* delivery 38; 'perfect' 37-8; production 69
speech and language: challenges 7; skills 7, 81-103; therapy 86, 92; trends in development 187-8
Speech and Language Therapists (SLTs) 6, 97-100, 163, 165-7, 171, 181-4, 190
speech-to-text programmes 190
stability balls 66
stammering 40
standing desks 66
stigma 178
Stock Kranowitz, Carol 194
story time 87
storytelling 124, 135
strengths-based approach 2, 129-30, 174, 185, 192; celebration of 129-30; challenging oneself 136, 138; contributions and 78; development of 143; focus on 48, 129-31; goal-setting 130, 174-5, 177; highlighting strengths 28; identifying strengths 154; importance of 153-4; individual 143; nurturing 155-6; scaffolding 45; support for strengths 194
stress: diagnosis-related 178
stress balls 65, 71, 122
structure 86-7, 118; *see also* routine
success: celebration of 47; communicative 99; envisioning 195; measurement of 142-3; opportunities for 130; redefining 151-2; small victories 47
support: culture of 152; inconsistent 166-7; individual needs 153; ripple effect 158-9
supportive learning environment 21, 46, 137
supportive network 145

tactile resources 61, 72
tactile sensitivities 14-15; *see also* touch
tactile under-registration 17
tailored interventions 191
tailored learning experiences 155
targeted strategies 145-6
taste 12, 20
teaching strategies 71
teamwork 46, 191

technology 151, 165, 170, 191; communication support 189-90; role of 193
textures 13, 14, 22, 54, 61, 65-6
therapists: role of 164; *see also* Occupational Therapists (OTs); Speech and Language Therapists (SLTs)
thinking time 88
time constraints 97
tone of voice 139
touch 11-12, 20
traditional assessments: criticisms 131-2
traditional methods: disadvantages 97-8
traditions 157
training 117
trauma: acknowledgement of 178-9; emotional 178-80; resources 179-80; sensitivity 179; support through 177-80; of uncertainty 178; understanding 178
triggers 57, 140, 171, 193
trust 148-9
turn-taking 83, 89-90, 96, 109

under-registration *see* sensory under-registration behaviours
understanding 7, 40, 76; comprehensive 190; growth and 158-9

verbal cues 121
vestibular sense 12, 15, 21, 53, 60
vestibular under-registration 17
video modelling techniques 190
virtual reality (VR) 193
vision *see* sight
visual cues 121
visual modifications 67
visual schedules 17-18, 32, 38, 60, 95
visual sensitivities 14
visual supports 28, 37-8, 44, 70, 96, 122-3, 140, 189
visual timetables 70
visual under-registration 16
Voice4U (app) 194

wall displays 66
weighted objects: blankets 119; lap pads 66, 71; *see also* deep pressure
welcoming environment 172-3
well-being: emotional 24, 56-7, 106, 125, 143-4, 158
WhatsApp 170
wobble stools 60, 66, 72, 122
workshops 179-80, 193

yoga 124

For Product Safety Concerns and Information please contact our EU representative GPSR@taylorandfrancis.com
Taylor & Francis Verlag GmbH, Kaufingerstraße 24, 80331 München, Germany

www.ingramcontent.com/pod-product-compliance
Lightning Source LLC
Chambersburg PA
CBHW060300240426
43661CB00060B/2846